Beckett

The Irish Dimension

To the memory of my husband

Beckett

The Irish Dimension

MARY JUNKER

WOLFHOUND PRESS

First published 1995 by WOLFHOUND PRESS Ltd
68 Mountjoy Square
Dublin 1
Ireland

© Mary Junker-Brennan 1995

British Library Cataloguing-in-Publication Data
A catalogue record for this book is available from the British Library

ISBN 0 86327 384 X

ACKNOWLEDGEMENTS

My first debt of gratitude is due to Professor Dr Paprotté of the Department of English,
Münster University, who supervised the Thesis, having approved the theme: *Samuel
Beckett: The Irish Dimension in Five of his Plays*; and given me a free hand to develop
and present it.

I am deeply grateful to Professor Dr Brendan Kennelly, Professor of Modern Literature, Trinity College, Dublin, for reading the text; for his encouragement and valuable
criticism; and later for assiduously working through the complete Thesis as the
officially designated External Examiner.

Heartfelt thanks to Mr Aedan O'Beirne, Blackrock, for keeping me abreast of Beckett
Studies with gifts of new publications and copies of relevant commentaries.

For his interest in the work and encouragement towards its completion my sincere
thanks to Mr Peter Wiborg of the Overberg Institute, Münster. Likewise my gratitude
extends to Mr Patrick Brennan, Naples, Florida, for his keen interest in the text, his
encouragement and firm support of the project.

Many thanks to Ms Irmgard Heitkötter who diligently typed the manuscript and
whose interest in Beckett enlivened its progress.

Heartfelt thanks to Mrs P Caha for her unstinted help and patient guidance through
the technical instructions of the promotion procedure.

For permission to quote the poem *Stone* by Dana Wynter I am grateful to *Ireland of the
Welcomes*.

To my daughters, Roseleen and Maureen, who were supportive, optimistic and
understanding, a final lasting Thank You.

Jacket photograph of Beckett: Courtesy of Gisèle Freund
Jacket design: Joe Gervin
Typesetting: Wolfhound Press
Printing: Cambridge University Press, UK

CONTENTS

PREFACE

Samuel Beckett died just before Christmas 1989, at the age of 83. His death brought numerous tributes to the man and his work, from around the world. It also brought to light two apparent 'trunk pieces' of deeply moving prose-poetry: *Stirrings Still* (1989), and *what is the word — Comment dire.*[1]

Both pieces of terminal writing, as it were, probe 'the same as ever' isolation and immensity of the human condition. Yet, in *Stirrings Still*, patience (one of the Twelve Fruits of the Holy Spirit) ripens in the darkness of despair:

.... And patience till the one true end to time and grief and self and second self his own.

A worthy tribute to Beckett is encapsulated in a line — a man whose work 'sings the shattered song of our time.'[2] Beckett's swansong, *what is the word — Comment dire* is a shattering search for the word to encompass the reality of old age, its fear of folly, and the faint mental sightings beyond it, as 'seeing' is reduced to 'glimpse':

afaint afar away over there what —
folly for to need to seem to glimpse
afaint afar away over there what —
what —
what is the word —
what is the word

The elusive *word* may be the one he forged in the smithy of his soul forty years before : where patience, tempered on the anvil of time, portrays the universal plight of Everyman 'till the one true end to time ... and self. ...' in *Waiting for Godot*.

The impact of *Waiting for Godot* was widely felt, though variously interpreted, when he received the Nobel Prize for Literature in 1969. For another twenty years he endured and articulated, to the point of silence, the enormity and futility of human existence. Yet, in his writings as in his life, total darkness did not endure... 'it in its turn went out.'[3] This glimmer of hope he retained up to his last breath, in *Stirrings Still*:

> For when his own light went out he was not left in the dark. Light
> of a kind came then from one high window.

The world would have this obtain for Beckett still. As one encomium concluded:'Godot is no longer waiting for Samuel Beckett'.

The theme of this work was inspired by a need to fill the void that seems to exist between seeing/reading Beckett's plays and fully understanding them. Frequently, people who are moved by a performance of one or other of his plays cannot explain lines of the dialogue that apparently secured their *involvement* in the play.

Understanding Beckett's dramatic poetry can only enrich that experience of involvement, and increase the enjoyment of a performance, by participating fully in the total 'creation' of the play.

NOTES

1   The poem appears courtesy of John Calder and Seán O Mórdha. The texts in French and English were recently given to Mr O Mórdha by the author as a contribution to a BBC film documentary on Irish poetry (Quoted from *The Irish Times*, 25, 26, 27 Dec. 1989).

2   John Banville, in *The Irish Times* of the same dates.

3   *Stirrings Still*.

Chapter One

UNDERSTANDING BECKETT

The sun shone, having no alternative, on the nothing new.

(Murphy)

The first line of Beckett's first novel, *Murphy* (1938), is, in retrospect, a metaphor for most of his subsequent writings, especially his plays, ever since he dramatised that line in *Waiting for Godot* a decade later. Just as the sun shines anew on the nothing new somewhere every day, Beckett's drama, exceeding fifty plays,[1] presents 'nice variations on an ever-reiterated theme',[2] the human condition.

'This dramatic astronaut'[3] sustains the interest by turning technology into a dramatic technique to portray aspects of human consciousness like variants of science fiction. He is as inventive with radio and television as he was in staging *Godot*, aptly 'demonstrating how the formal techniques of these media — camera movement and perspective in film, voice-over and close-up in television — provide multiple ways to stage a self-confrontation'.[4]

'And what he has himself examined remorselessly is identity, and the question of being.'[5]

Since Beckett could use tape-recording or television techniques to articulate the two voices of self, he felt no need for two or more characters to recall the experiences that compel him to write. However, the anonymity he claimed for these memories became untenable, as more was written about his life and time in Ireland up to 1932, and of the family bond that drew him back again and again until 1950.[6]

Consequently, the critics' philosophical, psychological and metaphysical approach to his work is giving way to a more realistic assessment of the influence and extent of that Irish background shimmering through his plays. One critic writes ...

> The Irishness in Beckett's work seems part of its vital core: the element which he himself sees as constituting in any work of art, its 'condensing spiral of need'.[7]

The autobiographical trend in Beckett's writing, earlier noted by a few critics, is now more widely recognised. With Beckett's blessing — and co-operation — it is authentically documented and illustrated in Eoin O'Brien's valuable book, *The Beckett Country*. It shows that Beckett's plays are not based on the no-man's land of fiction, but on his observations and lasting impressions of life in his native country.

Beckett's plays, like those of any other dramatist, should be interpreted in the light and knowledge of the conditions that inspired them. These conditions comprise 'inner' and 'outer' reality.[8] For Beckett, 'inner reality' is distilled from memories, experiences, and observations, drawn from the 'outer reality' of the Irish landscape, sky and multiple sea settings along the two-thousand-mile coastline of inlets and bays.[9]

Particular attention is given to *language* in these plays. Beckett's dramatic, telegrammatic language merely fosters the notion that he is aloof, abstruse, and extremely difficult to understand.

His aloofness is in fact shyness;[10] his abstruseness is deliberate;[11] and as for understanding Beckett, Alvarez wrote,

> Yet even now [1973] his total output is still relatively small and is becoming, as it were, even smaller; it is also forbiddingly difficult and certainly becoming more difficult.

The Beckettian paradox that less is more, since he substituted depth for length, is amplified in *The Beckett Country*.

The increasing 'lessness'[12] as a dramatic technique in his later work is exemplified in three one-man plays considered here: *Krapp's Last Tape*; *Eh Joe*; and *That Time*. The 'difficult' aspect of Beckett's technique in all five plays — opacity, obscurity, ambivalence — is lessened by fuller understanding of the language, lore, and 'soul-landscape'[13] that characterise his Irish plays.

The subject of this study is the Irish background of his work as reflected in five of his plays written over the third quarter of this century:

1. *Waiting for Godot* (1952)
2. *All That Fall* (1956)
3. *Krapp's Last Tape* (1958)
4. *Eh Joe* (1966)
5. *That Time* (1976)

In the Prologue to his book, *Beckett/Beckett* (1977), Professor Vivian Mercier, who comes 'from the same rather philistine Irish Protestant background' as Beckett, writes:

> Beckett is unique, as we all are, but he has not descended from another planet.[14]

Reassured that he is not one of 'the little green men' from outer space, although he holds the green passport of the Emerald Isle,[15] we can begin to understand Beckett by going back to his Irish roots, the soil that nourished them, and the landscape in its varied and violent beauty his mature writing assumes.

In four of the five plays considered here, the landscapes — mountains and bays, parks, plains, racecourse and rock landmarks — affecting for good or ill the actions of his 'people' are within walking distance of Foxrock, Dublin, where Beckett was born on Good Friday, April 13, 1906.

The symbolism of the day and date of his birth pervades the first play, *Godot*, which also has significant points of location in the Irish landscape, e.g. the reference to Connemara 'abode of stones',[16] on the western seaboard. Its rocky mountain range, the Twelve Bens,[17] is so-called from the twelve conical quartzite peaks rising in characteristic dominance against the fury of the Atlantic.[18] Imagery of contest, dominance and resistance, metaphors for stones, and figurative language for the origin of plutonic rocks abound in the text of a menial's protest.[19]

Beckett provides his characters with an Irish setting not only for sentimental reasons, but as a basis for his own intellectual protest.

Like the two-faced stone idol in Celtic mythology[20] he faces both ways. The bifocal vision of his Irish mind determines the shape of his art, and as Hesla tells us: the shape of Beckett's art is the shape of the dialectic.[21]

Beckett's twenty-five impressionable years in Ireland left images that persist, and are embossed on his writings.

> But Ireland is most important to Beckett as an inheritance to deny, or a set of appearances to go behind, or a range of authorities to disagree with.[22]

To understand why Beckett should look back in anger on the country he left in 1932, for an uncertain future in foreign parts, it must be said that by then Ireland had become 'foreign' to him, politically, culturally, and spiritually.[23] It remained for him to turn his up-ended world into literature: which he has been doing ever since. The enduring crisis of identity is what he seeks to solve in his Irish plays.

In his essay 'Beckett: the Demythologising Intellect', Richard Kearney concludes:

> Beckett's entire literary oeuvre embodies a modern critique of traditional notions of 'identity' – whether it concerns the self, being, language, God or one's sense of national belonging. His aim, I suggest, is less a nihilistic deconstruction of sense into non-sense than a playful wish to expose the inexhaustible comedy of existence.[24]

Samuel Beckett's long life is not exactly a text-book example of 'the inexhaustible comedy of existence'. The laugh implicit in the comedy he creates is, in his own words —

> ... the dianoetic laugh, down the snout — Haw! — So. It is the laugh of laughs, the *risus purus*, the laugh laughing at the laugh, the beholding, the saluting of the highest joke, in a word the laugh that laughs — silence please — at that which is unhappy.[25]

This, 'the mirthless laugh'[26] is the 'mode of ululation'[27] Beckett enjoys as he continues to demythologise, declare, declaim, and demonstrate the dual-vision of the Irish mind,[28] into his ninth decade.

Finally, 'Do not try to understand everything, lest you thereby be ignorant of everything.'[29] The bit we shall never understand is that which by right belongs to Beckett's soul, to his uniqueness — which he keenly felt as separateness, suffered as loneliness, and interpreted as rejection — and to his genius as a creative artist. It is the earnest we must give him if we want him to go on writing, as a covenant of our faith in the sincerity of his art.

In his chapter 'Ireland/The World', the author who has contributed much to understanding Beckett concludes:

> He has travelled farther than most men towards the centre of his own being; more important still, he has been able to come back and 'record his findings'.
> We who read his books and watch his plays have been able to recognise ourselves in this or that part of his findings and thus are or ought to be prepared to take the rest on trust.
> Beckett's universality, in the last analysis, does not depend on

impatriation or expatriation, on Irishness, Frenchness or cosmopolitanism: it depends on the paradox of a unique self that has found its bedrock in our common human predicament.[30]

NOTES

1 Vivian Mercier writes that 'the *complete* dramatic works are at least fifty in number', in 'Poet and mathematician', *Hermathena*, No. CXLI, Winter 1986, p. 66.

2 Jacobsen, Josephine and Mueller, William R., *The Testament of Samuel Beckett*, 1966, p. 109.

3 A title bestowed on Beckett by theatre historian Micháel O hAodha, on presenting *Godot* at the Abbey (1969).

4 Roche, Anthony, 'Beckett's contexts', *Hermathena*, No. CXLI, p. 74.

5 Foreword by A. Norman Jeffares, Ibid., p. 8.

6 Bair, Deirdre, *Samuel Beckett A Biography*, 1978, London: Picador edition, Pan Books, 1980.

7 O'Brien, Eóin, 'Introduction', *The Beckett Country*, The Black Cat Press, Dublin, in association with Faber and Faber, London, 1986, p. xxiii.

8 Knowlson, James, 'Foreword', in O'Brien, *The Beckett Country*, p. xvii.

9 Ibid., pp. 306 - 309.

10 Alvarez, A., *Beckett*, London: Fontana/Collins, 1973, pp. 9, 10.

11 Ibid., p. 79.

12 Beckett applied this technique to the prose piece — *Lessness* (1970) — translated by the author from his French publication, *Sans* — literally 'without' — in 1969. London: Calder and Boyars, 1970.

13 See *Watt* (1944) for Beckett's 'home thoughts from abroad', Paris: Olympia Press, 1958, p. 249.

14 Mercier, Vivian, *Beckett/Beckett*, Oxford University Press, New York (1977), Prologue, p. x.

15 *Irish University Review*, Spring 1984, p. 20.

16 *Godot*, p. 44.

17 *Ben* is the Gaelic word for mountain.

18 *Ireland of the Welcomes*, Vol. 34, No. 1, 1985, p. 26.

19 *Godot*, p. 43, 44.

20 'Carved in stone long before the birth of Christ, this two-faced idol stands on Boa Island in Lough Erne, Co. Fermanagh' (*Ireland of the Welcomes*, 1985).

21 Hesla, David H., *The Shape of Chaos: An Interpretation of the Art of Samuel Beckett*, Minneapolis: University Press, 1971.

22 Mays, J.C.C., 'Young Beckett's Irish Roots', *Irish University Review*, Spring 1984, p. 21.

23 Mercier, *Beckett/Beckett*, pp. 25 - 35.

24 Kearney, Richard (ed.), *The Irish Mind, Exploring Intellectual Traditions*, Dublin: Wolfhound Press, 1985, p. 293.

25 *Watt* (1944), pp. 46, 47. Beckett wrote *Watt* in English while working (disguised as a labourer) in the Vaucluse near Avignon. Paris: Olympia Press, 1958.

26 Ibid.

27 Ibid.

28 James Joyce called it a faculty that allows 'two thinks at a time': Kearney, *The Irish Mind*, p. 10.

29 Advice which Democritus (c. 460 - 357 B.C.) gave his disciples. See Webb, Eugene, *The Plays of Samuel Beckett*, London, 1972, p. 17.

30 Mercier, *Beckett/Beckett*, p. 45.

Chapter Two

BECKETT'S LITERARY
AND CULTURAL HERITAGE

Great literature is seldom the product of a 'pure' or isolated cultural
situation, but springs rather from the encounter of different ways of
life and thought ....
To understand literature, then, is to understand the traditions involved and how they interact .... Yet the work of art is also particular
to the poet, his time, and his traditions; and the paradox is that the
better we understand the particular circumstances and meanings of
a poem the better we can also share its universal qualities.[1]

Samuel Beckett is a beneficiary of three cultures, Irish, English, and
French, and their traditions. His work is a unique amalgam of all three,
leavened with his own personal vision of the universe, and 'a strain of
anarchism'[2] that determines that vision. This strain expands as the urge to
write seized him convulsively, after 1945.

The scope of Beckett's creative impulse is summarised by Richard Ellmann thus:

First he was a poet who wrote short stories, then a novelist who
wrote plays .... Each foray into a more stark and final apprehension
necessitated another; he was impatient with his own modes of
pursuit, which became increasingly outlandish as he strove to come
closer to the total expression of his experience.[3]

As poet, Beckett made his first impact on the literary scene with the grotesque satire[4] *Whoroscope* (1930). This long poem (ninety-eight lines) about *Time*, won him a cash prize,[5] and the recognition he needed as an aspiring writer among the international, fiercely competitive literary élite of pre-war Paris. Nancy Cunard wrote of *Whoroscope* in 1959:

> ... What remarkable lines, what images and analogies, what vivid colouring throughout! Indeed what technique! The long poem, mysterious, obscure in parts ... was clearly by someone very intellectual and highly educated.[6]

The poem did not sell well, but it brought Beckett new contracts, including the *Proust* (1931) commission. It was his first published book; and at twenty-four, 'Whoroscope seemed to him a talisman of good things to come'.[7]

Twenty years later, Time, wrapped in an obscure pun — *Godot* — proved a reliable talisman in the making of a playwright.[8] Cunard's comment on the poem, 'mysterious, obscure in parts ...' is universally made on the play, wherever it is read or created. Time, flying kites, symbols, images and analogies are the basic themes of Beckett's autobiographical plays. By 'flying kites' I mean:

> (1) Time as an analogous bird of prey, a predatory agent preying on man's mental faculties, e.g. memory and understanding; and sapping the senses, such as seeing and hearing, that sustain them.
> (2) Flying a kite to test opinion or float an idea.[9]

The mutations of time are clear, too, in assessments of Beckett and his work. 'Our approval is not the nutrient his gift craves' wrote Hugh Kenner in 1973.[10] 'To be understood, to be accepted, are Beckett's deepest needs ...' wrote a psychiatrist, Patrick Wakeling, in 'Looking at Beckett: The Man and the Writer' (1984). His plays reveal 'the nature of his inner self' and 'the ways in which he is perceived by himself .... Beckett knows he is a misfit and feels in his bones the ache of loneliness and despair ... In order to be understood at all, he has had to write in the fashion we have come to recognise'. From his biographer we learn that the tramps, clowns, alcoholics, failures and misfits are, singularly and collectively, the tormented, often demented Samuel Beckett. Through his 'characters' he is 'expressing as honestly as he can, his own experience'. He is flying a kite, testing our understanding, tolerance and forbearance. 'He throws himself upon the mercy of the discerning, inviting our compassion and, perhaps, disarming our criticism'.[11]

Criticism of Beckett is softened by the general belief that Dante and

Descartes are the dominant figures in his 'personal mythology':[12] hence his cosmic philosophy and abstruse language, also the far-fetched reasoning of his protagonists.[13] As a graduate in Italian and French he was fascinated by the two men, and used their works to add substance to his own, and occasionally as an alibi. The hero in *Dante and the Lobster* (1932), the Dublin student Belacqua, notable for indolence and sloth, is Beckett himself. This story is just part of a novel, *Dream* (1932) in which the main character Belacqua is 'the barely fictionalised Beckett' from childhood to the disinterested lecturer at Trinity College.[14]

The influence of Descartes on Beckett's work is so pervasive that his heroes have been described as 'a succession of suffering Cartesians'.[15] Cartesian ideas on the relation between mind and body — the time-lapse between decisions taken and the actions called for — find effective expression in his plays. The well-calculated slowness of action marks the razor's edge between impatience and suspense that draws the audience into *involvement* in the play. An example of this in *Godot* is the delayed action in helping Pozzo up from the floor after Vladimir and Estragon had decided to help him.[16]

The fact is that in mind and body Beckett was himself a good example of Cartesian dualism. Like Belacqua, Dante's indolent lutemaker, his 'characters' just pluck the strings of the Beckettian lute.

The Joycean Influence

The dominant figure in Beckett's early adult life and work as a writer is James Joyce. From their first meeting in Paris in 1928, Joyce's influence on the young, lonely, emotionally immature *lecture* grew to the Pozzo-Lucky dimension of master and slave. Beckett was indeed on a lead:[17] Joyce commanding him to *think* and dance attendance on himself as he 'gradually took over his life and turned him into a man-of-all-work'.[18] Beckett 'was awed by Joyce'[19] and in need of a father figure for his own mental stability, (he was referred to as 'the splendidly mad Irishman ... who wanted to commit suicide ...'),[20] he 'formed an intense emotional attachment and expected that Joyce would do the same'.[21] Joyce was adept at converting adulation into allegiance and allegiance into assistance, and he 'had little need for relationships except when they could be useful to him'.[22]

The Joyce/Beckett relationship, that of 'a professor and his trusted research assistant',[23] was mutually beneficial. Beckett did the detailed

research for *Finnegans Wake* (1939) during the first two years, 1928-1930 —
as 'a willing but unpaid servant' of the author.[24] His expressions went
directly into the book, and Joyce acknowledged this in a sarcastic paragraph, praising and punning, as he sensed competition in the intelligence
and wit of his 'servant':

> Sam knows miles bettern me how to work the miracle ...
> Illstarred punster, lipstering cowknucks ....[25]

From Joyce, Beckett learned by example and precept 'how to work the
miracle'. Joyce's advice to him and other young Irish writers abroad is
firmly expressed in a letter to one of them, Arthur Power:

> You are Irishmen and you must write in your own tradition. Bor-
> rowed styles are no good. You must write what is in your blood and
> not what is in your brain .... For myself, I always write about Dublin
> because if I can get to the heart of Dublin I can get to the heart of all
> the cities of the world. In the particular is contained the universal.[26]

None of them took his counsel, 'to cull their own biographies, examine
their own relationships and write about the people they knew',[27] more
literally than did young Beckett. He did this most successfully and effectively in his plays.[28] In his 'own tradition' he wrote *Waiting for Godot* and
All That Fall; and he culled his own biography for *Krapp's Last Tape, Eh Joe*
and *That Time*. His own 'styles' mean for Beckett 'the techniques of disguise
and concealment that infuse his later writings'.[29] When a piece of writing
becomes too autobiographical he disguises it, as in *Eh Joe* (Move 7),[30] or
withholds publication of it. In the latter case the piece is classified as another
'trunk' manuscript, of which he had many.

The break with Joyce in 1930 saddened him profoundly. Whether or not
he had earned the wrath that made him *'persona non grata* to Joyce',[31] Beckett
'was desolated by his loss of Joyce', but could not reverse or repair the
events that caused it.[32] With hindsight, the rift was a blessing in disguise
for Beckett. Ironically, this became apparent even as he brooded over his
loss. It was 'the bust-up with Shem' that resulted, within weeks, in his
writing *Whoroscope* — as a therapy for the acute depression the banning
from Joyce's home and presence had effected.[33]

Beckett's 'loss of Joyce' meant that he found himself: *his* stream of
consciousness ran faster and deeper, to overtake the Space Age and embrace
the consciousness of all humanity. In whatever genre he chose he could
follow his own teaching in *Proust*:

> The only fertile research is excavatory, immersive, a contraction of
> the spirit, a descent. The artist is active, but negatively, shrinking

from the nullity of extra-circumferential phenomena, drawn into the core of the eddy.[34]

However, his mentor's influence lingered on, with *Dream* and other narratives, rendering to Joyce the sincerest form of flattery, up to the demise of Murphy, the anti-hero of his first novel, *Murphy* (1938).[35]

The Irish Literary Tradition

The Irish Literary Revival made little conscious impression on young Beckett. The trend of his studies and his brief lectureship immersed him in French and Italian literature.

The central tradition of Anglo-Irish literature since 1890 has three compact literary cycles, each of roughly thirty years' duration. The first dynamic and most important phase extended from about 1890 to 1920. Romanticism, idealism, and the reawakening of national cultural consciousness were its spur.[36] The Celtic Revival and the founding of the Abbey Theatre in 1904 mark its main achievements. The second literary phase from 1920 to about 1960 is said to be 'revisionary'.[37] The establishment of the Irish Free State — now the Irish Republic — in 1922, partly realised the dream of nationhood and replaced it with a sober realism. The Irish language revival went on apace, and soon the noble Anglo-Irish dreamers of the Celtic Twilight[38] passed the torch to a new and critical generation of bi-lingual Irish writers.

As J.C.C. Mays explains:

> The prophets of a new nation were overtaken by the critics of it; the influence of Yeats was succeeded by that of Joyce, and as the one was taken as a pastoral dreamer so the other was taken principally to be the author of essays in urban realism. A protestant Ascendancy background was overtaken by a native Catholic one, and prose set the pace.

The third literary phase from 1960 to 1986 cannot yet be fully assessed, but this cycle may well prove as fruitful and dynamic as the first. Possibly, a European dimension will be seen to enrich the bifocal Anglo-Irish traditions. This phase is already distinguished by a creative explosion of new poetry and drama depicting the psychological reality of social change. Its imprint on the banner of literary excellence can only be judged in the perspective of time and space.

Beckett belonged to the second generation of the Irish Literary Revival writers — the critical, even reactionary cohorts led by James Joyce. They regarded W.B. Yeats, Lady Gregory, Douglas Hyde and the rest of the Celtic Twilight visionaries as 'Antiquarians'. Beckett had eminent companions in his protest against the ideals that inspired the writings that initiated the literary movement. His friend Thomas McGreevy and other writers, all of them better known than Beckett was at that time, felt that the Irish Literary Revival was too narrow: the 'tradition' excessively indigenous.

Beckett rejected it outright in his 1934 article, 'Recent Irish Poetry'. But the article betrayed a feature of his dialectic. As Vivian Mercier says: 'It revealed that Beckett knew enough about the Gaelic tradition to mention Oísin, Cuchulain, Maeve, *Tír na nOg*, the *Táin Bó Cuailnge*, and 'the Crone of Beare'... he even quoted the opening words of 'Gile na Gile' ('Brightness of Brightness') in Irish.'[39] This knowledge is reflected frequently in his writings.

This group of critical intellectuals had an alternative tradition that engaged their energies. They wished to revive and expand the Irish-European literary and cultural connection, severed for centuries by an alien Government antipathetic to Irish culture at home, and actively opposed to Irish links with learning abroad.[40] Beckett and McGreevy were, of course, well-read in the French literary tradition, having lived, lectured, and published some of their writings in Paris. They felt drawn to the casual life-style of the literati there. Unencumbered by family, they were 'not tied'[41] to Ireland, where their 'alternative tradition' had no impact on the march of a nation. They took their pens — and Ireland with them — back to Paris, to join Joyce and his circle at the hub of the literary *avant-garde* in the thirties.

The Irish-European literary and cultural connection 'was never the same after that'.[42] Beckett has long since moved the frontiers of that connection beyond Europe to most of the world, and they are still moving.[43]

The French Literary Tradition

The French literary tradition is reflected in every genre of Beckett's work. His very first play in any language, *Le Kid* (1931), a parody of Corneille's *Le Cid* (1636), was written in French, when he was a Lecturer in French at Trinity College, Dublin. Beckett played the part of Le Kid's father, Don Diegue, in the performance by the Modern Language Society at the Peacock Theatre. The first production was 'a howling success', but the furore that followed his Professor's anger over the parody stunted Beckett's obvious talent as a comic actor. The second performance 'was a disaster'.[44]

Beckett's favourite French author was the poet and tragic dramatist, Jean Racine (1639-99). 'Beckett has studied the work of Racine more than that of any other dramatist, Shakespeare included.'[45] Racine's influence is felt in his plays. The circular structure, lack of action, vague location, and the paired characters in *Waiting for Godot*, reflect the classical silhouette of Racine's dramaturgy.

'All creativity consists in making something out of nothing ....' (Tout l'invention consiste à faire quelque chose de rien ....') wrote Racine in the preface to his tragedy Bérénice, in which nothing happens for five acts.[46] This is true of *Waiting for Godot*, 'a play in which nothing happens, *twice.*'[47] The Racinian profile is so clear in Beckett's drama that Mercier styles him 'a latter-day Racine'.[48]

From Racine's 'extremist Jansenism', according to which God is hidden, 'so hidden that it is impossible to know his will' or to have 'the slightest indication of whether we are damned or saved',[49] we follow the trail to Jean-Paul Sartre's Existentialism, shimmering through Beckett's plays.[50] Sartre's masterpiece *Huis clos* (1944) — called *No Exit* in English, *Geschlossene Gesellschaft* in German — has linguistic and structural parallels in *Waiting for Godot*.[51]

Beckett and Sartre had much in common, apart from being contemporaries — Sartre was born in 1905. They were both associated with the Ecole Normale Supérieure in 1928-30, and both were 'on the trot' (Beckett's term for being in the French Resistance) in the war. The philosophers Hegel, Husserl and Heidegger influenced them, Sartre to a greater extent than Beckett. Both dramatists, though by different routes, came to the movement now called The Theatre of the Absurd.[52]

Jules Renard (1864-1910), was one of Beckett's favourite casual writers. Renard's *Journal Intime* gave him ideas that he turned into a technique and 'used later with great success in *Waiting for Godot* and *Krapp's Last Tape*.[53]

His Protestant Heritage

A very important part of Beckett's cultural heritage is his Protestant religion. His pronouncements give the impression that he is, at best, an agnostic.

Denying suggestions of a religious meaning in *Godot*, he said: 'Christianity is a mythology with which I am perfectly familiar, and so I use it. But not in this case!'[54] This may illustrate Beckett's 'fecund double-mindedness',[55] or prove that, 'A Truth in art is that whose contradictory is also true'![56] For none of his plays has more orthodox Christianity in the dialogue and its interpretation than this play, whose characters ponder the purpose of life in relation to the mystery of the first Good Friday. Declan Kiberd said of Beckett, 'As a writer, he is as religious as they come, a man whose entire *corpus* constitutes a latter-day *Book of Job* .... Like all his major works, *Waiting for Godot* is a meditation on the problem of pain and suffering.[57]

Beckett found Irish Protestantism lacking in spiritual depth. 'At the moment of crisis it has no more depth than an old school tie' he said.[58] From the spiritual side of religion Beckett garnered little from 'the piety of his devout mother'.[59] Bair (p. 25) says she:

> gave an impression of religious rigidity to her neighbours and fellow parishioners; ... but her own feelings were governed by the rote performance of ritual observance and not by any true belief.

Whether or not Beckett's lack of 'true belief' merits his designation as 'the atheist from Paris', or 'an agnostic from Dublin',[60] his strict Protestant upbringing in Catholic Ireland left an indelible mark on his psyche. This was compounded by the fact that political upheaval, and reversal of the 'ascendancy' status synonymous with Protestantism, marked a decade in Irish history — 1916-1926 — when Beckett's identity would normally crystallise in the old mould of a minority ruling class. Religious rigidity at home, and nationally the imposition of (to him) an alien if ancient language, culture, and authority, 'have been a formative intellectual influence'.[61] His frustration was later distilled into his writing in variants of protest, parody, and self-pity, ostensibly 'expressed by his characters on behalf of the human race'.[62]

In his work the tenets of the Protestant faith are manifest on three levels basic to his integrity as a writer:

1. His familiarity with the Bible texts, whether he preaches or parodies them. If the latter, his arguments display an even wider knowledge of the historical allegorical meaning of the texts, and of scholarly treatises on them.[63] Yet, his portrayal of God shows that: 'The God of the Bible is, for Beckett, a God of paradox and apocalypse, a *Deus Absconditus* who sends mysterious messengers, perhaps even his son, but never comes Himself.'[64]

2. The Protestant work-ethic — which he scorns. His early fiction — if that is what it was — mocks the morality and dignity of work, the necessity of effort, and the principal of reward.[65] Beckett's heroes are lazy, and spend much time and wit extolling the virtues of indolence. The most obvious one is 'freedom' from the discipline of work, the natural desire for self-sufficiency is appeased, and that can only be 'the Protestant thing to do'.[66] In short, Beckett demythologises the Protestant work-ethic with the mythology of self-sufficiency. It is just one aspect of Beckett's *negative theology.*[67]

In *Waiting for Godot*, idleness is creative; and the wisdom of doing nothing is stressed early in the play. The tramps had just abandoned the idea of hanging themselves 'while waiting',[68] and searching for a suitably effortless way of passing the time till Godot would come:

Vladimir: Well? What do we do?

Estragon: Don't let's do anything. It's safer. (p.18)

Dan Rooney spurned the practice of work, effort, and reward. In 'moments of lucidity' he told himself:

> that by lying at home in bed, day and night, winter and summer, with a change of pyjamas once a fortnight, you would add very considerably to your income.[69]

3. The Puritan conscience — which he cherishes. Beckett confided to his friend, Thomas McGreevy, that an inherited streak of puritanism was 'the straightforward and dominant part of his personality'.[70] His dramatic use of this scion of his Protestant heritage is obvious in the text and technique, and in the ordered presentation of his plays. If the Protestant work-ethic goes against the rhythmic grain of his being, his innate puritanism flows in the stream of consciousness protesting the foibles of man forever striving to be God.

> He writes, he'd have us believe, in a kind of anguished trance; far from being contrived, the fine symmetries grow secretly.[71]

So wrote Hugh Kenner, an old friend of Beckett, on the eve of his eightieth birthday.

Declan Kiberd cites Beckett as the puritan testifier:

> For the Protestant ethic of work, he has substituted the Puritan ethic of relentless self-exploration, and produced the most striking testimony of our times to the need for human sufferings to be at once experienced and unexplained.[72]

This 'relentless self-exploration' forms part of the text in all five plays of this study, but it is most merciless in the one-man plays, where the protagonists are puppets of Beckett himself.[73]

According to Hugh Kenner: 'Beckett's work draws on two spiritual traditions by which history has shaped the specifically Protestant character: the personal testimony, and the issueless confrontation with conscience.[74] 'Confrontation with conscience' is common to all Christians, but its resolution is not. The Catholic confession is a dialogue with a priest, 'a ritual conversation',[75] ending with absolution. The Protestant confession is made to oneself in the form of a monologue, which is unending — 'issueless' without absolution, 'because no man can absolve, and touch with God has either been lost or not initiated'.[76]

A valid confession presupposes an intention of reform ('a firm purpose of amendment'). In Beckett's monologues there are moments of seeming conversion, repentance or regret, discernible in tone or facial expression. But Krapp's last line: 'No, I wouldn't want them back';[77] and Joe's 'little sneer'[78] recant rather than repent of the guilt content of the play. Thus the monologue goes on in the next play, with *Listener* making a final 'general confession', and wondering about 'something the dust said ... come and gone was that it something like that ... come and gone ...'.[79] Was that his absolution?

Furthermore, it is the puritan conscience that dictates:

(a) The symbolic simplicity of his stage settings. They are stripped of all theatrical trappings, 'like bleak low-church altars'.[80]

(b) The economy of language to the point of meanness, and the deliberate difficulties he inserts into the meagre script he presents, which are aspects of his dramatic use of puritanism. He does not suffer the toil of writing so that his readers or audience need make no effort in the realisation of the play. The human condition they depict makes puritans of us all — the suffering of being knows no religious divide.

(c) Lastly, the constant reminder that they are only plays, and that this was a mere lapse in his strict puritan aversion to play-acting, implicit in the grin on the actor's face at the fade-out.

> By breaking the dramatic illusion to exert the actor's self at the expense of his role, these plays articulate the puritan case against *mimesis* in art and remind us of the common puritan fear that the integrity of the self is violated by play acting .... Beckett's plays are a slow-motion re-enactment of the puritan closing-down of the theatres.[81]

NOTES

1 Lucy, Sean (ed.), *Irish Poets in English*, 1973, Mercier Press, Cork and Dublin, pp. 15, 16.

2 Mays, J.C.C., Young Beckett's Irish Roots, *Irish University Review*, Spring 1984 (Special Issue on Samuel Beckett), p. 31.

3 'Samuel Beckett: Nayman of Noland' pp. 80, 81, in Ellman, *Four Dubliners: Wilde, Yeats, Joyce, and Beckett*, Hamish Hamilton, London, 1987, first published in the USA, 1986, by Library of Congress, Washington.

4   The poem is a satire on the life and thought of René Descartes (1596 - 1650). Macabre humour permeates this dramatic monologue. Its grotesque imagery can only provoke a 'hollow laugh'. 'The hollow laugh laughs at that which is not true, it is the intellectual laugh.' *Watt* (Paris 1953), p. 49. See Mercier, Vivian, 'Macabre and Grotesque Humour in the Irish Tradition', in *The Irish Comic Tradition*, Oxford University Press, 1969, pp. 47 - 49.

5   Nancy Cunard and her newly established Hours Press had offered 1000 francs (ten pounds sterling) for the best poem written on the subject of time. Beckett heard about the contest only hours before the deadline of midnight June 15, 1930. He wrote the poem, and walked across Paris to deliver it before dawn. It won him the prize and some publicity.

6   Bair, *Samuel Beckett*, p. 95.

7   Ibid., p. 98. 'Whoroscope' was a pun on the Greek *horo* (hour).

8   He always kept the original French text as a talisman.

9   *The Penguin English Dictionary* (1965), p. 403.

10 *A Reader's Guide to Samuel Beckett*, London, 1973, p. 159.

11 *Irish University Review*, Spring 1984, p. 7.

12 Murray, Patrick, *The Tragic Comedian: A Study of Beckett*, Mercier Press, Cork, 1970, p. 33.

13 Murray, op. cit., p. 40.

14 Bair, *Samuel Beckett*, pp. 130 - 134.

15 Murray, *Tragic Comedian*, p. 36.

16 *Waiting for Godot*, pp. 78 - 84.

17 Just as Lucky was put on a rope by Pozzo (*Godot*, p. 21).

18 Bair, *Samuel Beckett*, p. 66.

19 Ibid.

20 Bair, op. cit., p. 64.

21 Bair, op. cit., p. 66.

22 Ibid.

23 Bair, op. cit., p. 67.

24 Bair, op. cit.

25 *Finnegans Wake*, p. 467.

26 Quoted in Bair, *Samuel Beckett*, p. 130.

27 Bair, op. cit., p. 130.

28 He began it with a novel, *Dream of Fair to Middling Women* (1932), a 'virgin chronicle' he preferred to call it, as it lacked the coherent structure of the novel. This was, until 1993, still a 'trunk' manuscript, being too 'immature and unworthy' for publication. See Bair, op. cit., pp. 129, 130.

29 Bair, op cit., p. 304.

30 In the play he refers to a 'flight' ticket, whereas in fact he did the actual journey by boat, back in 1931.

31 Bair, *Samuel Beckett*, p. 102.

32 Bair, op. cit., pp. 89 - 93.

33 Ibid., 'Joyce, in tones of icy rage, informed Mr Beckett that he was no longer welcome in his home or his presence'.

34 Quoted from Mercier, *Beckett/Beckett*, p. 4.

35 Deane, Seamus, 'Joyce and Beckett', *Irish University Review*, Spring 1984 (Special Issue), pp. 57 - 68.

36 The Celtic Revival was the fruit of political failure to obtain 'Home Rule' for Ireland in 1886. Thwarted in the political field the Irish turned to the revival of their language and culture. That in turn led to the events that won Independence in 1922.

37 Mays, 'Young Beckett's Irish Roots', p. 27. See *Irish Poets in English*, pp. 30 - 33.

38 W.B. Yeats (1865 - 1939) coined the term 'Celtic Twilight'. It was inspired by a poem or ballad by Samuel Ferguson (1810 - 1886) called 'The Fairy Thorn'. The rediscovery of Gaelic literature and folklore following a *silence* that accrued from the Famine of 1845 - 47, inspired the Irish Literary Revival.

39 Mercier, *Beckett/Beckett*, p. 22.

40 Dowling, P.J., *The Hedge Schools of Ireland*, Mercier Press, Cork, 1968, p. 38 - 39.

41 *Waiting for Godot*, p. 20.

42 *That Time*, p. 11.

43 Esslin, Martin, *The Theatre of the Absurd*, London, 1982, p. 39.

44 Bair, *Samuel Beckett*, p. 114.

45 Mercier, *Beckett/Beckett*, p. 74.

46 Ibid.

47 Vivian Mercier's criticism of the play, after a performance at the Pike Theatre, Dublin. The critique was headed 'The Uneventful Event', and appeared in *The Irish Times*, 18 February 1956.

48 Mercier, *Beckett/Beckett*, p. 87.

49 Ibid., p. 82.

50 Esslin, *Theatre of the Absurd*, pp. 22 - 28.

51 Mercier, *Beckett/Beckett*, p. 84.

52 Esslin, *Theatre of the Absurd*, p. 24.

53 Bair, *Samuel Beckett*, pp. 106 - 107.

54 Bair, *Samuel Beckett*, p. 327.

55 Kearney, Richard (ed.), *The Irish Mind*, Wolfhound Press, Dublin, 1985, p. 10.

56 Wilde, Oscar, 'The Truth of Masks', *Complete Works of Oscar Wilde*, Latest reprint, London, 1981, p. 1078.

57 Kiberd, Declan, 'Samuel Beckett and the Protestant Ethic', *The Genius of Irish Prose*, Mercier Press, Dublin, 1985, p. 121.

58 Bair, *Samuel Beckett*, p. 25.

59 Kiberd, op. cit., p. 122.

60 Kearney, 'Beckett: the Demythologising Intellect', in *The Irish Mind*, p. 279.

61 Ibid.

62 Mercier, *Beckett/Beckett*, p. 237.

63 Kearney, *The Irish Mind*, pp. 279-287.

64 Ibid., p. 277.

65 Kiberd, *The Genius of Irish Prose*, pp. 123, 125.

66 *All That Fall*, p. 21. Miss Fitt, forced to support Mrs Rooney on her arm, said (*resignedly*) 'Well, I suppose it is the Protestant thing to do.'

67 Kearney, *The Irish Mind*, p. 278.

68 *Waiting for Godot*, p. 17.

69 *All That Fall*, p. 33.

70 Kiberd, *The Genius of Irish Prose*, p. 127.

71 Kenner, Hugh, 'Beckett at 80', published in A Supplement to *The Irish Times*, Saturday, April 12, 1986. Kenner, a well-known Beckett scholar is author of *A Reader's Guide to Samuel Beckett* (1973).

72 Kiberd, *The Genius of Irish Prose*, pp. 129-30.

73 *Krapp's Last Tape, Eh Joe*, and *Listener* are largely autobiographical.

74 Kenner, *A Reader's Guide to Samuel Beckett*, p. 134.

75 Kiberd, *The Genius of Irish Prose*, p. 127.

76 Kenner, op. cit., p. 134.

77 *Krapp's Last Tape*, p. 20.

78 Under Beckett's direction in the Stuttgart S.D.R. production of *Eh Joe*, about ten years ago, Joe wore 'a little sneer' for the fade-out. It gave another twist to the interpretation of the play.

79 *That Time*, p. 16.

80 Kiberd, *The Genius of Irish Prose*, p. 124.

81 Ibid.

Chapter Three

THE IRISH DIMENSION
IN THE FIVE SELECTED PLAYS

The pervasive Irishness of these five plays is three-dimensional in respect to: Location; Evocation; Language.

Location

Location is not only the geographical locale, or some geological symbol of endurance, e.g. a stone or a cliff that forms the 'setting', but the history, sociology, and cultural minutiae inseparable from it. Stones have a meaning in his plays, as they did in Celtic mythological literature.[1]

Sometimes the location is clearly and correctly stated, e.g. Connemara in *Godot*, or the Portrait Gallery and Foley's Folly in *That Time*. Occasionally, as in *Eh Joe*, Beckett uses the local names for familiar places, like 'the Green' for St. Stephen's Green, Dublin, and 'the Rock' for the White Rock Strand, a popular bathing place in Killiney Bay, near his home.

When the location is too near home, as in *All That Fall*, or the events disclosed are too near his heart, as in *Krapp's Last Tape*, he will disguise the place-name, e.g. Foxrock Station is called 'Boghill'; or leave the precise location vague, as in the Baltic setting of the boat love-scene in *Krapp*. Be it land or seascape,[2] bog,[3] or beach,[4] the location motivates the characters, and inspires their nostalgic yearnings to 'Be again, be again'.[5]

Evocation

Evocation[6] emanates from location, and the people who inhabit that location at a particular moment in time. He also cherishes vivid memories of places and times he roamed alone — or with the family dog. Old Krapp's longing to 'Be again ...' among the scenes (Croghan), the sights (the red-berried holly), and the sounds (church bells), of his youthful wanderings in the Wicklow Mountains,[7] illustrates the inter-relationship between location and evocation in Beckett's Irish plays. Evocation gradually replaced location as his absence from Ireland lengthened; perhaps he was aware, too, that builders and bulldozers were turning parts of his Dublin into a memory.[8]

Yet despite, or because of, his absence from Ireland since 1950 he recalls aspects of his life there with crystal clarity, recording 'memorable' and 'never to be forgotten' events that inspired his writing.[9] At times evocation is so startling that he has to insert a *Not I* formula of denial or diminished guilt.[10] Memory is eventually dimmed by time; and this aspect of the human condition is the theme of the last play of my study — *That Time* (1976).

Language

Beckett turned to play-writing to escape the tedium of prose. 'I began to write *Godot* as a relaxation, to get away from the awful prose I was writing at the time', he said.[11] It is Beckett the poet that comes through in his 'Irish plays', as is manifest in his personal mythology and in his language.

Personal Mythology

On a poet's need of a personal mythology, the poet Brendan Kennelly writes,

> A poet without a myth is a man confronting famine. Like the body,
> the imagination gets tired and hungry: myth is a food, a sustaining
> structure outside the poet that nourishes his inner life and helps him
> to express it.[12]

Beckett's personal mythology is so personal that each of the five plays — in varying degrees autobiographical — is an odyssey in quest of an identity. Yet the identity, the real self he seeks, in expressing 'his inner life', emerges as two selves, their divergence widening with each play, till in *Eh Joe* one self is straining to hear the other. Finally, in *That Time* 'the true-self has split into many other selves',[13] and the myth is indistinguishable from the man.

That is the identity Beckett settled for in the end. The myth gives the man an aura of mystique, which he relishes. He has let it be known that he 'likes all these lies and legends — the more there are, the more interesting I become'.[14]

Poetic Diction

Language is noted as the third dimension of Irishness only because it requires a more comprehensive investigation than do location or evocation. Like these, language is considered separately in each of the five plays. But since language as a first dimension accounts for the *impact* of Beckett's plays,[15] I will outline the general characteristics of that dimension, of which the Irish plays supply the particular.

'Since Beckett is primarily a poet, there is no aspect of his work which is not poetically relevant.' The authors of *The Testament of Samuel Beckett* set down 'three ways in which his poetic sensibility functions': (1) intensification; (2) disparity; (3) intimation.

(1) The poetry of intensification, in which observation is the consuming passion; and 'this is Beckett's closest approach to the poetry of joy':

> Any intense vision celebrates the nature of the thing observed, be that nature what it may. Even if the object of his scrutiny is sombre or revolting, Beckett has here succeeded in escaping the cage of self, in his celebration of *seeing*. ...
>
> The poetry consists not in the poet's own creation drawn from the scene or object described but in the intensification of the thing itself' ...[16]

Examples of this 'celebration of seeing' abound in all five plays. It may mark a climax or turning-point in the character's consciousness, or foreshadow an intensification of the human predicament. Whichever it is, the protagonist and the play are 'never the same after that never quite the same'.[17]

Examples are immediately obvious in:

1. Pozzo's poetic description of the sky, as he 'explained the twilight' with theatrical élan. (Act I). Pozzo came back blind in Act II.[18]

2. Mrs Rooney's lyrical commentary on the view from the station platform. Her celebration of seeing extended to celebration of sight...

> I stand here and see it all with eyes ... (the *voice* breaks) ... through eyes ... oh if you had my eyes ... you would understand ... the things they have seen ... and not turned away ....[19]

3. Krapp's 'vision' on the end of the jetty on 'that memorable night in March' (1946).[20] Inspiration for tomes of creative writing had its

genesis in the celebration of seeing.[21]

4. A sombre instance of the celebration of seeing is the elusive line that hastens the climax of *Eh Joe*: 'Sees from the seaweed the tide is flowing' ...[22] It is decisive in the girl's eventual suicide.

5. Listener's revelation in the Portrait Gallery, as he observed 'a vast oil black with age and dirt ... behind the glass'. When he 'peered' through the glass he was awarded with an apparition that so affected him he was 'never the same after that'.[23]

(2) The poetry of disparity, or antipoetry, 'in which the element of poetry is revealed by the careful use of suitable opposites'.[24] The counterpoint of the poetry of intensification, it appears as an anti-climax, or a series of repetitions with a slight change of emphasis, till, the cycle complete, the original statement seems absurd or insignificant. 'The entire laborious order collapses back into chaos ...' Less subtly but more frequently it marks a raffish display of comedy. 'This is the poetry of the clown; and this is the bulk of Beckett's poetry.'

Traits of the clown are assumed or implied in all five plays, and the poetry of disparity expresses itself in various forms: music-hall banter, nuances of irony and sarcasm, inferences bordering on the macabre. Beckett throws the audience a line of involvement in the form of antipoetry. A veteran director of his plays writes: 'Direct references to the audience abound in some of the plays, usually comments in a vein humorous, and mildly disparaging or sarcastic.'[25] He cites examples from *Waiting for Godot*, which include:

> Estragon (surveying the scene, *with his back to the auditorium.*)
> Estragon: Charming spot. (*He turns, advances to front, facing auditorium.*) Inspiring prospects. (*He turns to Vladimir.*) Let's go.

This is Vladimir's cue to throw the now famous Beckettian line to the whole world: 'We're waiting for Godot'.[26]

All That Fall has no visible audience, but the poetry of disparity pervades the dialogue: 'Beckett wants to offer the ear as much variety as possible'.[27] Language he highlights through a variety of voices, each revealing its owner's character and social tendencies. 'Beckett's brief and pointed characterisations of these people are satiric but not bitter.'[28] Mercier finds 'the closest thing to poetry .... is the long comic speech by Miss Fitt about her absent-mindedness....'[29]

> Ah yes, I am distray, very distray, even on week-days, Ask Mother, if you do not believe me. Hetty, she says, when I start eating my

doily instead of the thin bread and butter, Hetty, how can you be so distray?...[30]

Krapp's Last Tape has bitter lines that enshrine in the poetry of disparity the haunting memory of his mother's death. The ledger entry ('at foot of page') reads: 'Mother at rest at last ... Hm ... The black ball ....'[31] Krapp-39, sitting by the canal, saw the blind in his mother's room go down. He was 'throwing a ball for a little white dog, as chance would have it'.

> I happened to look up and there it was. All over and done with, at last. I sat on for a few moments with the ball in my hand and the dog yelping and pawing at me. (*Pause.*) Moments. Her moments, my moments. (*Pause.*) The dog's moments. (*Pause.*) In the end I held it out to him and he took it in his mouth, gently, gently. A small, old, black, hard, solid rubber ball. (*Pause.*) I might have kept it. (*Pause.*) But I gave it to the dog.[32]

Eh Joe has its most sardonic lines of antipoetry concentrated in Move 5:

> How's your Lord these days? ... Still worth having? ... Very fair health for a man of your years ... Just that lump in your bubo ... Till one night ... 'Thou fool thy soul' ... Put your thugs on that ... [33]

That Time has examples of the poetry of disparity in that all three sets of passages A B C end with an anti-climax. Symbolic are these lines in the romantic B passage:[34]

> ... alone on the towpath with the ghosts of the mules the drowned rat or bird or whatever it was floating off into the sunset till you could see it no more ... (p. 14)

(3) The poetry of intimation, ... 'in which a shadow or an echo implies what is not stated.'

> Its chief characteristic is a sense of advent — of something larger, more significant, more revealing than anything we have so far been told, which is about to occur.[35]

The language is that of the poetry of intensification; 'but there is here a shadow, a stillness, a kind of preparation'. The fact that it is a preparation for something which does not occur 'makes it only more distinct'. A quality common to all the passages of intimation, is 'the absence of something foreshadowed'.[36]

This 'shadow' or an 'echo' can be conveyed by a *phrase* or a *word*. 'The poetry forms from the phrases' echo'.[37] Every 'little canter'[38] in the dialogue of *Waiting for Godot* glows with the poetry of intimation. One of these, a poet writes, 'achieves the condition of music; it is sublime ...'[39]

> Estragon: All the dead voices.

Vladimir: They make a noise like wings.
Estragon: Like leaves.
Vladimir: Like sand.
Estragon: Like leaves.
Silence.
Vladimir: They all speak together.
Estragon: Each one to itself.
Silence.
Vladimir: Rather they whisper.
Estragon: They rustle.
Vladimir: They murmur.
Estragon: They rustle.
Silence. (pp. 62, 63)

In *All That Fall*, Schubert's *Death and the Maiden* is the intimation, the shadow, and in retrospect the echo of the plot.[40] The musical image, recalled three times in different contexts, 'contributes to the building of a compound image of the death of daughters'.[41] The imagination returns to that image after Dan's laconic line: 'Nip some young doom in the bud' (p. 31).

Krapp's Last Tape has a passage where the 'luminance of intimation'[42] emanates from the image of a lover's eyes: 'one of his favourite images as an artist is that of the human eye'.[43]

Krapp: ... The eyes she had!... Everything there .... Everything there, everything on this old muckball, all the light and dark and famine and feasting of ... (*hesitates*) ... the ages! (p. 18)

In *Eh Joe* the 'sense of advent' is clear, as the Voice echoes Krapp's tribute to 'the eyes she had!' (Move 7). It foreshadows the final scene in Move 9.

... The green one ... The narrow one ... Always pale ... The pale eyes
... Spirit made light ... To borrow your expression ... ... Eh Joe? ...
There was love for you ... (p. 19)

That Time exemplifies the poetry of intimation, in that it demonstrates more forcibly and poignantly than any of the other plays the quality common to all of them — 'the absence of something foreshadowed': each intent as unreachable as 'the glider passing over ....'[44]

Meaning and Mutability

Within this poetic triangle, in the theatre Beckett uses language as he uses lighting, to create an illusion of reality. Conversely, he uses language to depict reality as a shifting mirage, elusive as the self split into perceiver and perceived, changing from moment to moment; hence capable of communicating only 'the experience of a single moment in the fullness of its emotional intensity, its existential totality'.[45] Esslin praises Beckett as one who restores 'one's faith in the power of the dedicated pursuit of truth and beauty'.[46]

How Beckett's language bends the truth he purports to seek, is expressed variously by other writers thus: 'Beckett's writing is calculated to arouse indecision in the reader.'[47] One of the many examples of this in *Waiting for Godot* is Vladimir's version of the Crucifixion, insisting that the four Evangelists 'were there — or thereabouts — and only one speaks of a thief being saved'.[48]

His words are 'shifty', writers affirm:

> If the single meaning of any word in Beckett is suspect, the key words shift their sense as a diamond shifts its colour. An example of this is the title of his most famous play.

They expand on this phenomenon, saying,

> So compelled is he by the echoes, facets, and refractions of words that they writhe in his grasp like mythical monsters; they reverse themselves, shift, and realign their letters.[49]

An illustration of this in his most famous play is: '... Godin ... Godet ... Godot ...'[50] Stressing Beckett's devious ways with words, they maintain that:

> Words are unreliable, as puns, as sounds. Also, as echoes. ...
> ... Beckett plays the old game of a word repeated until it ceases to mean, until it becomes a sound.[51]

All these comments on Beckett's words are verified in his own; with a faint strain of truth and beauty coming through them, too.

On Beckett's relationship with words, Beckett has the last word:

> Over, over, there is a soft place in my heart for all that is over, no, for the being over, I love the word, words have been my only loves, not many. Often all day long as I went along I have said it, and sometimes I would be saying vero, oh vero ...[52]

Within this professed passion for words Beckett's other literary idiosyncrasies are manifest. As Seamus Deane put it:

> The ramifications of his sentences — statements countered by negatives, reservations, denials, interruptions and digressions — lead the reader into a labyrinth from which there is no escape because, even when the speaker changes, he reproduces the same sort of maze built around the same never-ending themes.[53]

In the context, 'over' *adverb*, means ended; past; finished. But that would make the statement too clear-cut and final to articulate the Beckettian 'logic of ambivalence'.[54] He shifts the sense of 'over' meaning ended/finished — as a diamond shifts its colour — to 'being over', which must mean: not ended or finished. 'The compulsion to stop is also a symptom of the dedication to going on.'[55]

'The being over' is a metaphor for the succession of endings that constitute life for Beckett's protagonists. 'Being over' is a verbal variation of *For To End Yet Again* (1976).[56] This is an unpunctuated repetitious *fizzle*, depicting the mirage of reality flickering in a distant desert between earth and sky. A sequence of diminishing images represent reality melting into memory. Memory withers into litter[57] ('the dung litter of laughable memory'), and soon becomes one with the grey dust of the desert sand.

In the compressed text, the line between reality and fantasy diminishes too, till like a Fata Morgana they dissolve, as they began, in the dark doubt of the mind ...

> For to end yet again skull alone in the dark the void no neck no face
> just the box last place of all in the dark the void.[58]

Possibly, *For To End Yet Again* is a postscript to *Watt* (1944).[59] Like the novel, the fizzle illustrates 'the dual impossibility of reducing reality to words and of transcending words towards reality.'[60]

Alec Reid writes: 'As a rule, Beckett's characters use ordinary words and short sentences.'[61] An exception to the latter is the unpunctuated text of *That Time*, where the sentences are as long as the play. Beckett uses 'ordinary words' with multiple nuances of meaning, contrived by puns,[62] word patterns,[63] and 'dissociated metaphor'[64] that keep the dialogue taut and intellectually demanding.

'Dissociated metaphor: metaphor that is never apparent and sometimes carefully disguised'[65] lies concealed in the text of each play. The construction is devised from a limited vocabulary in which certain key words are repeated so as to create a magical (poetic) aura around the text. Mostly, they are words of sensory significance like feel,[66] touch,[67] hands,[68] eyes,[69] or heart, head, and feet. Occasionally, they are words of seeming insignificance such as 'bog' and 'Board' in *Waiting for Godot*.[70]

Beckett's dramatic recycling of words — his much criticised *repetition* — keeps the audience *involved*, yet free to 'create' the play, each in the light of his own experience. Martin Esslin's comment on compression in Beckett's poetry can apply to his plays:

> A single line may carry multiple meanings, public and private allusions, description and symbol, topographic reference, snatches of overheard conversation, fragments in other languages, Provencal or German, the poet's own asides ... learned literary allusions together with brand names of cigarettes or shop signs in Dublin. Four

lines may thus require four pages of elucidation, provided, that is, that the full information were at hand ...[71]

The research on the inspirational and territorial background of the five selected plays examined here is an endeavour to provide some of that necessary information.

NOTES

1 See Appendix II, 'Stone in the Mythology of Ireland'.

2 *That Time*, pp. 11, 13.

3 *Godot*, p. 15.

4 *Eh Joe*, p. 21.

5 *Krapp's Last Tape*, p. 19.

6 A calling forth or out; summoning; an evoking. To evoke: to call forth or out — from the Latin *e*, out + *voco*, call. Reviving memories of places, etc.

7 *Krapp's Last Tape*, p. 19. See O'Brien, *The Beckett Country*, p. 71.

8 This is depicted realistically in *That Time*.

9 *Krapp's Last Tape*, pp. 15, 16.

10 In *Not I* (1973), the narrator, although telling her own story of her life, does not use the first person pronoun, but speaks of 'she', thereby detaching herself from the autobiographical facts she relates. See Bair, *Samuel Beckett*, pp. 524, 525.

11 Cohn, Ruby, *Back to Beckett*, Princeton, N.J., 1976, p. 129.

12 Kennelly, Brendan (ed.), *The Penguin Book of Irish Verse*, 1970, p. 42.

13 Wakeling, 'Looking at Beckett – The man and the writer', *Irish University Review*, Spring 1984, p. 16.

14 Bair, *Samuel Beckett*, p. 13.

15 Cohn, *Back to Beckett*, p. 272.

16 Jacobsen, Josephine, & Mueller, William R., *The Testament of Samuel Beckett*, London, 1966, pp. 49, 51.

17 *That Time*, p. 11.

18 *Waiting for Godot*, pp. 37 - 39, 77.

19 *All That Fall*, pp. 23, 24.

20 *Krapp's Last Tape*, pp. 15, 16.

21 Bair, *Samuel Beckett*, pp. 298, 301.

22 *Eh Joe*, p. 20.

23 *That Time*, pp. 10, 11.

24 Jacobsen and Mueller, *Testament of Samuel Beckett*, pp. 49, 55.

25 Barnes, Ben (Resident Director of the Abbey Theatre), 'Aspects of Directing Beckett', *Irish University Review*, Spring 1984, p. 72.

26 *Waiting for Godot*, pp. 13, 14.

27 Mercier, *Beckett/Beckett*, p. 148.

28 Lyons, Charles R., *Samuel Beckett*, London, 1983, p. 77.

29 Mercier, op. cit., p. 148.

30 *All That Fall*, p. 20.

31 *Krapp's Last Tape*, p. 11.

32 Ibid., p. 15.

33 *Eh Joe*, pp. 18, 19.

34 In the B passages that concern young love, he introduces the incongruous imagery of 'the dead rat' (p. 12), and 'the drowned rat floating off into the sunset' (p. 14). For the symbolism of rats see — *Brewer's Dictionary of Phrase and Fable*, p. 749. Like a drowned rat means looking exceedingly dejected. Ibid. As Listener was 'alone on the towpath' — the girl had vanished — he probably was feeling exceedingly dejected.

35 Jacobsen and Mueller, *Testament of Samuel Beckett*, p. 49.

36 Ibid., p. 59.

37 Ibid., p. 50.

38 *Waiting for Godot*, p. 65.

39 Derek Mahon, 'A Noise Like Wings: Beckett's Poetry', *Irish University Review*, Spring 1984, pp. 91, 92.

40 Bair, *Beckett*, p. 403.

41 Lyons, *Samuel Beckett*, p. 87.

42 Jacobsen and Mueller, *The Testament of Samuel Beckett*, p. 50.

43 Mercier, *Beckett/Beckett*, p. 131.

44 *That Time*, p. 15.

45 Esslin, *The Theatre of the Absurd*, p. 91.

46 Esslin, Martin, *Meditations: Essays on Brecht, Beckett, and the Media*, London, 1980, p. 109.

47 Deane, Seamus, 'Joyce and Beckett', *Irish University Review*, Spring 1984. Special Issue, p. 59.

48 *Godot*, p. 12. Beckett knows full well that not one of the Evangelists was there, in the sense of being present. The Gospels were written much later, the earliest in AD 70.

49 Jacobsen and Mueller, *The Testament of Samuel Beckett*, pp. 31-33.

50 *Waiting for Godot*, p. 36.

51 Jacobsen and Mueller, op. cit., p. 33.

52 *From an Abandoned Work*, (1956); *Breath and Other Short Stories*, (1971), Faber and Faber, London, p. 47.

53 Deane, 'Joyce and Beckett', *Irish University Review*, p. 65.

54 Kearney, *The Irish Mind*, p. 14.

55 Deane, op. cit., p. 65.

56 Written in French in 1975 and first published as *Pour finir encore* by Editions de

Minuit in 1976, it belongs to the group of short texts Beckett called his *Foirades* or *Fizzles*, when he translated them into English. First published in English, 1976, John Calder Ltd., London.

57 Ibid., p. 13.

58 Ibid., p. 11.

59 Bair, *Samuel Beckett*, pp. 278 - 281.

60 Kearney, *The Irish Mind*, p. 291.

61 Reid, Alec, *All I Can Manage, More Than I Could: An Approach to the Plays of Samuel Beckett*, Dublin, 1968, p. 24.

62 Jacobsen and Mueller, *The Testament of Samuel Beckett*, p. 32.

63 Deane, 'Joyce and Beckett', *Irish University Review*, Spring 1984, p. 65.

64 O'Connor, Frank, *A Short History of Irish Literature*, New York, 1967, p. 200.

65 Ibid.

66 *Krapp's Last Tape* (the scene with the ball), p. 15.

67 *Eh Joe*, p. 21.

68 Ibid.

69 Mercier, *Beckett/Beckett*, Chapter 6 Eye/Ear, pp. 118 - 159.

70 This example of 'dissociated metaphor' is explained under *Language* in *Waiting for Godot*, later in this work.

71 Esslin, *Meditations*, p. 11. See O'Brien, *The Beckett Country*, pp. xx, xxi.

Chapter Four

WAITING FOR GODOT

Waiting for Godot (1952), Beckett's most famous play, was written between October 9, 1948 and January 29, 1949, as a brief respite from the tedium of the novels he was writing at the time.[1] He found the change to writing for the stage 'a marvellous, liberating diversion'.[2] To flee 'the impasse of self-confrontation and revelation into which his novels had led him',[3] to freelance fantasy; to drink from the wishing well of his mind the curative water of hope that, 'Tomorrow everything will be better',[4] was such an act of gay abandon that he called the play, 'a tragicomedy in two acts'. The tragedy was, of course, the human condition, worsening despite 'the strides of physical culture',[5] sport, medicine and philosophy.[6] Comedy was a synonym for waiting for the miracle which tomorrow must bring. The action in the play — the antics they play to fill the void[7] till tomorrow comes — was calculated to 'recreate a circus-cum-vaudeville atmosphere in a dramatic experience of total simplicity ... he wanted it to be good commercial theatre, traditional yet different and effective.'[8] By contrast, the dialogue is not simple, nor particularly funny, despite 'certain crudities of language' which Beckett likes so much that he 'would not consent to their being changed or removed.'[9]

Originally written in French, *En Attendant Godot* 'sprang full bloom from Beckett's head in a very short time'. According to his biographer, it was written at a time during which Beckett wanted something very much and wished for time to pass. 'With the play, he was killing time until both publishers and the public would recognise the importance of his fiction.' For him, writing is like a game, 'much like chess: plotting moves, foreseeing changes and intellectualising interactions'.[10] No wonder both Acts end in checkmate![11]

Writing about reality (waiting), as if it were fantasy, Beckett discovered a fact he exploited in later plays:

> ... that the presentation of any event as if it were theatre creates theatre; the frame of the stage is almost all that is needed to give symbolic power to the inconsequent, the casual, the insignificant.[12]

This dramatic tactic gives the play a textual lightness and thematic simplicity absent in his novels. However, the apparent banality of parts of the dialogue stems from his plotting moves to keep the script surface slippery for the clown image to uphold the tradition of the Absurd.[13]

How the play recaptures the tradition of the Absurd will be considered later. Notable is the fact that its initial rejection and subsequent acclaim represent a progress record on the popular acceptance of:

> the philosophy of the Theatre of the Absurd, in which the world is seen as a hall of reflecting mirrors, and reality merges imperceptibly into fantasy.[14]

This fascinating play, written while waiting, about waiting, now became a metaphor on waiting, and soon Beckett experienced the suffering of being a playwright. Waiting for publication meant accepting rejections.[15]

It was published by Les Editions de Minuit, Paris, in 1952, and first published in English by Grove Press, New York, 1954, with changes and polish incorporated by Beckett into his own English translation. By the time the definitive edition appeared in 1965, the play had been refined and revised on stage and in print over some sixteen years.

Waiting for production was a dénouement worthy of a play in itself. Six producers said 'No' to *Godot*, the last two 'calling it among other things, in-comprehensible, boring, too highbrow or too deep'.[16] The seventh, ac-tor-producer Roger Blin, 'expressed cautious interest in the play'. He did not understand *Waiting for Godot*, but he liked it. Nevertheless Beckett could envisage 'indefinite periods of waiting while Blin scoured Paris for money and a theatre, with no guarantee of success'.[17]

In the summer of 1950 Blin and Beckett met for the first time, to talk about the play. At first, Blin wanted to stage *Godot* as a circus, for his initial reading of the play merely registered images of clowns. 'The dialogue, which he called '*oui-non*', reminded him of circus one-liners, and he thought a circus would insure the necessary understanding his actors would need to bring to such a play.' Beckett could no more contemplate the idea than argue with Blin and 'upset a still delicate relationship'.[18] He guided the conversation from stage clowns to stage playboys. Blin had appeared in a French production of the renowned *Playboy of the Western World*,[19] and in their shared admiration for Synge's play they returned to *Godot*. The circus idea had evaporated. Deirdre Bair writes:

> At this point, it suddenly occurred to Blin that a circus would not only cost more money than he could ever hope to scrape together, but would also distract from the pathos and humour of the action unfolding on the stage and what should be paramount in the audience's mind — the dialogue.[20]

In late 1951, with *Godot* still in search of a theatre, Beckett sent typescripts of the play to more than thirty theatre directors in and around Paris without success. On January 29, 1952, Blin's financial hurdle was cleared by a letter from the Minister of Arts and Letters, offering him a grant of 750,000 francs to facilitate the production of what he called 'an astonishing play'.

Productions and Reception

The first production, on January 5, 1953, was at the tiny Théâtre de Babylone, on the Boulevard Raspail. It was directed by Roger Blin, who also played Pozzo.[21] Beckett, co-director from the beginning of the rehearsals, escaped to his country home at Ussy to 'face his opening night jitters' there. After that, avoiding first night performances of his play became a tradition for him. The little theatre (now defunct), with only 230 folding chairs, was full to capacity, for word had got round the Left Bank literati that it was 'an experience not to be missed'.[22]

Those who did not miss the experience did not quite know what they had experienced — a hoax, a scandal or an outrage! Roger Blin was besieged by a public demanding to know 'What does it mean!'[23] The reaction of the Paris audience to the first production is recalled by Martin Esslin:

> Beckett first aroused attention by a *succès de scandale*. ...Was it not an outrage that people could be asked to come to see a play that could not be anything but a hoax, a play in which nothing whatever happened! People went to see the play just to be able to see that scandalous impertinence with their own eyes and to be in a position to say at the next party that they had actually been the victims of that outrage.[24]

Meanwhile, Beckett remained secluded in Ùssy for two weeks after the first performance, resolutely refusing to face the press or the public. His only regret about that performance was that his stage directions had been modified: Estragon 'had only dropped his trousers as far as his hips, thus undercutting the effectiveness of Vladimir's admonition that he should raise them'.[25] (The last few lines of Act II). In a hastily written letter to Blin, Beckett complained:

> One thing troubles me, the pants of Estragon ... he keeps them half on. He mustn't. He absolutely mustn't. It doesn't suit the circumstances. As for the laughter which would greet their complete fall, there is nothing to object to in the great gift of this touching final tableau ... The spirit of the play, to the extent to which it has one, is that nothing is more grotesque than the tragic.... Just be good enough to reestablish it as it is in the text... that the pants fall completely around the ankles. That might seem stupid to you but for me it's capital.[26]

Blin and Latour (Estragon) complied, and from the second performance the pants fell to his ankles exactly as directed in the text.

The French cast in that memorable production was:

Pozzo — Roger Blin
Vladimir — Lucien Raimbourg
Estragon — Pierre Latour
Lucky — Jean Martin

Serg Lecointe played the small boy. The cast, like the setting, was determined by the lack of money. The entire production was a marvel of ingenuity, simplicity and improvisation.[27] The play ran for four hundred performances at the Théâtre de Babylone, and was later transferred to another Parisian theatre.

The first British production, at the Arts Theatre Club, London, on August 3, 1955, was directed by Peter Hall. It followed a long battle with the Lord Chamberlain who took offence at certain words in the text, and insisted they be changed or removed.[28] To secure his eventual approval Beckett compromised with the Lord Chamberlain — 'Fartov' became 'Popov' and Mrs Gozzo had 'warts' instead of 'clap'. Beckett resisted several deletions, and remained adamant that 'the pants of Estragon' should drop to the ankles in the final tableau. Soon afterwards the Lord Chamberlain was dropped, too, on a consensus that official censorship of literature was an anachronism.[29]

As in Paris, the cast comprised able people who were not among the leading actors in the English theatre at the time. The Knight-actors refused to take part in the play.[30] With hindsight it is symbolic — though certainly unintentional — that Peter Hall, going beyond Beckett's directions for the décor, 'added a dustbin and miscellaneous rubbish to the required tree'.[31] Another timorous innovation was that he titled and typed Vladimir and Estragon as 'tramps'.[32] The tramp stamp, which is reductive and misleading, has adhered to their image ever since.

Peter Bull, who played Pozzo, described the first night:

> Waves of hostility came whirling over the footlights, and the mass exodus, which was to form such a feature of the run of the piece, started quite soon after the curtain had risen ...

The entire popular press dismissed the play as rubbish. Milton Shulman of the *Evening Standard* headed his review, 'Last Night's Theatre, Duet for Two Symbols'. He said it was 'another of those plays that lift superficially to significance through obscurity ... his symbols are seldom more demanding than a nursery version of Pilgrim's Progress' (London, August 1955). *Punch* deemed it 'a bewildering curiosity' (10 August 1955). *The Daily Telegraph* (London, August 1955), headed the critique, 'Obscure Play is Oddly Moving; West End Transfer'; yet W.A. Darlington called it 'admirable as a serious highbrow frolic, but would not do for the serious play-going public.

Beckett, in Ussy, received the first reviews the day after they appeared. He wrote to McGreevy:

> The shopkeepers seem to be making mincemeat of London. ... I am tired of the whole thing and the endless misunderstanding. Why do people have to complicate a thing so simple I can't make out![33]

Within days, reports by two leading English theatre critics swayed public opinion, and sent people flocking to the theatre to see *Godot*. In an article called 'New Writing', Kenneth Tynan wrote in the *Observer*, 7 August 1955: 'It will be conversational necessity for many years to have seen *Waiting for Godot*.' Harold Hobson, writing in the *Sunday Times*, London, 7 August 1955, called his piece, 'Tomorrow', and said: 'Go and see *Waiting for Godot*. At the worst you will discover a curiosity, a four-leaved clover, a black tulip; at the best something that will securely lodge in a corner of your mind for as long as you live.' Beckett called Hobson's review touching and courageous, and said he read it with emotion.[34] On 12 September, the play moved to the Criterion Theatre, and attracted capacity audiences until May 1956.

In December 1955, Beckett was in London, and saw every performance for five successive nights, together with the American, Alan Schneider, who was to direct the Miami production in the New Year. Schneider wrote:

> My fondest memories are of Sam's clutching my arm from time to time and in a clearly-heard stage whisper saying: 'It's ahl wrahng!

He's doing it ahl wrahng!' about a particular bit of stage business or the interpretation of a certain line ...[35]

On January 3, 1956, *Godot* opened in Miami at the height of the holiday season. Directed by Alan Schneider, and produced by Michael Myerberg who had advertised the play as 'the laugh sensation of two continents', there were great expectations among the glittering audience, which included Tennessee Williams.

By the end of the first act two-thirds of the audience had left. The next day a queue formed early at the box office, not to buy tickets but to demand refunds. The press reflected the hostility openly displayed by the audience. The mildest report, in the Miami *Herald*, was headed 'Mink clad audience disappointed in *Waiting for Godot*'. After two weeks Myerberg cancelled the show. He fired Alan Schneider. It was later he learned that it was not the direction that was 'ahl wrahng', but the audience who 'expected a farcical comedy, which *Waiting for Godot* of course is not.'

Undaunted and wiser, Myerberg took the play to New York in the spring. There he sought an entirely different audience. In the *New York Times* he appealed for seven thousand intellectuals to support the play, saying: 'This is a play for the thoughtful and discriminating theatregoer.... I respectfully suggest that those who come to the theatre for casual entertainment do not buy a ticket for this attraction.' The play ran for more than one hundred performances, to audiences who stayed after it ended for panel discussions of the play's meaning.

Waiting for Godot had its Irish première at the Pike Theatre, Dublin, on October 28, 1955. Directed by Alan Simpson, the play was presented neat from Beckett's pen; not, as in London, from the blue pencil of the Lord Chamberlain. Beckett's 'crudities of language' were retained; the 'artistic integrity of the piece' was preserved; and the 'integral performance'[36] Beckett wanted was realised. A critic conceded that the Pike, in contrast to the London production, followed the text with 'pious exactitude'.[37]

Simpson gave the production a distinctively Irish atmosphere: Vladimir and Estragon cantering 'in broad Dublin dialect', and the character of Pozzo interpreted as an Anglo-Irish gentleman. The critical comment on this was:

> ... It sounded strange at first and the laughs seemed to come more from the intonation than the text, but the added humour helped the audience to bear the more searing portions of the play...

Questioning Simpson's innovation, the critic goes on:

> It seems evident that the author had in mind a universal rather than a regional application of his vision of mankind in perpetual

expectation, desperately endeavouring to fill the hiatus between birth and death.[38]

To accord with the socio-historical casting of Pozzo, Lucky wore the cast-off footman's livery of the Georgian age.

The cast in that first Irish production was:

Pozzo — Nigel Fitzpatrick
Vladimir — Dermot Kelly
Estragon — Austin Byrne
Lucky — Donal Donnelly
A Boy — Seamus Fitzmaurice

The Pike production was an extraordinary success. The play ran on into the spring, with more than a hundred performances at the Pike Theatre.[39] It transferred to the larger Gate Theatre for a short run, before going on a tour of eight towns and cities throughout the country. It finished up at Dun Laoghaire on June 10, with a record of over one hundred and fifty performances, during which Lucky was played by five different actors; Pozzo and the Boy by two each.

The Irish dimension in Simpson's interpretation of *Godot* led inevitably to the play being translated into Irish. Beckett was 'unexpectedly pleased about this'.[40] In November 1971, Alan Simpson directed the Irish translation — *Ag Fanacht Le Godot* — by Liam O'Briain and Seán O' Carra, in the national Gaelic theatre, Galway. It was later played at the Peacock[41] in Dublin, 26 - 27 February 1972.

The production of *Ag Fanacht Le Godot* was just as successful as the original *Waiting for Godot* that naturally reached a wider public. A writer who has seen both, reporting on the Irish *Godot*, says: 'I can say that Simpson brought out the lyricism and the humour of the play in a restrained, homely manner: it was a warm, unsophisticated but moving production.'[42] The performance was reviewed in the *Irish Times* of March 1, 1972 by Dominic O'Riordáin. He was impressed with how well the play translated, in rhythm and diction. Writing in Irish, he made an interesting observation, which translates:

Until I saw *Godot* in Irish I didn't properly understand how exactly Beckett takes hold of the Irish literary heritage. Because he is the (legendary) clever craftsman of humour, humour sexual and macabre, as ancient as the *Tain* and as fresh as *Finnegans Wake*.[43]

The privilege of a producer or director, to present *Waiting for Godot* as he understands the text, accounts for the varying interpretations it has survived in the thirty-three years of international presentation. Directors continue to experiment with Beckett's 'curiosity', finding new depths of wisdom and wit in the simplicity of the Absurd where 'The clown is scholar; the scholar clown.'[44]

The Berlin Schiller Theatre presented the definitive *Godot* at the Abbey Theatre, Dublin, on April 17, 1977. That interpretation 'made mime supreme, and dialogue simply a part of the symbiotic whole', reported the *Irish Times* next day.[45] *Mime* secured audience involvement in the creation[46] of the play. The dialogue, in German, came over as *verbal nonsense*, another essential of the Absurd.[47] The novel performance was well received.

Innovations in a 1982 Dublin production by Director Ben Barnes revealed the 'absurd' simplicity of some sections of *Godot*.[48] Looking for the physical rather than literary meaning, seemingly unimportant lines were given significance and a viable interpretation.[49]

Waiting for Godot, described by its author as 'a play that is striving all the time to avoid definition',[50] has inspired countless attempts at definition; but no definitive key has yet come from the swelling ranks of Beckett scholars. One of them stated: 'No key exists that will unlock the enigmas of this play'.[51] It is a statement as defeatist as Estragon's opening line — 'Nothing to be done', and prompts Vladimir's reply — ...'be reasonable, you haven't yet tried everything' (p. 9).

His biographer says: 'It is difficult to say which came first, the play or the title.' 'Beckett will never discuss the implications of the title.' His answers to theories about its meaning eliminated a few of them at the outset: 'If I knew who Godot was, I would have said so in the play', or, 'If Godot were God, I would have called him that'. He is insistent that the name did not come to him through other famous playwrights: Balzac, Strindberg, W.B. Yeats. In short, he claims 'Godot' as his own brainchild, and insists — 'I meant what I said' (in the play).[52]

In *The Testament of Samuel Beckett* we read:
> ... Beckett's titles are often intimately associated with the nature of his revelation. A name, thus, is more than a name; it intimates an entire revelation, a mysterious knowledge implicit in, but not defined by, the name itself. Beckett's titles intimate tone, mood, orientation. The pun or wordplay is a defiant clue.[53]

Beckett's two literary masters, Marcel Proust (1871-1922)[54] and James Joyce (1882-1941), explored the mystery of Time. In praise of both, Marcel Brion, one of Joyce's twelve apostles,[55] contributing to *Our Exagmination*, wrote that Proust: '... made of time the essential dimension of his work

— *temps perdu* and *temps retrouvé* .... In his books time is a character like the others — I might even say more than the others. Time is at the centre of his work like a sort of lighthouse with turning signals....'[56] Showing how *Ulysses* (1922) elucidates 'the mystery of the relativity of time', he continues:

> If time remains external to Proust, if he gives it an existence apart,
> isolated from his characters, for Joyce, on the contrary, it remains
> the inseparable factor, the primary element at the base of his work.
> This is why he creates his own time, as he creates his vocabulary and
> his characters.[57]

Beckett forged these two 'received' techniques into a new dramatic instrument,[58] within the fluid form of the Theatre of the Absurd. As in Proust, in this play, time is a character like the others — even more than the others. He named this character with a Joycean pun on the Irish word for endless time — Go deo — Godot — Eternity. ('The pun or wordplay is a defiant clue.')

Having launched the word 'Godot', Beckett could do anything he liked with it! He could mould the word and the audience as he wished, using 'Godot' like a Juggler's patois, while striving all the time to avoid definition of it. He took the audience on a theatrical paper-chase, laying one false trail after another, up to the end of each Act, when words reverse their meaning:

> Estragon: Well, shall we go?
> Vladimir: Yes, let's go.
> *They do not move.* (p. 54)
> Act I
> Vladimir: Well? shall we go?
> Estragon: Yes, let's go.
> *They do not move.* (p. 94)
> Act II

Thus, by instinct or intent, Beckett upheld a basic tenet of the Theatre of the Absurd, namely, that 'what *happens* on the stage transcends, and often contradicts, the *words* spoken by the characters'.[59]

Location

Waiting for Godot is not a conventional play, in which characters relate to one another within a chosen plot, setting, and code of behaviour. It is as if Beckett is playing it by ear all the time. The setting is nowhere and every-where — a road, a tree, a bog. It is so vague, they even argue as to whether it is a tree, a bush or a shrub, for the leaves are dead. The outlook is bleak

as they try to find their bearings, and reason out[60] why they are there.
The undifferentiated landscape of *Godot* holds no detail that would
give Vladimir or Estragon a personal connection to the location.[61]

Location must be gleaned from the dialogue: a character recalls other
places, and their imprint on this consciousness. For the Irish location, Lucky
has very clear recollections of Connemara — 'abode of stones ... the air the
earth the sea ... (p. 44) the skull in Connemara ... (pp. 44, 45). Connemara is
the western portion of Co. Galway, extending from Lough Corrib to the
Atlantic (27 miles long, variable breadth — maximum 7 miles — covering
68 square miles). It is a region of outstanding beauty. Half of Lucky's
garbled speech proclaims its superb scenic grandeur.[62] It has inspired many
famous paintings.

Lucky's raving is Beckett's reminiscence of the fantastic scenic diversity
of the Connemara landscape. His lines accord with the actual physical
features that make it famous. They may sound chaotic but they ring true.
Connemara — 'abode of stones who can doubt it ...' (p. 44).

The 'capital' of Connemara is called Clifden — the anglicised form of *An
Clochán* — *The Stepping Stones*. 'Steinweg and Peterman'[63] now come to
light: they follow the first reference to Connemara in his crazy speech.
Granite, a plutonic rock, underlies the lowlands of the region.[64] Quartzite,
a metamorphic rock, forms the conical peaks of the Twelve Bens.[65] This
group of twelve mountains occupying a circular area, six miles in diameter,
is the dominant feature of the Connemara landscape. The Twelve Bens are
bounded on their southern and eastern sides by a chain of lakes.

Lucky's lines pick out details of lake and mountain scenery, and his
jumbled images reflect the process of their creation and formation.[66]

> ... plunged in fire whose fire flames ... will fire the firmament that is
> to say blast hell to heaven so blue still and calm... (p. 43).

Intimating the scenic area around *Recess*,[67] he refers to the great glaciated
valley of Glen Inagh:

> ... in the plains in the mountains by the seas by the rivers running
> water running fire the air is the same ...
> ... and then the earth in the great cold the great dark the air and the
> earth abode of stones in the great cold... (p. 44).

Recess has Connemara green marble quarries,[68] to which Lucky dedicates
one line: 'the earth abode of stones in the great deeps...' (p. 44).

Four times, in the context of Connemara, Lucky mentions 'the air'. Three
of them concern the well known quality of pure air in the region. The air is
so bracing that the road from *Roundstone*[69] to Clifden (11 miles) has been

called the 'Brandy and Soda Road'. The fourth reference reads: '... on land on sea and in the air ...'(p. 44). The theme of Lucky's homily is that 'in spite of the strides' on land on sea and in the air, man is in full decline — man 'is seen to waste and pine ...' (p. 43).

An historic stride 'in the air' was the first non-stop flight across the Atlantic — from Newfoundland to Ireland — June 14-15, 1919.[70] After 15 hours 57 minutes in the air, the plane landed in a bog near Clifden. Hailed as a great feat of endurance for men and machine, it was the world's first leap into the powered aviation era. The spot in Connemara where the pioneers landed is marked by a memorial in the form of an aircraft fin, together with a cairn,[71] erected in 1959 by Irish International Airways.

One of the most puzzling lines in Lucky's speech — which, scholars now admit, 'is far from being gibberish'[72] — is:'... the skull the skull in Connemara...' (pp. 44, 45). He repeats the word *skull* eight times, in the context of 'Connemara ... abode of stones'. He is shouting his text, 'the skull alas the stones' as the other three overpower him (p. 45).

The 'skull' in Connemara is in fact, a stone — *The Turoe Stone*[73] — an anthropomorphic image of pagan worship, dating from around 279 B.C.

> The Turoe Stone (pronounced tew-roe) in Co. Galway is a powerful piece of western granite about 4 feet high, its dome decorated in a great welter of swirling curves, like the tattooed spirals of a Maori head.[74]

That the 'skull' refers to the Turoe Stone is indicated earlier, in Lucky's stammered reference to the Academy of Anthropometry. Typically, Beckett presents the word Turoe (tew-roe) half disguised as Testew.[75]

> ...as a result of labours left unfinished crowned by the Acacacaca-demy of Anthropopopometry of Essy-in-possy of Testew and Cu-nard it is established beyond all doubt all other doubt than that which clings to the labours of men ... (p. 43).

The statement 'beyond all doubt' qualified in the same line by 'all other doubt than...' means that there is no such thing as 'beyond all doubt'. It reflects the ambivalence of the oracular divinations 'uttered forth' (p. 42) at some great pagan Celtic ritual round the Turoe Stone — 'the skull the skull in Connemara' (p. 45).

'Abode of stones' fits innumerable districts in Connemara. But as he links the remark with 'the year of their Lord six hundred and something' (p. 44), Beckett must be referring to the ecclesiastical remains of three foundations that flourished there in the seventh century.

Near Clifden, along the coast, is *Omey* where 'abode of stones' marks the ruins of the *College* and *Church of St. Feichin*. Here (at Castle Kirk), the stones, called 'St. Feichin's Stones' have the dubious distinction of being the most famous and effective cursing stones in the country.[76] It is worth noting that 'abode of stones' is mumbled four times after Lucky's cursing frenzy has overtaken his laconic ranting about the philosophical premise (*esse est percipi*), maintained by Bishop Berkeley (1685 - 1753), another churchman, who flourished a thousand years later.

Two other stone oratories dating from 'the year of their Lord six hundred and something', seventh century Celtic churches built and roofed with stone, are to be seen in Connemara. Off the coast of *Carna*, on a small island called *Oileán Mhic Dara* (St. Mac Dara's Island) is a beautiful stone-roofed oratory named like the island after St. Mac Dara. Part of the roof, a primitive window and a fine lintelled doorway remain. Boatmen passing the island dip their sails three times in honour of the saint.

At *Annaghdown*, on the eastern shore of Lough Corrib, are the ruins of a castle and an ancient church, once the seat of a bishopric founded by St. Brendan the Navigator in the sixth century. St. Brendan[77] also founded an abbey at Clonfert, Co. Galway in A.D. 558. On the site of the abbey a cathedral in Irish-Romanesque style, introduced in the twelfth century, was built there. The ruins of the cathedral, famous for its fine doorway, a porch-like composition of multiple arches springing from colonettes and topped by a decorative pediment of stone sculptured human heads, is a splendid example of Irish-Romanesque architecture. The human heads decoration is of Armenian influence, and dates from the seventh century introduction of eastern ideas into the Celtic church.

Beckett has good reason to associate Connemara with, among things, 'the year of their Lord six hundred and something'.

Evocation

The play is autobiographical to a greater extent than is at first apparent. As more is known about Beckett's early life, it becomes clear that his suffering and sentiments are recalled in the dialogue of *Godot*. His biographer says:

> While it is every bit as biographical as the novels, and is in places even less disguised than they, it somehow transcends his life and becomes the most separate entity of all his writings. It is unique because it is so deeply rooted in his life and experience, while at the same time the text stands by itself, having universal meaning for a worldwide audience.[78]

Apart from the associations made with points of location, Connemara and

Dublin (implied as the home of 'Peterson's System Pipe'), he preserves memories of his father in the characters' costumes — hats, coats and tie.[79]

His walking tour of Connemara in 1931 is recalled in Lucky's sermon, and naturally concerns feet and comfortable footwear:[80] 'in the stockinged feet in Connemara in a word ...' (p. 44) The 'word' is *pampootie*, a shoe without heels and made of rough hide, worn by men in parts of Connemara and in the Aran Islands. Made to measure, it fits comfortably.

Evocation inspired the concept of his main characters. A Connemara connection with Beckett's 'tramps' is illustrated in a picture in the Tate Gallery, London. According to Derek Mahon,

> There hangs in the Tate a picture by Jack B Yeats,[81] oil on canvas, entitled 'Two Travellers'. The 'travellers' — 'tinkers' as they used to say — are ragged figures on a road in Connemara.... and it seems evident to me that 'Two Travellers' provided at least one point of departure for Didi and Gogo in *Waiting for Godot*. ...

Furthermore, he sees as evocative of Beckett's Protestant, specifically Church of Ireland home environment, 'Didi's parsonical peroration' in *Godot*.[82]

> Vladimir: Let us not waste our time in idle discourse! Let us do something, while we have the chance! It is not every day that we are needed ... To all mankind they were addressed, those cries for help still ringing in our ears! But at this place, at this moment of time, all mankind is us, whether we like it or not ... (p. 79).

I think Didi's sermon more accurately expresses Beckett's own theology: that is, his *negative theology*.[83]

> ... What are we doing here, *that* is the question, and we are blessed in this, that we happen to know the answer. Yes, in this immense confusion one thing alone is clear. We are waiting for Godot to come (p. 80).

Pozzo's cries for help still ringing in his ears,[84] Vladimir goes on:

> Or for night to fall. (*Pause.*) We have kept our appointment, and that's an end to that. We are not saints, but we have kept our appointment. How many can boast as much? (p. 80).

To which, speaking for all mankind from Adam[85] through Eternity, Estragon replies, 'in a manner at once reductive and expansive':[86] 'Billions.' Billions then, have kept their appointment — 'To wait for Godot' (p. 93). Godot alone is the defaulter. 'He' has not kept his appointment. For Beckett, on the theological plane, Godot is the symbol of the absent God. One of the tenets of Beckett's negative theology is that: 'God is totally other and transcendent, absent from the workings of the world and of men.'[87]

Beckett's exploration of negative theology pervades his first novel, *Murphy* (1938).[88] The third novel, *Watt* (1944) — written in his wartime hideout in the Vaucluse in southeast France — recounts his futile search for the *Deus Absconditus*.[89] Since this sentiment is merely reiterated here it can be classified as Evocation in *Waiting for Godot*.

Language

Beckett 'claims the author's right to create an opaque text that is difficult for the reader to understand'.[90] He does this in *Godot* by the use of arcane language and information; the Irish language; and Hiberno-English.

Arcane Language

This is juxtaposed with familiar words or names and parochial inferences e.g. the words 'corpses', 'skeletons' and 'charnel house' do not refer to the dead and the past but to the living in the present. They are conscious theatrical jokes directed at the audience. Interpreted in the physical rather than literary sense, 'the corpses and skeletons are the audience, still and spectral from the actors' point of view, negatived shapes (a charnel house) from behind that barrage of lights'.[91]

There are many examples of arcane language in Lucky's speech: ...'divine apathia divine athambia divine aphasia'... (p. 43) meaning respectively, insensibility to suffering; imperturbability; inarticulate, inability to communicate. Simple phrases, 'no matter what matter the facts are there' (p. 44) may seem commonplace, but they proceed from Lucky's earlier reference to Bishop Berkeley.[92] They allude to the Bishop's doctrine that matter does not exist; hence the name of his philosophical premise — *immaterialism*.

Simple words, e.g. *bog*, and *Board*, are transposed by 'dissociated metaphor'[93] into arcane language in *Godot*. The word 'bog' occurs early in Act I, as Vladimir and Estragon, trying to find their bearings in the bleak landscape, wonder whether they have not 'come to the wrong place' (p. 14).

> Estragon: In my opinion we were here.
> Vladimir: (*looking round*). You recognise the place?
> Estragon: I didn't say that.
> Vladimir: Well?
> Estragon: That makes no difference.
> Vladimir: All the same ... that tree ... (*turning towards the auditorium*) ... that bog (p. 15).

Ostensibly a jocular reference to the audience,[94] 'that bog' also intimates location[95] and reorientation. Doubt about 'the place' now dispelled is replaced by doubt about the time. ...

> Estragon: You're sure it was this evening?
> Vladimir: What?
> Estragon: That we were to wait.
> Vladimir: He said Saturday. (*Pause.*) I think.
> ....
> Estragon: (*very insidious*). But what Saturday? And is it Saturday? Is it not rather Sunday? (*Pause.*) Or Monday? (*Pause.*) Or Friday? (p. 15).

The word 'Board'[96] occurs in Act II in a setting similar to Act I, except the tree is in leaf. Blind Pozzo and Lucky (now dumb), are on stage with Vladimir and Estragon. Confusion about time — whether it is morning or evening — and place reigns once more:

> Estragon: I'm going.
> Pozzo: Where are we?
> Vladimir: I couldn't tell you.
> Pozzo: It isn't by any chance the place known as the Board?
> Vladimir: Never heard of it.
> Pozzo: What is it like?
> Vladimir: (*looking round*). It's indescribable. It's like nothing. There's nothing. There's a tree.
> Pozzo: Then it's not the Board.[97]
> Estragon: (sagging). Some diversion![98]

The word 'Board' here refers to the Irish Turf Development Board or *Bord na Móna*. Beckett's flash of comic relief, 'that bog', in Act I, now has its parallel in 'the Board', in Act II (p. 87). Only Pozzo — the landowner — mentions 'the Board', i.e. the Turf Development Board: *Bord na Móna*.[99] Estragon's subtle pun on the word 'Board' shows that he, like Vladimir, 'never heard of it'.

Six pages of incisive dialogue separate the two words: *bored* (p. 81) and *Board* (p. 87). As Vladimir and Estragon 'weigh the pros and cons' (p. 80) of helping Pozzo, now prostrate on the ground crying 'Help!' and 'Pity!', reason returns to their deliberations. ...

> Vladimir: We wait. We are bored. (*He throws up his hand.*) No, don't protest, we are bored to death, there's no denying it. Good. A diversion comes along and what do we do? We let it go to waste. Come, let's get to work! (*He advances towards the heap, stops in his stride.*) In an instant all will vanish and we'll be alone once more, in the midst of nothingness!
> *He broods* (p. 81).

The words 'bored' and 'diversion' are all Estragon remembers of Vladimir's vibrant reasoning. Estragon's forgetfulness is itself a recurrent diversion in the play: it prompts his own comment....

> Estragon: That's the way I am. Either I forget immediately or I never forget (p. 61).

Estragon forgets immediately whenever the issue requires intellectual reflection. He never forgets sensory impressions whether of pleasure[100] or pain.[101] Vladimir and Estragon are 'bored to death' (p. 81). But the relief implicit in the 'diversion' Vladimir seeks (to help Pozzo to his feet), vanishes too, since, keeping him on his feet means carrying him. ... (p. 84).

> (*Pozzo sags between them, his arms round their necks.*)
> Estragon: How much longer must we cart him round?
> ... ... We are not caryatids! (p. 86).

Pozzo's remark on the *Board* (p. 87), is heard as a reference to the *bored* weariness of the 'caryatids': Pozzo's supporting figures. Estragon's response — already quoted — mimics Pozzo and Vladimir in mock resignation ... Estragon: (*sagging*). Some diversion! (p. 87).[102]

Irish Language

The Irish language is used in the form of: (a) Pure Irish words: *bladar* — flattery or coaxing; *blathering* — talking, pleasantry; *dudeen* — a small clay pipe.

> Estragon: Ah stop blathering and help me off with this bloody thing (p. 10).
> Estragon: ... He's lost his dudeen (p. 35).

(b) Puns on Irish words: *Godot* is a pun on the Irish word, *Go deo* — Eternity.

> Vladimir: We're waiting for Godot (p. 14).

This line, the first meaningful reference to their lives, is intoned like an incantation ten times, as it threads its way through the play, giving it the cohesion of mystery, with a strain of archaic verbal magic.[103] Vivian Mercier points out that ...

> ... word play originates in verbal magic and becomes wit as the magical elements gradually wither away ... word play in its other sense — play *with* words rather than *on* words — is an important element in the Old Irish spells and incantations given by Whitley Stokes and John Strachan in *Thesaurus Palaeohibernicus*, ii (Cambridge 1903), 248-50

and that ...

> Irish wit, in English as well as Gaelic, has never broken its ties with word play: as Joyce so vividly exemplifies, the favourite form of witticism in Ireland is still the pun.[104]

To stress the fact that *waiting* and *blathering* are synonymous, and that *time* is not clock time but cosmic time, he provides a fusion of concrete and poetic imagery in Act II.

The tree, pronounced 'dead' the day before (Act I) is now 'covered with leaves' ... 'in a single night!' (p. 66). Unable to explain the phenomenon on the basis of lineal time, they agree by inference to dispense with lineal time, for the time being. The accepted meaning of words was also suspended ... 'yesterday evening it was all black and bare'. (p. 66) 'Yesterday' could mean yesteryear: clock time was immaterial within the cosmic timelessness of eternity — Go deo — Godot. In the ensuing dialogue, 'yesterday', now freed from the hair-spring shackles of the clock, is the key word.

> Estragon: I tell you we weren't here *yesterday* ....
> Vladimir: And where were we *yesterday* evening according to you?
> Estragon: How do I know? In another compartment. There's no lack of void.
> Vladimir: Good. We weren't here *yesterday* evening. Now what did we do *yesterday* evening?
> Estragon: Do?
> Vladimir: Try and remember.
> Estragon: Do ... I suppose we blathered.
> Vladimir: About what?
> Estragon: Oh ... this and that, I suppose, nothing in particular. Yes, now I remember, *yesterday* evening we spent blathering about nothing in particular. That's been going on now for half a century (p. 66).

For half a century they had been blathering/waiting. Any activity (or inactivity) of such duration is often referred to in Ireland as lasting *Go deo*, for an eternity. Godot when first mentioned by Vladimir meant time past. But Estragon was quick to turn it into future time. It gave a new dimension to their inactivity. They could go on now 'blathering about nothing in particular'. They had freed themselves from the discipline of time and meaningful language. Language could now mean anything they wished it to mean.

The immediate result was that Godot began to project a human — or superhuman-image. Godot became 'He', at once: 'Vladimir: He said by the tree'.[105] They gave Godot a personality, and assumed a relationship to that personality. It relieved their feeling of anonymity. *They* were 'beginning to mean something'.[106] An identity could be established in a dream world.

Thus *Waiting for Godot* upholds and exemplifies the old tradition of the Theatre of the Absurd, which includes: 'the literature of dream and fantasy, which often has a strong allegorical component.'[107] The strong allegorical component is contrived initially by the pun on *Go deo.*

Go deo may indicate various moods, meanings, and shades of meaning:

(a) *Go deo* in the context of Time (always future time) means;[108] For ever, eternity, always, to the end of time. Elliptically in reply to a question, e.g. When will you marry? *Caithin a phósfair? Go deo* means, *Never*. It has a positive if slightly exaggerated meaning in sentences such as: *Mairfidh sé go deo* — He will live *for ever*.

(b) *Go deo* as an interjection can indicate sorrow, pity, disgust. *Faire go deo* means Alas alas! shame! or everlasting shame! In Lucky's long, unpunctuated speech the nuance is clear:

> I resume alas alas on on ....
> I resume alas alas abandoned, unfinished ...
> .... the skull alas the stones ... unfinished .... (pp. 44, 45)

That could read:

> I resume Godot Godot on on — 'Hypothetical imperative'
> I resume Godot Godot abandoned unfinished — that is, still waiting for Godot.
> .... the skull Godot the stones ....
> unfinished ....: — just another way of saying Go deo or eternity goes on unfinished.

(c) *Go deo* as an expletive is used to express frustration or resignation. In that case it has the accented form —

Go deo deo or *Go deo na ndeor*, meaning: For ever and ever life's crosses lie waiting, and bearing life's crosses is part of the process of Waiting for Godot. As *Vladimir* said: 'To every man his little cross .... Till he dies ... And is forgotten' (p. 62).

Go deo na ndeor — literally, till the end of tears (in this valley of tears), life's trials, disappointments and tears are part of the human lot. One reminder from

> Estragon: 'We always find something, eh Didi, to give us the impression we exist?' (p. 69).

Lucky weeps on hearing that Pozzo wants to sell him.

> Pozzo: He's stopped crying. (*To Estragon*) You have replaced him as it were. (*Lyrically*) The tears of the world are a constant quantity. For each one who begins to weep, somewhere else another stops (p. 33).

(d) *Go deo* indicating compassion or sympathy is used as a soothing expression, for example, when a small child is distressed after a little fall, the catastrophe of a broken toy, or other such calamity.

Hiberno-English

> Hiberno-English is a distinctive form of speech which reflects the centuries-old relationship between the two languages of Irish and English in Ireland.
>
> Irish has influenced the vocabulary, syntax, idioms, and pronunciation of Irish speakers using English, and the English language has succumbed to these transformations, while at the same time exhibiting the usual effects of a language cut off from its country of origin and, in consequence, developing at a different rate and in different ways.[109]

Beckett uses this linguistic heritage sparingly, but with studied dramatic effect. In the 'oui-non' dialogue of *Godot*, it is spoken occasionally by Didi and Gogo. It usually signifies relief, or relaxation of tension in their relationships. Twice they 'celebrate' their reunion with the very Irish expression:

> Vladimir: ...Get up till I embrace you (p. 9). (Act I)
>
> Vladimir: ...Come here till I embrace you (p. 58). (Act II)
>
> Estragon: ...We're not tied? ... To your man (p. 21)

'Your man' or 'Yer man' is a common Hiberno-English idiom. (cf. Irish *mo dhuine*, 'my man').[110]

Beckett stresses the difference in pronunciation between Irish and English speakers of English in a jesting illustration of it:

> Vladimir: Calm yourself.
>
> Estragon: (*voluptuously*), Calm...calm... The English cawm (p. 16).

The Irish idiom has regional variations.[111] Beckett lapses into the Dublin idiom, naturally, in his Irish plays. Eoin O'Brien points out that: The Dublin idiom is used often by Beckett, sometimes almost imperceptibly and always with subtlety. In fact, the use of the Dublin or Irish idiom gives to many of Beckett's 'placeless' writings an unmistakable Irish identity ...' He cites as examples of the Dublin idiom in *Godot*:

1. The use of the 'double-mister':[112]

   > Estragon: Mister ... excuse me. Mister ...
   >
   > Pozzo: You're being spoken to, pig! Reply! (*To Estragon.*) Try him again.
   >
   > Estragon: Excuse me, Mister, the bones, you won't be wanting the bones?
   >
   > *Lucky looks long at Estragon.*
   >
   > Pozzo: (*in raptures.*) Mister! (*Lucky bows his head.*) (p. 27)

2. Colloquial Dublinese: He says that —

   > The words 'ballocksed' and 'amuck', as used in *Godot*, could be straight from a Dublin street conversation:[113]

> Vladimir: That Lucky might get going all of a sudden. Then we'd be
> ballocksed.
> Estragon: Lucky?
> Vladimir: He's the one who went for you yesterday.
> Estragon: I tell you there was ten of them.
> Vladimir: No, before that, the one that kicked you.
> Estragon: Is he there?
> Vladimir: As large as life. (*Gesture towards Lucky.*) For the moment
> he is inert.
> But he might run amuck at any minute (p. 79).

3. Perversion of pronunciation.[114] He writes:

> The exaggerated perversion of well-known French sayings is a
> favourite verbal past-time in Dublin, and Estragon is no stranger to
> the practice —[115]
> Estragon: Oh tray bong, tray tray bong.
> Pozzo: (*fervently*). Bless you, gentlemen, bless you!
> (*Pause.*) I have such need of encouragement!
> (*Pause.*) I weakened a little towards the end, you didn't notice?
> Vladimir: Oh perhaps just a teeny weeny little bit (p. 38).

Here, the perversion of pronunciation is, in effect, 'Verbal nonsense' — one
of 'the age-old traditions of the Theatre of the Absurd'.

It follows one of 'the music-hall routines with hats in *Waiting for Godot*',
and 'clowning relies on verbal nonsense as well as on abstract scenic effects.
Beckett's Dublin idiom establishes *Waiting for Godot* in the realm of 'pure'
abstract theatre in the Theatre of the Absurd.[116]

There are Irish speech mannerisms, such as Vladimir's exaggeration at
the beginning of Act I, ... 'We should have thought of it a million years ago,
in the nineties (p. 10).
Estragon asks Vladimir about the tree they wait at ...

> Estragon: What is it?
> Vladimir: I don't know. A willow (p. 14).

Towards the end of Act I the stage is dark, except for the moon *shedding a
pale light on the scene.* Estragon ... *contemplates the moon.*

> Estragon: Pale for weariness.
> Vladimir: Eh?
> Estragon: Of climbing heaven and gazing on[117] the likes of us (p.
> 52).

The Irish idiom, 'the likes of us,' frequently used by Beckett,[118] comes from
the Celtic word, *leithéid* — the like, plural *leithéidí* — the likes or such as.[119]

The Text and the Technique

The principal structural characteristic that the absurdist plays share
is their opacity. Each presents obstacles that interfere with the
spectator's immediate comprehension.[120]

Beckett ensures the opacity of this play with a linguistic chess game —
'intellectualising interactions'[121] and exploiting its manifold possibilities.
The obstacles are provided by an array of symbols, and a sequence of images
that demand the imagination, and compel the audience's *involvement* in the
play.

Although the play is constructed around symbols, Beckett's counsel to
each of eight directors planning simultaneous performances in eight German cities, in late 1953, was: 'go easy on the symbols — and the clowning'.[122] He never ceases to warn: 'The danger is in the neatness of
identifications'.[123] Yet many of the symbols can be identified in his personal
life, and in earlier writings.

Symbols are image-makers. They embellish ideas. They prevent language, particularly the English language, from being 'abstracted to
death'.[124] In *Godot*, they constitute a line of communication between author
and audience, which abstruse language fails to do. By their commonplace
character the symbols foster involvement in this 'strange' play.[125]

The symbols he employs are objects of everyday use: shoes, hats, coats,
watch, pipe, beard; or common features of a quiet, rural setting: road,
stones, tree, bog, horse. Some of them serve as status symbols in the
portrayal of character,[126] or as vehicles of satire on clichés,[127] or to mock a
philosophical premise.[128] Many of the symbols have clichés attached:

> road — Pozzo: 'The road is free to all.' (p. 23)
> stones — Lucky speaks of 'Steinweg and Peterman' (p. 44) —
> referring to life's stony path and rock obstacles.
> tree — Vladimir: '... A willow'. (p. 14) The cliché, a weeping willow,
> is implied as the tree is 'dead'....
> Estragon: 'No more weeping'. (p. 14)
> The status symbols indicate present and possibly past claims to
> respectability. Among them are, obviously: hats — bowler hats,
> suggesting middleclass businessmen, stockbrokers, staid profes-
> sional men, or even landlords away from Ascot. They may also mark
> 'displaced persons' from these ranks[129] (of whom there were many
> after the war).

The image of Godot he wishes to convey with the *beard* is of something
— or someone, for the beard is also part of the decoy — very old. A *white*

beard indicates the ultimate in time or age. It is an intimation of time immemorial, of something, possibly ethereal, as old as God. There is a great deal of myth and symbolism surrounding the *beard*.[130] He uses the symbol of manly dignity and the imagery of age-old wisdom associated with the *beard* to create a sense of awe, respect, and reliance.

'Godot': The Mystery and the Mirage

Having given 'Godot' the bearded face of a sage; the fleeting image of a saint; and twice, the timorous figure of a boy, Beckett exploits other areas of disguise as the taut dialogue shuttles back and forth from apparent banalities to ponderous, profound truths.

While hats are tossed and shoes are traded in seemingly meaningless ritual, numerous flares dropped along a false trail burn themselves out, but throw no light on the identity of the guru whose command held them captive or the liberator who might set them free. The hint of a god or saint lurking in 'Godot' is clear in:

> Estragon: What exactly did we ask him for?
> ....
> Vladimir: Oh ... nothing very definite.
> Estragon: A kind of prayer.
> Vladimir: Precisely.
> Estragon: A vague supplication.
> Vladimir: Exactly. (p. 18).

As mystery and mirage succeed each other in a whirligig of short, sharp exchanges between the two, Vladimir imagines he hears a noise outside. It is another stroke in the art of decoy.

> Vladimir: I thought it was he.
> Estragon: Who?
> Vladimir: Godot.
> Estragon: Pah! The wind in the reeds.
> Vladimir: I could have sworn I heard shouts.
> Estragon: And why should he shout?
> Vladimir: At his horse. (p. 19).

Traditionally, a horse, or more poetically, a steed, is a figurative name for Time. A galloping white horse is an age-old euphemism for death.[131]

The linguistic chess game is best seen in the subtle moves ('intellectualising interactions') he initiates with the pipe. The pipe — a Kapp and Peterson[132] — apart from being a status symbol for Pozzo, has a promotion cliché he tries to justify: 'The Thinking Man smokes a Peterson's Patent Pipe'.[133] Beckett seizes on this as an invitation to 'tease out'[134] the Cartesian axiom, *Cogito ergo sum* — I think therefore I am.

> Beckett was fascinated by the Cartesian project to free the thinking
> self from all external constraints. ... The Cartesian self exists because
> it thinks — *cogito ergo sum* — and seeks to remain an autonomous
> substance entirely independent of material reality. The *cogito* aspires
> to the condition of an eternal and self-sufficient being far removed
> from corporeal and temporal decay...[135]

Beckett uses every nuance of the *cogito* to show that this idealistic vision
of spiritual freedom is untenable, since it ignores the material reality of the
ergo sum — the fact that the 'thinker' has a body. Flights of fancy or of fantasy
begin and end on earth, as Pozzo demonstrated, and murmured: 'That's
how it is on this bitch of an earth' (p. 38). Pozzo's pipe established him
symbolically as a 'thinking man', completing his image as 'the self-sufficient
being'. (His social status as land and slave owner was clear.)

> Pozzo: *(having lit his pipe)* The second is never so sweet ... *(he takes
> the pipe out of his mouth, contemplates it)* ... as the first, I mean. *(He puts
> the pipe back in his mouth)* But it's sweet just the same (p. 28).

Following the introduction of the pipe with its cliché, and its slogan,[136] *think*
is the key word in the dialogue for the next dozen pages; till Lucky's
astonishing 'think' provides endless food for thought, and further insight
into Beckett's demythologising intellect.[137]

In every nuance of the word 'think' Beckett implies the existence of
'external constraints'.

> Pozzo: *(To Vladimir)* Think twice before you do anything rash. (p.
> 29).
> Vladimir: *(To Estragon)* I think he's listening. (p. 29).
> Pozzo: Well, that's what I think. (p. 31).
> Pozzo: You wouldn't think it to look at me, would you? (p. 33).
> Vladimir: I don't think so. ... I don't know. (p. 34).

Pozzo's image, dented by his sobbing, and shouting ... 'I'm going mad' ...
(p. 34), is temporarily restored by his image-maker, the pipe.

> Pozzo: *(calmer)* Gentlemen, I don't know what came over me. For-
> give me. Forget all I said ... What have I done with my pipe?
> ......
> Pozzo: What can I have done with that briar? (p. 35).
> Estragon: He's a scream. He's lost his dudeen.
> *Laughs noisily.*
> Pozzo: I've lost my Kapp and Peterson!
> Estragon: *(convulsed with merriment)* He'll be the death of me! (p. 35).

Of the four bowler-hatted men on the stage, Estragon alone is not seeking intellectual identity.[138] Creature comforts are his concern, and even 'the bones' satisfies one of these. (p. 27). He therefore takes an impish delight in mocking the symbol of 'The Thinking Man'. He also takes a gram of sweet revenge for Pozzo's scornful refusal to allow him to take the bones in the first place.[139]

However much Pozzo tried to reconstruct his image, with excuses for his lapse, and his expensive 'briar', the edifice collapsed anew under the satirical connotation of the Irish word 'dudeen'. *Dudeen* demoted the pipe and the owner, Pozzo. Dudeen is an old Gaelic word (Dúidín) for a clay pipe.[140] But the word implies more than that.

The clay pipe is white and complete; but a dudeen is a short, grey (from use), truncated pipe, composed of the head (bowl) and a stump of a stem which a very old man or woman pulls at or sucks, whether it is 'out'[141] or not. Clay pipes are given out (with tobacco) to the neighbours who come to a 'corpse house' or to wakes[142] in Ireland up to the present day.

The dudeen diminished Pozzo's stature in that, despite his recovery of the landlord's self-confidence,[143] his 'scene' showed that he had 'feet of clay', and his haughtiness was a smoke-screen round a man as 'lost' as any of them; even more in need of encouragement[144] and the warmth of human sympathy. Soon he was begging to be allowed stay a little longer — on his own land.[145] Pozzo's shattered pipe-dream as it were makes shards, too, of the cliché on the vanity of human wishes: 'The Thinking Man smokes a Peterson Patent Pipe'. Other symbols, signs, or even proofs of the 'thinking man' must be found.

Observing 'the play's characteristic rhythm',[146] Pozzo, now composed, remarks:

> Pozzo: He subsides. (*Looking round.*) Indeed all subsides. A great
> calm descends. (*Raising his hand.*) Listen! Pan sleeps. (p. 36)

'Pan sleeps' — arcane language marking the return of the leitmotif — Think. But, the repetition of the word, *think*, in different mouths is 'an ironical device for pointing a contrast',[147] not of status but of genuine intellectual acumen.

In the context, the word Pan[148] can mean one or all of the definitions below. If interpreted linguistically, 'Pan sleeps' means, everything sleeps; peace reigns. If he is referring to the god of Greek mythology, 'the deity displayed in creation and pervading all things', then 'Pan sleeps' means that time — night following day — and universal movement in general, are suspended until Pan wakes up again. Hence the reaction:

Vladimir: Will night never come?

All three look at the sky. (p. 36)

Pozzo: You don't feel like going until it does?

Beckett is also remembering the Miltonic lines in praise of Pan:

Universal Pan,

Knit with the Graces and the Hours in dance,

Led on the eternal spring.

Milton: *Paradise Lost*, IV, 266.

References to the Graces[149] and the Hours[150] in dance,[151] are knit into the ensuing dialogue, in the form of puns and dissociated metaphor. The criteria of the 'Thinking Man', and the concept that 'Thought is free' are subtly and satirically explored.

Pozzo's inspiration left him, his lyrical explanation of 'the twilight' (p. 39) failed to break the boredom of waiting, and he wants to put on a 'turn' for[152] 'these honest fellows who are having such a dull, dull time' (p. 39). Pozzo will have his 'knook'[153] entertain them.

Pozzo: ...(*He picks up the whip.*) What do you prefer? Shall we have him dance, or sing, or recite, or think, or —

Estragon: Who?

Pozzo: Who! You know how to think, you two?

Vladimir: He thinks?

Pozzo: Certainly. Aloud. He even used to think very prettily once, I could listen to him for hours.[154]

... Well, would you like him to think something for us? (p. 39)

Estragon: I'd rather he'd dance, it'd be more fun? ...[155]

Vladimir: I'd like well to hear him think.

Estragon: Perhaps he could dance first and think afterwards, if it isn't too much for him.

Pozzo: By all means, nothing simpler. It's the natural order.[156]

Vladimir: Then let him dance.

Pozzo: ... Dance, misery!

... *Lucky dances. He stops.*

Estragon: Pooh! I'd do as well myself. ...

Pozzo: He used to dance the farandole, the fling, the brawl, the jig, the fandango, and even the hornpipe.[157] He capered. For joy. Now that's the best he can do. Do you know what he calls it? (p. 40).

Estragon: The Scapegoat's Agony.[158]

Vladimir: The Hard Stool.[159]

Pozzo: The Net.[160] He thinks he's entangled in a net.

The three disparate names for Lucky's joyless caper have one common inference — external constraint! They have other associative links in the arcane language pattern of his extended parody of *cogito ergo sum*; and the Cartesian vision of spiritual freedom.

'The Net' is Joycean metaphor for whatever restricts the freedom of the soul. In the *Portrait* Joyce wrote:

> The soul is born..... It has a slow and dark birth, more mysterious than the birth of the body. When the soul of a man is born in this country there are nets flung at it to hold it back from flight. You talk to me of nationality, language, religion, I shall try to fly by those nets.[161]

The intellectual affinity between Vladimir and Lucky noted in Vladimir's desire 'to hear him think', extends to the emphasis on their hats.[162]

> Vladimir: (*to Pozzo*). Tell him to think. (p. 41)
> Pozzo: Give him his hat.[163]
> ....
> He can't think without his hat.[164]
> ....
> It's better to put it on his head.
> ....
> Vladimir: I'll put it on his head. (p. 42)
> Pozzo: ... Think pig! (*Pause. Lucky begins to dance.*) Stop! (*Lucky stops.*)
> Forward! ... Stop! ... Think!
> Lucky: On the other hand with regard to —[165]
> Pozzo: Stop! ... Back! ... Stop! ... Turn!
> (*Lucky turns towards auditorium.*) Think!

As Lucky's speech poured from his soul 'truth of the first water' (p. 33), the 'nets flung at it to hold it back from flight' only caught the adamantine fact that man is in full decline ... 'progress' is his destruction.

Vivian Mercier stresses the aural and poetic impact of Lucky's monologue:[166]

> The most striking speech in the whole play, Lucky's monologue when ordered to think, rivets our attention at first by its shocking mixture of seeming sense and evident nonsense, mingling reflections on 'the existence ... of a personal God ... with white beard ... outside time without extension ...' with nonsense syllables 'quaquaquaqua.' ....
> ... But as an audience loses the thread of the progressively more disrupted sentence, it ceases to try to understand and is swept away by the verbal torrent which, in English, breaks down into the heavily accented dimeters already noted in Beckett's free verse:
>
>   /   /
> the air the earth

/   /
the sea the earth

/   /
abode of stones

/ /
in the great deeps

/   /
the great cold

/   /
on sea on land

/   /
and in the air

/
I resume

/   /
for reasons unknown

/   /
in spite of the tennis

/   /
the facts are there

/   /
but time will tell. ...

The poetic dimension appeals to a theatre audience, few of whom may have read the play. But a careful *reading* of Lucky's speech reveals an astounding mixture of evident sense and seeming nonsense.

Martin Esslin marks 'Lucky's farrago of chaotic nonsense ... as an indication that language has lost its function as a means of communication...'[167] The fact is, that Lucky *is* communicating his message to Vladimir, Estragon, and Pozzo, as their reaction to it clearly shows. Beckett's directions prove this:

> *During Lucky's tirade the others react as follows:*
> (1) *Vladimir and Estragon all attention, Pozzo dejected and disgusted.*
> (2) *Vladimir and Estragon begin to protest, Pozzo's sufferings increase.*
> (3) *Vladimir and Estragon attentive again, Pozzo more and more agitated and groaning.*
> (4) *Vladimir and Estragon protest violently. Pozzo jumps up, pulls on the rope. General outcry. Lucky pulls on the rope, staggers, shouts his text. All three throw themselves on Lucky who struggles and shouts his text.* (p. 42)

Pozzo is incensed that his ironic 'Think!' command to a slave, should boomerang; with Lucky in reality the 'thinking man', proving 'beyond all doubt' that spiritual freedom can 'fly by those nets' of human bondage.[168]

The formal and thematic sequence charted by two other critics of Lucky's sermon do not accord with Esslin's 'farrago of chaotic nonsense' appraisal of it. Anselm Atkins, writing in *Modern Drama*, sees the formal structure thus:

> (a) unfinished protasis of a theological or philosophical argument,
> (b) an incomplete fragment of a rational argument which is the last half of an objection to the unfinished demonstration of the first;
> (c) a second objection parallel to the earlier one which lapses into aphasia.

Horst Bruer, the German critic, notes the thematic order as follows:

> (a) Absence of God;
> (b) Shrinking of man;
> (c) World as chaos.[169]

While God, man, and the world are its main themes, Lucky's speech is not conclusive on any one of them. The 'absence of God' is not the premise of his discourse, but rather the presence of God. The co-existence of a 'personal God' with the problem of pain and suffering in the world is the rationale he examines here. He cannot reconcile the presence and passivity of God. Seeming nonsense is inevitable when erudition is discharged at top speed, and 'when the mechanism of the record (as it were) breaks down into helpless repetition'.[170] In *Waiting for Godot*, repetition refines the fabric of cohesion.

Certain key words and phrases repeated with spellbinding rhythm are driven into the subconscious. They have a good logical context within the broad concept of 'free association' in the Theatre of the Absurd. But at the end it is obvious that these words derive in some peculiar way from the *word*, and the *meaning* of 'Godot'/Eternity. Their real meaning is conveyed by collocations of images and sounds which recur in the play, and together with other fragments converge and crystallise into a magical reflection of reality. In the last analysis they 're-establish' contact with 'multiple reality' in the sense Ionesco envisaged.[171]

The groundwork of reality on which Lucky weaves his pattern with strands of his absurd tirade is laid in the first lines:

> Lucky: Given the existence ... of a personal God ... outside time ... (p. 42)

The basic concept on which he begins to 'think' is that God has been there from all eternity. The key words/phrases, the strands which he uses repeatedly in the pattern are: *in a word; time will tell; unfinished; I resume; alas.*

Repetition of key words and phrases in Lucky's speech

Words/Phrases	Logical context	Magical approach	Recurring in Text
1. In a word (5 times)	in short, brief	'word' is *Godot* *Go deo*/Eternity	44 times in all 13 times before 31 times after Lucky's diatribe, the *word* 'Godot' is mentioned but not defined
2. Time will tell (5 times)	'time' solves, heals and reveals	Here 'time' is 'dissociated metaphor' for *Go deo*/Godot	20 times or more, all of them as oblique references to *Go deo*: 'In the fullness of time' (p. 82) 'Time flows again already' (p. 77) 'It'd pass the time' (p. 83) 'The blind have no notion of time' (p. 86)

Words/Phrase	Logical context	Analogies and parallels in the Play	
3. Unfinished (7 times)	not completed, not realised, abandoned, interrupted.	Lucky's tirade was 'left unfinished' when he collapsed Estragon's sleep was interrupted twice when Vladimir woke him up Estragon's dreams were unfinished Their stories were unfinished	

Words/Phrase	Logical context	Analogies and parallels in the Play
(cont'd)		Pozzo's lyrical description of the firmament is unfinished (his inspiration leaves him) (p. 38)
		The whole play is a catalogue of unfinished labours or activities. e.g. their attempt to console Lucky; their attempt to help Pozzo; and the bargain they were trying to strike with Pozzo, for 200 francs was also left unfinished
4. I resume (8 times)	begin again, or continue	Vla:...And I resumed the struggle (p. 9) They resumed their friendship twice Vla: Come here till I embrace you (p. 58) Vla: We could start all over again perhaps (p. 63) Est: Let's pass on now to something else (p. 75) Vla: We have to come back tomorrow ...To wait for Godot (p. 93).
5. Alas, alas	Pity! Too bad!	Accepting that *'Godot'* is *Go deo*, then every reference to the human condition is analogous, within the context of the play, to 'alas alas' *Go deo* as an interjection can indicate sorrow, pity, complaint
		Faire go deo means exactly: Alas! alas!

Words/Phrase	Logical context	Analogies and parallels in the Play
		In Lucky's speech this key word is associated with tears
		This is extended, indeed anticipated by Pozzo: 'The tears of the world are a constant quantity. For each one who begins to weep, somewhere else another stops' (p. 33)

At the end of his supposedly senseless tirade, Lucky puts the five key words into two lines which succinctly express, albeit in metaphor, the total reality portrayed in *Waiting for Godot*.

... but time will tell I resume alas alas on on ...

... in a word I resume alas alas abandoned unfinished ... (pp. 44,45).

Within the context of eternity time heals and reveals, but 'The essential doesn't change' (p. 21). Time goes on and mankind resumes the struggle. His labours cannot be otherwise than 'unfinished' in *Go deo*.

But 'unfinished' is just an arc of the circle in the orbicular structure of Beckett's universe. 'I resume' completes the circle. Significantly, Lucky repeats this eight times (once more than 'unfinished') in his chilling homily. *I resume*, the declared response to an inner command to continue, to resume the struggle, Beckett calls the 'hypothetical imperative': 'Charming things, hypothetical imperatives!'[172]

The striking circularity of the play was stressed in rehearsals for its first production — co-directed by Beckett with Roger Blin — in Paris, January 5, 1953, to the extent that:

Originally the play was to be staged in the round, so that Pozzo could make circles as he walked and talked to enhance the idea of circularity in the play, i.e. that the end was the same as the beginning, and the repetition of the waiting would go on indefinitely. However, this seemed to express too concrete an idea for Beckett, and he insisted that circularity be suggested but not clearly apparent.[173]

The Word 'Godot' is Made Flesh in Act I

The whole image-making process is calculated to create an impression that not only Vladimir and Estragon but the entire world is waiting for Godot.

An aura of authority, benevolence and masterly competence is built into the image of the personality who is regarded as a redeemer. The very name 'Godot' is as charismatic as the image, for the sensory impact of the word 'Godot' is an evocation of God, or of the gift and power of the Holy Spirit. This enhances the prestige and credibility of the saviour they await, but also tends to put their expectations on too high a plane for the sobering intrusion of reality.

Furthermore, as in the case of the Word in St. John's Gospel, the word 'Godot' has a different connotation for each of the four characters, Vladimir, Estragon, Pozzo and the Boy. The response varies according to their particular interpretation of the *word* and the image it creates for each one of them.

Beckett wrote in his essay on Proust: 'The only world that has reality and significance is the world of our own latent consciousness'. Vladimir, a Christian and a man of thought, is deeply conscious of the fact that life has a purpose and man a destiny. But the world's priorities are based on a complex order in which the individual is a nonentity; his welfare dependent on a catalogue of pressure groups and factors over which he has no control.

In one of the many 'canters' in the dialogue, Beckett names some of them:

Estragon: What exactly did we ask him for? ....
....
Vladimir: Oh ... nothing very definite. ....
Estragon: A vague supplication.
Vladimir: Exactly.
Estragon: And what did he reply?
Vladimir: That he'd see.
Estragon: That he couldn't promise anything.
Vladimir: That he'd have to think it over.
Estragon: In the quiet of his home.
Vladimir: Consult his family.
Estragon: His friends.
Vladimir: His agents.
Estragon: His correspondents.
Vladimir: His books.
Estragon: His bank account.
Vladimir: Before taking a decision.
Estragon: It's the normal thing. (p. 18)

Here Beckett realistically portrays the social and bureaucratic chain of command through which 'a vague supplication' passes, and how difficult it is for man 'to assert his prerogatives' (p. 19) if he has any.

No wonder the next lines read:

> Estragon: We've no rights any more?
>
> ....
>
> We've lost our rights?
> Vladimir: (*distinctly*). We got rid of them (p. 19).

The Flesh is Made Word in Act II

The Flesh — and by implication all mankind — represented by the four struggling, vaguely hopeful human beings in the play is made word, Godot, in the play. They are synonymous with *Time*. Time changes, so do they. Time tempers people. Pozzo was tempered on the anvil of Time. Time teaches: Vladimir and Estragon saw in the end that life had a purpose, and that they could fulfil their mission without the redeemer Godot. They discovered that they were not rejects or underprivileged but privileged to be at a moment in time and place indispensable, capable, and, as Pozzo said, 'Made in God's image' (p. 23). One may be corrupted by Time, but, like hope, human dignity springs eternal in the human breast. Time can cure as well as corrupt.

Martin Esslin (without knowing Irish) says, that whether Godot is meant to suggest a supernatural agency or a mythical human being is of secondary importance. He insists that:

> The subject of the play is not Godot but waiting, the act of waiting as an essential and characteristic aspect of the human condition. Through our lives we are always waiting for something, and Godot simply represents the objective of our waiting — an event, a thing, a person, death. Moreover, it is in the act of waiting that we experience the flow of *time* in its purest, most evident form. If we are active, we tend to forget the passage of time, we *pass* the time, but if we are merely passively waiting, we are confronted with the action of time itself.[174]

Vladimir and Estragon were for the most part passively waiting for Godot to come. 'He' did not come. He would never come.

In an analysis of this play Professor Eugene Webb wrote:

> Being, as Aristotle said, a creature that desires to know, man cannot endure for long the absence of meaning. And meaning, in its most basic sense, is pattern .... *Waiting for Godot* is the story of two vagabonds who impose on their slovenly wilderness an illusory, but desperately defended pattern: waiting .... They are men seeking meaning in an absurd universe.[175]

Esslin wrote ten years earlier (1961): 'The act of Waiting for *Godot* is shown as essentially *absurd*. Admittedly it might be a case of '*Credere quia absurdum est'*, yet it might even more forcibly be taken as a demonstration of the proposition *'Absurdum est credere'*.[176]

Undoubtedly it is a case of 'Credere quia absurdum est', *Glauben wiel es absurd ist*. This built-in mechanism or Divine faculty in man 'to believe because it is absurd' has made human progress possible down through Time itself, to the Age of the Micro-chip, the Satellite and the Nuclear Age. 'Credere quia absurdum est' *is* Waiting for Godot: Eternity. If it were taken as a demonstration of 'Absurdum est Credere' which is naked nihilism, Vladimir would not be agonizing over the discrepancies among the Evangelists in the Gospels. He believed despite the alleged disagreement in the four accounts of the Crucifixion. He found 'meaning' in that mystery — a meaning called *Hope*, his only life-line.

Following an exhaustive analysis of the play in a chapter entitled 'Samuel Beckett: The search for Self', Martin Esslin concludes: 'That *Waiting for Godot* is concerned with the hope of salvation through the workings of grace seems clearly established both from Beckett's own evidence and from the text itself.'[177]

In his final assessment of the play, Eugene Webb writes:

> Even if time stands still, man cannot. Pozzo, after his vision of the emptiness and futility of human life, revives his Lucky and cries, 'On!' though they have nowhere to go and nothing to carry but sand. Vladimir and Estragon too go on in their own way, but the critic must resist the temptation to interpret this as an affirmation on the part of the play of hope or human fortitude ...
> In the universe of this play, 'on' leads nowhere.[178]

The two opposing views of the meaning of the play accrue from the fact that, as another critic put it: 'Beckett writes of hope in images of despair'.[179]

The images of two men waiting on the stage, as the curtain falls on Act I and Act II, illustrate this. In the context of both Acts, the identical curtain line ... 'Yes, let's go' (pp. 54, 94) is a metaphor for despair. *They do not move.* — the proof of hope — is the immortal message of Waiting for Godot — Waiting for *Go deo* — Waiting for Eternity.

Finally, this 'astonishing play'[180] about Time, is itself timeless, as Eoin O'Brien states unreservedly:

> *Waiting for Godot* is a timeless play. No detail dates the drama or its message to any age. It will adapt to the theatre of the future as readily as it has done to the twentieth century stage. As it is timeless, so too, it is placeless, demanding little more for its setting than a strange tree, a country road and desolation. Beckett removed most, but not

quite all, detail that might permit identification of place in *Godot*. He wishes to create, as Con Leventhal so aptly put it, 'a cosmic state, a world condition in which all humanity is involved.[181]

NOTES

1 He had just finished the second part of his trilogy — *Molloy, Malone Dies*, and *The Unnamable*.

2 Bair, *Samuel Beckett*, p. 323.

3 Ibid., p. 325.

4 *Godot*, p. 52 (Vla. 'Tomorrow everything will be better').

5 Ibid., p. 43.

6 Ibid., p. 43, 44.

7 Ibid., p. 66 (Est. 'There's no lack of void').

8 Bair, op. cit., p. 326.

9 Quoted from Beckett's letter to Alan Simpson on giving him the rights to do the play — *Godot* — in Dublin in 1955. See *Irish University Review* 1984, p. 104.

10 Bair, *Samuel Beckett*, pp. 323, 325.

11 The word is used in its figurative sense: complete defeat or frustration. (*The Penguin English Dictionary*, p. 120.) The curtain lines of Act I and Act II are identical: 'Yes, let's go. *They do not move.*'

12 Mercier, *Beckett/Beckett*, p. 25.

13 Esslin, *The Theatre of the Absurd*, p. 318.

14 Ibid., p. 388.

15 Bair, *Samuel Beckett*, p. 340.

16 Ibid., p. 336.

17 Ibid., p. 341.

18 Bair, *Samuel Beckett*, p. 342.

19 The play by John Millington Synge (1871-1909) premièred at the Abbey Theatre, Dublin, in January 1907. Its portrayal of the anti-hero, Christy Mahon, caused riots and controversy that helped to make the *Playboy* and the Abbey (founded 1904) famous.

20 Bair, op. cit., p. 342.

21 Blin did not want this role; he would have cast himself in the role of Lucky, but Beckett insisted he played 'the gross, fat Pozzo' (Bair, p. 356).

22 Bair, *Samuel Beckett*, p. 362.

23 Ibid., p. 363.

24 Quoted from Bair, op. cit., p. 363.

25 Bair, *Samuel Beckett*, p. 362.

26 Ibid.

27 Ibid., p. 357.

28 Bair, *Samuel Beckett*, p. 376.

29 To protest the censorship Beckett decided not to go to England for the first production in London.

30 Bair, op. cit., p. 381.

31 See Fletcher, John et al., *A Student's Guide to the Plays of Samuel Beckett*, London, 1978, p. 39.

32 Ibid.

33 All reviews quoted in Bair, *Samuel Beckett*, p. 383.

34 All reviews quoted in Bair, *Samuel Beckett*, pp. 383-4.

35 All reviews quoted in Bair, *Samuel Beckett*, p. 385.

36 This was Alan Simpson's expressed wish, issued with a warning that the language of *Godot* might upset some people. See Murray, Christopher, 'Beckett's Productions in Ireland: A Survey', *Irish University Review*, Spring 1984, p. 104.

37 Ibid., p. 105.

38 Ibid., A.J. Leventhal is the critic quoted here.

39 The Pike Theatre, a converted coach-house, could seat only fifty-five people. The stage was just twelve feet by twelve. It was started by Alan Simpson in 1953, when 'basement' theatres were appearing as an alternative to the Abbey and the Gate theatres. The Pike introduced *avant-garde* plays by Beckett, Tennessee Williams, Pinter, Ionesco.

40 Bair, *Samuel Beckett*, p. 400.

41 The Peacock Theatre is the experimental theatre attached to the Abbey. It can seat 156 people.

42 Murray, 'Beckett Productions in Ireland: A Survey', p. 106.

43 Ibid., p. 107.

44 Jacobsen and Mueller, *The Testament of Samuel Beckett*, p. 30.

45 Murray, 'Beckett's Productions in Ireland: A Survey', p 117.

46 Beckett called the first run-through of a text with actors a 'realisation' of the play; when performed publicly, he said that it had been 'created'. See Reid, *All I Can Manage, More Than I Could*, p. 19.

47 Esslin, *The Theatre of the Absurd*, p. 340.

48 Barnes, 'Aspects of Directing Beckett' pp. 73 - 76 and 82 - 86.

49 Ibid., p. 82. For example, two pages of inanities about the carrot (pp. 20, 21) are shown to be 'dissociated metaphor' for the popular theory that eating carrots is good for the eyesight.

50 Bair, *Samuel Beckett*, p. 327.

51 Lyons, *Samuel Beckett*, p. 44.

52 Bair, pp. 323-40.

53 Jacobsen and Mueller, p. 64.

54 For Proust's influence on Beckett's early and mature writing, see Bair, *Samuel*

Beckett, p. 99.

55 Joyce asked twelve friends to write essays in praise or promotion of *Work in Progress*, that later became *Finnegans Wake* (1939). The volume of essays, Joyce called: *Our Exagmination Round his Factification for Incamination of Work in Progress* (1929).

56 Ibid., p. 27.

57 Ibid., p. 28, 29.

58 Beckett 'uses language like an instrument, the emotions seething beneath'. Mays, 'Young Beckett's Irish Roots', *Irish University Review*, Spring 1984, (Special Issue), p. 30.

59 Esslin, *The Theatre of the Absurd*, p. 26.

60 See Vladimir's 'reasoning' on this question in his soliloquy, pp. 79, 80, 81.

61 Lyons, *Samuel Beckett*, p. 21.

62 Beckett knew the area very well. With his elder brother, Frank (and their dog), he went on a three weeks walking tour of Connemara, in the late summer of 1931 (Bair, *Samuel Beckett*, p. 117).

63 Two of the most obvious puns in the play. Beckett spoke German. Stone and rock are personified here.

64 See Appendix II, *Stone in the Mythology of Ireland* — Granite.

65 Ibid. Quartzite forms the conical peaks of many rocky mountains around the coast of Ireland.

66 Herries Davies, G.L., 'The Making of Ireland', *Ireland of the Welcomes*, Vol. 34, No. 1, 1985, p. 22.

67 Situated amid superb lake and mountain scenery, 13 miles south east of Clifden, Recess is a favourite angling resort. On one side is Glendalough Lake, on the other Derryclare Lough, north of which Lough Inagh stretches along the great glaciated valley of Glen Inagh, separating the Twelve Bens from the Maamturk Mountains.

68 Marble is of course, hard crystalline limestone capable of being highly polished.

69 Roundstone is a quiet coastal resort, beautifully situated on Bertraghboy Bay. The road from there to Clifden runs close to the shores of Ballyconneely Bay and Mannin Bay. The route is renowned for its varied scenery as much as for its rarefied atmosphere.

70 Two Englishmen, Alcock and Brown, flying a converted Vickers Vimy twin-engined bomber, made the hazardous 1890 mile flight from Newfoundland to Ireland, and made a soft landing on a Connemara bog.

71 A heap of stones raised as a landmark or memorial.

72 Fletcher, et al., *A Student's Guide to the Plays of Samuel Beckett*, p. 63.

73 See Appendix II, *Stone in the Mythology of Ireland*.

74 Harbison, Peter, 'The Turoe Stone', *Ireland of the Welcomes*, Vol. 34, No. 1, 1985, p. 26.

75 See Bair, *Samuel Beckett*, p. 95, for Beckett's divinations with words.

76 Power, Patrick, *The Book of Irish Curses*, Mercier Press, 1974, p. 32.

77 *Encyclopedia of Ireland*, Dublin, 1968, pp. 301, 402.

78 Bair, *Samuel Beckett*, p. 326.

79 Ibid., pp. 328-9. 'Beckett insisted that the characters wear bowler hats, similar to those his father had always worn... he was absolutely adamant... so Blin agreed.' 'Beckett suggested, then insisted, that they wear black coats also similar to those worn by his father.'

80 Ibid., p. 328. 'From his childhood, Beckett had suffered from recurring problems with his feet ... As a young man, he suffered from all the afflictions he bestowed upon his fictional characters, and as an adult in France, the problems of his feet were magnified by the ill-fitting French shoes he wore.'

81 Jack B Yeats (1871 - 1957), although more renowned as a painter, was also a playwright. He was a close friend of Samuel Beckett. They first met in 1930. *Godot* and Jack Yeats's play *La La Noo* (1942) have dramatic features in common. (See *Beckett/Beckett*, p. 25.)

82 Mahon, Derek, 'Enigma of the Western World' (the poet's tribute to Beckett for his eightieth birthday), *Observer*, 13 April 1986.

83 Kearney, *The Irish Mind*, p. 278.

84 Pozzo's eighth unanswered cry of 'Help!' (p. 80) immediately preceded these lines.

85 Estragon said his name was 'Adam' (p. 37).

86 Mahon, 'Enigma of the Western World'.

87 Kearney, *The Irish Mind*, p. 278.

88 Ibid., p. 280.

89 Ibid., p. 286.

90 Lyons, *Samuel Beckett*, p. 2.

91 Barnes, 'Aspects of Directing Beckett', p. 73.

92 George Berkeley (1685-1753). A great Irish philosopher, ranked with Aristotle, Descartes and Hegel. His fame rests on numerous and novel philosophical treatises, essays and theological writings. His name is foremost among the great empiricists and idealist philosophers of the Age of Reason. In Europe Berkeley is seen as the father of modern idealism.

93 The technique of linking two or more associated facts concealed below the surface of the text; each fact represented in the text by one word, e.g. bog or Board. Joyce was a master of the technique. See O'Connor, *A Short History of Irish Literature*, pp. 200 - 205.

94 Barnes, 'Aspects of Directing Beckett', p. 72.

95 O'Brien, *The Beckett Country*, p. 68.

96 Critics, puzzled by the word 'Board', occurring almost out of context in Act II, assumed that Beckett was referring to 'the boards', meaning the stage.

97 Trees do not grow in bogland. The flora of raised bogs consists of *Sphagnum* (bog-moss) species, *Andromeda polifolia* (bog rosemary) and *Oxycoccus palustries* (cranberry).

98 Both 'bog' and 'Board' have satirical overtones in *Godot*. This reflects an opinion held by the opponents of the Turf Development Board in the early years of the scheme, 1946 - 1949. Newspapers were reporting on some aspect of Bord na Móna almost daily during the months Beckett spent in the 'liberating diversion' (Beckett's words: See Bair, p. 323) of writing this play... October 1948 — January 1949. Estragon's snide remark, 'Some diversion!' refers to the current theme, 'the Board', and to Vladimir's earlier speech (p. 81).

99 'Bord na Móna — the Irish for Turf Board — is a semi-state body which evolved in 1946 from the Turf Development Board. It is the State's agency for the purpose of developing the bogs, and extracting turf on a commercial basis. In its forty years existence it has successfully exploited 200,000 acres of bogland which help to keep the home fires burning, and this has greatly reduced the bill for imported fuel. For most Irish people, the main function of Bord na Móna is to provide those compressed briquettes which are wonderful for keeping a fire aglow in the family grate. But any gardener world-wide will tell you that Bord na Móna produces superb peat-moss which loosens the soil. An amazing five million tonnes of peat are marketed each year and one sixth of Ireland's electricity is generated from peat, so that it is no wonder that Bord na Móna pays its way without subsidy. For years, many countries have looked to Bord na Móna for leadership and advice on the winning of turf, and the Bord provides a thriving consultancy in the Americas, Asia and Africa. It is now recognised as one of the leaders in developing the technology and machinery for the processing of the world's peat resources.' (*Ireland of the Welcomes*, Vol. 36, No. 3, 1987, p. 36)

100 *Waiting for Godot*, p. 12. He remembers maps of the Holy Land. 'Coloured they were. Very pretty ...'

101 Ibid., p. 60. 'I remember a lunatic who kicked the shins off me. Then he played the fool.'

102 Beckett infers that there is no 'diversion' from the boredom of waiting; just an exchange of one burden for another.

103 Mercier, *The Irish Comic Tradition* (1962), pp. 3 - 4.

104 Ibid., pp. 6 - 7.

105 p. 14. In Act I the leafless tree indicates time — 'the season' — *yesterday* (3 times) is stressed, and tomorrow (twice), but the *present* offers only doubt and uncertainty; expressed by Vladimir to Estragon: 'Nothing is certain when you're about.' (p. 14).

106 *Endgame*, p. 27.

107 Esslin, *The Theatre of the Absurd*, p. 328.

108 Dinneen, Rev. P., *An Irish-English Dictionary*, Dublin, 1970, p. 328.

109 Dolan, T.P., 'Samuel Beckett's Dramatic Use of Hiberno-English', *Irish University Review*, Spring 1984, p. 46.

110 Dinneen, *Irish-English Dictionary*, p. 379.

111 O'Farrell, Padraic, 'Leinster', in *How the Irish speak English*, Mercier Press, Cork, 1980, p. 9-27.

112 O'Brien, *The Beckett Country*, pp. 252-3.

113 O'Brien, op. cit., p. 254.

114 In *All That Fall*, this idiomatic characteristic is exercised by Miss Fitt: 'Ah yes, I am distray, very distray, even on week-days' (p. 20).

115 O'Brien, *The Beckett Country*, p. 254.

116 Esslin, *The Theatre of the Absurd*, p. 328.

117 Estragon is quoting from Shelley's 'To the Moon' ... ('Art thou pale for weariness/Of climbing heaven and gazing on the earth ...')

118 *Eh Joe*, p. 17.

119 Dinneen, *An Irish-English Dictionary*, p. 657.

120 Lyons, *Samuel Beckett*, p. 17.

121 Bair, *Samuel Beckett*, p. 323.

122 Ibid., p. 369.

123 Beckett, Samuel, in his essay: 'Dante...Bruno. Vico...Joyce'. *Our Exagmination Round his Factification for Incamination of Work in Progress* (1929), p. 3.

124 Ibid., p. 15.

125 Bair, op. cit., p. 361.

126 Pozzo, flaunting his pipe and watch, referred to his land and manor house (pp. 28, 46).

127 Pozzo jests at the slogan, 'Smokes Sweet', used to promote sales of his special brand of pipe (p. 28).

128 Beckett uses another cliché about Pozzo's 'briar' (p. 35), to parody a Cartesian premise.

129 Mercier, *Beckett/Beckett*, pp. 46 - 53.

130 Among the Jews, Turks, and Eastern nations generally the beard has long been regarded as a sign of manly dignity. To cut it off wilfully was a deadly insult, though shaving it was a sign of mourning among Jews. No greater insult could be offered a man than to pluck or even touch his beard, hence the phrase *to beard one*, to defy him, to contradict him flatly, to insult him. By touching or swearing by one's own beard one's good faith was assured. There are at least a dozen idioms on *Beard* in current English. One is Chaucerian: '*To make one's beard*', which means, to have one wholly at your mercy, as a barber has been holding a man's beard to dress it. An Elizabethan idiom: '*To lie in one's beard*' was a way of stressing the accusation. The lie was devastating. Persius (A.D. 34 - 62) styled Socrates (470 - 399 B.C.) *Bearded Master* (Magister barbatus) under the notion that the beard is the symbol of wisdom. (*Brewer's Dictionary of Phrase and Fable*, Cassell & Company Ltd., London, p. 85).

131 *Brewer's Dictionary of Phrase and Fable*, p. 467.

132 The history of the world-famous pipe as recorded in their leaflet, under the heading: *A Champion 'Piper'*: Over 100 years ago, Charles Peterson arrived in Dublin from Riga, and for many years might be seen in Kapp's miniature workshop in the front window in Grafton Street, turning everything he could lay his hands on into Pipes, cigar holders, and such like. It was here that he gave the public the first clue to the theory of 'how the fly got into the amber' by giving demonstrations in softening and bending that substance over the flame of a candle. Realising the fact that Dublin was the slave to the primitive and fragile 'Francis Street meerschaum' wherewith to offer incense to 'My Lady Nicotine', he produced an ideal 'incense receptacle', to wit, 'Peterson's System Pipe', which

revolutionised smoking from Francis Street to 'Frisco'. Unlike Peter the Great, he did not return across the Baltic with his invention, but in order to meet the growing demand, he formed a company and established a factory, where at present over a hundred hands are employed in the making of 'incense holders' for the worshippers of the 'Sublime Weed' throughout the world.

133 Written on the front of the amber-coloured leaflet, illustrated by a philosopher's head, and his pipe.

134 Kearney, *The Irish Mind*, p. 267.

135 Ibid., p. 270.

136 The slogan on the first inner page of the leaflet on Kapp and Peterson Pipes, reads: 'Smokes Dry / Smokes Cool / Smokes Sweet.'

137 This is considered comprehensively by Kearney in his essay: 'Beckett: the Demythologising Intellect' in *The Irish Mind*, Wolfhound Press, Dublin, 1985.

138 Barnes, 'Aspects of Directing Beckett', p. 76.

139 Pozzo: ... the bones go to the carrier. He is therefore the one to ask (p. 27).

140 Wie die Tonpfeife im Stutenkerl.

141 Pozzo's pipe was out — 'I'm out' he said (p. 29) and so was his train of thought and his vocabulary. There is a marked connection between the pipe and his 'stream of consciousness'.

142 'Wakes', in *Encyclopedia of Ireland*, pp. 111, 112.

143 Mercier *Beckett/Beckett*, pp. 52, 53. 'Pozzo would be immediately recognised as a landlord in a play about Victorian Ireland.'

144 Pozzo: I have such need of encouragement! (p. 38).

145 Pozzo: If you asked me perhaps. ...
     If you asked me to sit down (p. 36).

146 Fletcher, et al., *A Student's Guide to the Plays of Samuel Beckett*, p. 44: '... the play's characteristic rhythm, which consists of the alternation between a burst of speech and activity on the one hand and a period of motionless silence on the other ...'

147 Fletcher, John, and Spurling, John, *Beckett: a Study of his Plays*, London, 1972, p. 65.

148 Pan (Gr. all, everything). The god of pastures, forests, flocks, and herds of Greek mythology; also the personification of deity displayed in creation and pervading all things. He is represented with the lower part of a goat and the upper part of a man; his lustful nature symbolised the spermatic principle of the world; the leopard's skin that he wore indicated the immense variety of created things; and his character of 'blameless' symbolised the wisdom which governs the world (*Brewer's Dictionary of Phrase and Fable*, p. 674).

149 The three Graces. In classical mythology, the goddesses who bestowed beauty and charm and were themselves the embodiment of both. They were the sisters Aglaia, Thalia, and Euphrosyne. (*Brewer's Dictionary of Phrase and Fable*, p. 411).

150 The Hours or Horae (L). Mythology. The three goddesses of the seasons and of natural and social order (Ibid., p. 553). The ancient Greeks had three seasons, spring, summer and winter (Homer and Hesiod); the fourth (autumn) appears first in Alcman. He was a Spartan lyric poet of the 7th century B.C. (Ibid., p. 1025).

151 The *danse champêtre*, invented by Pan, quick and lively. The dancers (in the open air) wore wreaths of oak and garlands of flowers (Ibid., p. 265).

152 This was a bonus Pozzo felt he should give them. Having 'given them the bones'

and 'talked to them about this and that', ... he says, 'what tortures me, is it enough?' (p. 39).

153 The word knook, coined by Beckett from *knout* (nowt) which is a Russian leather-thonged whip, refers to the master-slave relationship between Pozzo and Lucky. Pozzo has the 'whip hand': the typical slave-driver insignia being the whip and the rope.

154 Lucky taught Pozzo 'all these beautiful things'... 'Beauty, grace, truth of the first water ...' (p. 33).

155 Estragon derives his happiness or suffering through the senses. Vladimir is intellectual, rational, serious.

156 A reference to The Hours or Horae, the goddesses of natural and social order.

157 Beckett underlines the artistic and international aspects of Lucky's cultural background.

158 See *Brewer's Dictionary of Phrase and Fable*, p. 802. The ancient ritual among the Hebrews for the Day of Atonement laid down by the Mosaic law was that one goat was sacrificed on the altar, while the other, laden with the sins of the high priest and his people, 'was taken to the wilderness and suffered to escape'. Similar rites are still common among primitive peoples. It was Lucky's unhappy lot to be Pozzo's scapegoat.

159 A typical Beckettian pun on the *Stool of Repentance*: 'The cutty stool, a low stool placed in front of the pulpit in Scottish churches', on which sinners sat during the service. After the service the penitent had to stand on the stool to receive the minister's rebuke (Ibid., p. 861).

160 Here is has the Dictionary meaning: 'That which entangles mentally or morally' See *Funk & Wagnalls Practical Standard Dictionary*, p. 768.

161 Joyce, James, *A Portrait of the Artist as a Young Man*, N.A.L. Signet Books, New York, 1916, p. 158.

162 Fletcher, et al., *A Student's Guide to the Plays of Samuel Beckett*, pp. 40, 41.

163 The hat on his head indicated his right to speak to 'superiors'. Many customs regarding rights and privileges revolve round hats or head covering for men. See *Brewer's Dictionary of Phrase and Fable*, pp. 438, 439.

164 In Lucky's case his bowler hat gave him status: intellectual status. He could now 'think very prettily' again, for Pozzo.

165 This line signalled the controversial nature of his discourse. It was the poet's revolt against the Establishment that enslaved him.

166 Mercier, *Beckett/Beckett*, p. 145.

167 Esslin, *The Theatre of the Absurd*, p. 87.

168 'It is, after all, Lucky's only opportunity to fly away beyond the constraints and limitations of his condition,' comment Fletcher, et al. in *A Student's Guide to the Plays of Samuel Beckett*, p. 62.

169 Fletcher, et al., *A Student's Guide to the Plays of Samuel Beckett*, pp. 61-2.

170 Quoted from Murray, 'Beckett's Productions in Ireland', p. 106.

171 Esslin, 'The Significance of the Absurd', *The Theatre of the Absurd*, p. 409.

172 *Molloy: Malone Dies: The Unnamable*, p. 87.

173 Bair, *Samuel Beckett*, p. 356.

174 Esslin, *The Theatre of the Absurd*, p. 49.

175 Webb, Eugene, *The Plays of Samuel Beckett*, London, 1972, p. 26.

176 Esslin, *The Theatre of the Absurd*, p. 56.

177 Esslin, op. cit., p. 56.

178 Webb, *The Plays of Samuel Beckett*, p. 41.

179 Higgins, Aidan, 'Foundering in Reality: Godot, Papa, Hamlet and Three Bashes at Festschrift', *Irish University Review*, Spring 1984, p. 96.

180 The French Minister for Arts and Letters in 1952 — Georges Neveaux, wrote to Roger Blin on 29 January 1952:

'Dear Roger:

You are indeed right to want to play *En Attendant Godot*. It's an astonishing play. Not necessary to tell you that I am strongly for you.'

The Minister approved the 750,000 franc (about $400) grant to Blin for the production of *Godot* (Quoted from Bair, p. 351).

181 O'Brien, *The Beckett Country*, p. 68. The Note on the source of the quotation from Leventhal, p. 354, No. 29, reads:- 'Leventhal, A.J., 'The Beckett Hero' in *A Collection of Critical Essays*, ed. Martin Esslin. Prentice Hall. New Jersey, 1965, p. 49.'

Chapter Five

ALL THAT FALL

All That Fall (1956), Beckett's first radio play, 'was written at the sugges-tion of the BBC, mainly because they had been impressed by *Waiting for Godot* in 1955'.[1] Beckett took some months to consider and assess the problems of writing for radio, but on July 18, 1956, his decision and enthu-siasm was conveyed by the Controller of the Third Programme to the Head of Drama at the BBC:

> I saw Samuel Beckett in Paris this morning. He is extremely keen to write an original work for the Third Programme ... I got the impres-sion that he has a very sound idea of the problems of writing for radio and I expect something very good.[2]

Now commissioned to write a play, Beckett set to work on the text that became *All That Fall*. He wrote it quickly, July-September 1956, in English, returning linguistically to his roots, and planting 'his third biblical seed'[3] in the pastoral byways of Foxrock. The biblical text that provides title and theme for the play comes from the *Psalms*: 'The Lord upholdeth all that fall and raiseth up all that be bowed down' (145: 14).

All That Fall was first broadcast on the Third Programme of the BBC on January 13, 1957. The author did not hear that one; his biographer tells us:

> On 13 January 1957, Beckett, in Ussy brooding over *Fin de partie* (Endgame), strained to catch the sound of the elusive BBC Third Programme so that he could hear the first broadcast of *All That Fall*, but the reception was so poor that he had to give it up.'[4]

The play's reception was gratifying for Beckett.[5] 'Critics immediately recognised the affinity between the works of Beckett and the medium of radio', and they expressed it in glowing terms. In *The Listener*, 24 January 1957, drama critic Roy Walker hailed it as a 'radio classic'. Writing in the *New Statesman*, 14 September 1957, Christopher Logue called it 'radio triumphant'. Another poet, Donald Davie, in effect praised Beckett's use of Hiberno-English, in making syntax 'parody itself', but went on to criticise the play because of its 'derivative slapstick' and 'trick ending'. Hugh Kenner touched on a deeper level of the play, in his comment that, 'radio proves to be the perfect medium for Beckett's primary concern: the relationship between words, silence and existence' (*Spectrum*, spring 1961).[6]

Beckett seemed to have done everything right in his first foray into radio drama. He had found his medium, and extended its frontiers. Since the play was so successfully created for radio, he never allowed the presentation of *All That Fall* in any other theatrical form or medium.

Location

Location has a wider significance in *All That Fall* than the mere 'setting', basic though that is to the whole atmosphere of this novel play. The characters have and proclaim an identity in relation to the place they inhabit, and the sociological factors it determines.[7]

Stating his preference for play-writing Beckett said: 'For me theatre is first of all a relaxation from work of fiction. We are dealing with a definite space and people in this space. That's relaxing.'[8]

In a radio play, the 'definite space' is indicated by the 'people in this space'. 'Words and sounds must create a sense of location.'[9] Fletcher and his co-authors say: 'This is the only play set in a named location, that of Boghill, an Irish suburb.' Later they consider Boghill — 'A possibly bawdy name ...'[10] Boghill is not a bawdy name, albeit a fictitious name. Eoin O'Brien writes:

> Beckett probably named the station Boghill because of the proximity
> of a bogfield known locally as 'the bog' lying between the chemist's
> shop and the Hainault Road.'[11]

I think 'Boghill' is 'dissociated metaphor'[12] for the Racing country in which the play is set. In Ireland, bog is synonymous with turf (peat).[13] 'The Turf' is a metaphor for — 'The racecourse; the profession of horse-racing, which is done on turf or grass.[14]

The events in *All That Fall* take place on the day of a race-meeting at

Leopardstown Racecourse. *A Lovely Day for the Races* was the original title of the play.[15] Despite its inherent sadness, the play has overtones of racing and betting excitement —

> Christy: Nice day for the races, Ma'am (p. 7)
> Mr. Tyler: Divine day for the meeting (p. 10)
> Lovely day for the fixture (p. 22)

Wild tips are floated for the Ladies Plate (p. 17). Boghill, adjacent to Leopardstown Racecourse,[16] is, Mrs Rooney informs us, part of the 'entire scene' which includes the racecourse (p. 23).

For whatever reason he elected to call it by 'the abhorred name',[17] *Boghill*, the play is set in his home place, Foxrock. Testifying to this area are two authors who know Beckett and the area well, and write: 'It is widely accepted that 'All That Fall' is set in Foxrock ....',[18] and:

> Foxrock Railway Station, now disused, which once served the ad-
> joining Leopardstown Racecourse as well as the village of Foxrock,
> can easily be recognised as the setting for the concluding pages of
> *Watt* and much of the action of *All That Fall*.[19]

To call the location by its real name would limit his poetic licence and cramp his dramatic technique. Attitudes to Boghill, and relationships within its community, provide material for character delineation and development, which in turn create the atmosphere that sustains the play in the medium he pioneers.[20] The name 'Boghill' is abhorrent to Dan, which means, since he cannot *see* the place, he is referring to the people there. Foxrock by any other name would revive memories of the life and way of life Beckett knew, and mostly enjoyed, in the years he was 'at home' there.

Evocation

Beckett's recollections of the place and people of his comfortable youth,[21] distilled through the filter of twenty harsh years abroad ('It is suicide to be abroad', p. 10), highlight the ordinary, the enduring features that are commonplace and mostly left unsung. He comments on the landscape, the sky and light, the country road and modes of conveyance that trundle along its dusty surface to the station. He extols the view from the platform in 'the poetry of joy'.[22]

Mrs Rooney is overcome by the beauty of ...

> The entire scene, the hills, the plain, the racecourse with its miles
> and miles of white rails and three red strands, the pretty little
> wayside station, ... and over all the clouding blue, I see it all ...
> ... (*the voice breaks*). (p. 23)

Mr Tyler feels thrice blessed on the road to the races. His remarks reflect the Beckett spirit:[23]

> What sky! What light! Ah in spite of all it is a blessed thing to be alive in such weather, and out of hospital. (p. 11)

Mrs Rooney, although 'not half alive nor anything approaching it', accepts the 'vile dust' with biblical stoicism...

> This dust will not settle in our time. And when it does some great roaring machine will come and whirl it all skyhigh again. (p. 12)

As for the means of transport Beckett introduces into the play: a hinny-drawn cart;[24] an old bicycle 'on the rim' (i.e. with a flat tyre); the stalling car, roaring engine, the 'grinding of gears', the 'scream of brakes' (p. 15), even the theatrical horn-blowing ... *Horn violently...* (p. 16); they are recollections as real to him as the 'fickle sky and light' that made Mr Tyler's day.

Beckett was a keen cyclist.[25] He made long bicycle trips through Co. Wicklow, in his student days; and is well acquainted with the vagaries of a bicycle on a bumpy country road. This knowledge he shares with us, through Mr Tyler ...

> '... My back tyre has gone down again. I pumped it hard as iron before I set out. And now I am on the rim. (p. 11)
>
> Mrs Rooney: Oh what a shame!

But that is not enough. Beckett expands on the personality of the bicycle,[26] which vies in complexity with Mrs Rooney's 'lingering dissolution' (p. 11):

> Mr Tyler: Now if it were the front I should not so much mind. But the back. The back! The chain! The oil! The grease! The hub! The brakes! The gear! No! It is too much!

Mrs Rooney completes the profile, calling the bicycle 'her' (p. 13). (*Mr Tyler rides off. Receding sound of bumping bicycle. Silence...*) Mr Slocum's 'limousine' soon *draws up beside her, engine running.* (p. 13)

The dialogue that follows, the pratfalls and slapstick, recall Beckett's comic use of the family car, in 1926, as recorded by his biographer. ...

> Bill bought an automobile that year, a Swift, and Beckett drove it around Trinity very badly but with enormous style. He shifted gears with sweeping, dramatic movements, and involved his entire torso in negotiating turns. He made blowing the horn a musical art and parking was an exercise in dance and mathematics with an occasional fillip from the latest Mack Sennet comedy ...[27]

Beckett is remembering, too, the 'humours' of a car. 'Two hundred pounds of unhealthy fat' (p. 30) added to 'her' load by Mrs Rooney's farcical entry, caused the stalling scene (p. 15). Like Christy's hinny in Maddy's presence, 'she refuses to advance' (p. 9).

> Mr Slocum: (*dreamily*). All morning she went like a dream and now
> she is dead. ...
> (*Pause. Hopefully.*) Perhaps if I were to choke her.
> (The car of course!)

Mr Slocum's mishaps en route are mild compared with Beckett's reckless driving record, in the borrowed Swift, thirty years earlier. Slocum only 'squashed' a hen and 'nipped' Maddy's 'nice frock' in slamming the car door. Beckett almost squashed one of Dublin's High Court Judges, who however lived to lecture him on the error of his ways ...

> One evening, after several hours in a favourite pub, Beckett was
> negotiating the Swift through the streets around Merrion Square ....
> The Swift rolled over a kerb and stopped only inches from one of
> Dublin's leading legal figures, Judge Eugene Sheehy. ... Beckett
> received a severe dressing down from the judge, who lectured long
> and eloquently on the dangers of reckless driving. This was not his
> first or only brush with the law; several times he lost the use of the
> car for legal infractions and several times Bill simply forbade him to
> drive it, which reduced him to the motorcycle... or, most humiliating
> of all, to an ordinary bicycle.[28]

The van that 'passes with thunderous rattles' (p. 10), along the road, recalls a service in country commerce familiar to Beckett. Mrs Rooney exclaims: 'Heavens, here comes Connolly's van!' (p. 10). The van delivered goods from Connolly's Stores,[29] in the nearby village of Cornelscourt, to the Beckett household.[30] His mother was a regular customer in Connolly's Stores; and he remembers going there with her at an early age:

> A small boy you come out of Connolly's Stores holding your mother
> by the hand.
> (*Company*, p. 12)

The 'bruitage' (sound effects) Beckett required of the BBC enhance the realism of the play.[31] At the station, the sound of an express train, 'the up mail', rushing through, contrasts with Beckett's well-remembered 'Slow and Easy'[32] suburban train — the down train carrying Mr Rooney — that *pulls up with great hissing of steam and clashing of couplings*. (p. 26).

Evocation in this play is vivid and authentic.[33] However, where it concerns his characters Beckett deliberately blurs the identity of people who were, after all, his neighbours. In *The Beckett Country*, Eoin O'Brien restores their original stature. *Christy*, the carter ('I suppose you wouldn't be in need of a small load of dung?' p. 8), was in fact the Beckett family gardener.[34]*Mr Slocum*, Clerk of the Racecourse, was in reality Mr Fred Clarke, Clerk of Leopardstown Racecourse.[35] Mr Slocum's greeting is, perhaps, jocular, but not flattering: Maddy remembers her romantic youth:

> Mr Slocum: Is anything wrong, Mrs Rooney? You are bent all
> double. Have you a pain in your stomach? (p. 13)
> Mrs Rooney: Well if it isn't my old admirer the Clerk of the Course,
> in his limousine.

Mr Barrell, the station-master of 'Boghill', was one Mr Thomas Farrell,[36] station-master of Foxrock, whose efficiency frequently won him first prize for the best kept station on the Dublin and South Eastern line. Hence, when the train was late, Mr Barrell responded testily to Mrs Rooney, and violently to his subordinates (pp. 17 - 19).

> Mr Barrell: (*testily*). What is it, Mrs Rooney, I have my work to do.
> (p. 19)
> ....

Mrs Rooney ridicules his award-winning management:

> Mrs Rooney: Before you slink away, Mr Barrell, please, a statement
> of some kind, I insist. ... We all know your station is the best kept of
> the entire network, but there are times when that is not enough, just
> not enough. (*Pause.*)
> Now, Mr Barrell, leave off chewing your whiskers, we are waiting
> to hear from you — we the unfortunate ticket-holders' nearest if not
> dearest.
> ....
> Mr Barrell: I know nothing. All I know is there has been a hitch. All
> traffic is retarded. (p. 25)

Thomas Farrell's father and grandfather had been, in their time, station-master at Foxrock.[37] Mrs Rooney reminds Mr Barrell ....

> You stepped into your father's shoes, I believe, when he took them
> off. ...
> I remember him clearly. A small ferrety purple-faced widower, deaf
> as a doornail, very testy and snappy. (*Pause.*) I suppose you'll be
> retiring soon yourself, Mr Barrell, and growing your roses. (*Pause.*)
> ... (p. 18)

The Gentility Syndrome

Mrs Rooney's claim to gentility isolates her in a community where 'gentility' is synonymous with 'ascendancy'. Hugh Kenner remarks, 'In her brief duet with the landscape we sense her terrible isolation':[38]

> Mrs Rooney: All is still. No living soul in sight. There is no one to
> ask. The world is feeding. The wind — (*brief wind*) — scarcely stirs
> the leaves and the birds — (*brief chirp*) — are tired singing. The cows
> (*brief moo*) — and sheep — (*brief baa*) — ruminate in silence. The dogs

— (*brief bark*) — are hushed and the hens — (*brief cackle*) — sprawl
torpid in the dust. We are alone. There is no one to ask. *Silence*
(p. 32)

Immediately after Maddy vowed to 'estrange them all', and tearfully be-
moaned their treatment of her in leaving her 'all alone' after the conventional greeting, she spied her co-religionist, Miss Fitt. She stopped sniffling,
and thought aloud: 'Oh there is that Fitt woman, I wonder will she bow to
me.' (p. 19)

Miss Fitt pretended not to know her, and was duly reproved:

'... Am I then invisible, Miss Fitt? Is this cretonne so becoming to me
that I merge into the masonry? ....'

Miss Fitt: Mrs Rooney! I saw you, but I did not know you.

Mrs Rooney: Last Sunday we worshipped together. We knelt side by
side at the same altar. We drank from the same chalice. Have I
changed since then? (p. 20)

Miss Fitt's reply, 'All I saw was a big pale blur ...' with an observation on
Mrs Rooney's appearance — 'So bowed and bent' (p. 20) drew the most
vehement — and authentic — claim to gentility: her high ancestral name!

Mrs Rooney: (*ruefully*). Maddy Rooney, née Dunne, the big pale blur.
(*Pause*) You have piercing sight, Miss Fitt, if you only knew it,
literally piercing. *Pause*. (p. 21)

An example of Beckett's cross-patterning of origins and attitudes as well as
words and word-sounds, is Maddy's volte-face in the matter of loyalty.
Having failed to impress with her enchanting language of 'ascendancy'
flavour, she resorts to her Irish ancestral name as an irrefutable status
symbol.

Unlike the surnames, Fitt, Tyler, Slocum and Barrell, both *Rooney* and
Dunne are old Irish family names with a distinctive family crest to illustrate
that fact.

Ireland was one of the first countries in which hereditary surnames
came into being.... There are some instances of hereditary Irish
surnames in the tenth century, and by the twelfth the system had
become widespread, though not yet universal. At that time Irish
(Gaelic) was the only language normally spoken in Ireland .... At
first the surname was formed by prefixing the word *mac* (son) to the
given name of the father or *ua*, later *ó* (grandson), to that of an earlier
ancestor.

The prefixes Mac and O were very widely dropped in the seven-
teenth and eighteenth centuries following the submergence of the
old Gaelic order and the introduction of the Penal Laws. It is of

interest to note that ... names are still to be found mainly in the areas to which they belonged in medieval times.[39]

O'Rooney is still found in Co. Down, Northern Ireland, and *O'Dunn* (Dunne) in Co. Laois, as well as in other parts of the country. Both families apparently dropped the 'O' so as to shade into the political landscape of 18th century Ireland. Eugene Webb misinterprets the significance of Maddy's maiden name, *Dunne*, and invests it with a symbolism that is unjust to her and to the play: dung and its synonyms. ....

> ...When Maddy Rooney — whose maiden name, Dunne (a pun on
> *dun* or *brown*), associates her as she was in her maidenhood with this
> image of potential fertility — fell into the ruin-y state that the play
> has shown to be the ultimate reality of all human life, her own life
> was left a 'manure heap', as she calls it at one point (p. 71), and a
> barren one at that.[40]

First of all the name *Dunne* or *O'Dunn* cannot be a 'pun' on *dun* or *brown* for it is pronounced Donne not *dun*. The Irish word *Donn* (dun) has several meanings:[41]

> Donn, *a.*, brown, brown-haired.
> Donn, *m.*, the heart of a tree.
> Donn, *m.*, a prince, a chief, a judge.
> Donn, *a.*, noble, princely.

There is no reason whatever to associate *Dunne, O'Dunn* or the Irish word, *Donn*, with manure, dung or any equivalent. If the Irish word *Donn* could symbolise Maddy's life and times, gentility and character, then it is in its *noble* sense. Her heroic endurance, loyalty to Dan, and *hope* despite all adversity — elements, age, ingratitude and isolation, that they would 'come safe to haven'. (p. 34)

Maddy's life, far from being a 'manure heap' — which she does *not* call it[42] — is a mountain of indomitable courage, tenacity and determination: the very essence of Beckett's 'Hypothetical Imperative'.[43] She turns her 'bizarre way of speaking' to good account. Ruby Cohn observes:

> ... Mrs Rooney's outworn phrases ring like crystal on a medium too
> often burdened with cliché ....
> She walks and talks past all obstacles. That is her way of saying No
> to Nothingness — to the Nothingness for which Dan obscurely
> hopes ....
> Maddy provides rare comic relief, in the oldest phallic kind of
> comedy. She may halt, lean, or falter, but she never falls.[44]

Gentility with reserves of such unconquerable spirit can neither destroy nor be destroyed.

Language

In *All That Fall*, a drama that exists only as language and sound, Beckett projects the 'soul-landscape'[45] of his 'people' and the landscape they traverse on the aural screen of radio, through differentiated strains of sound. The imagery they register in the mind's eye forms a realistic picture of his Irish environment, painted with the broad brush of local linguistic apartheid.[46]

Like the artistic structure of the play,[47] language divides into three sections. The first consists of Mrs Rooney's florid language with its resonant lyricism; her archaic expressions;[48] and the benign malice of her repartee.[49] She finds her way of speaking 'very...bizarre'. Whether the admission is prompted by pride or pain is unclear: Christy does not reply when she asks –

> Do you find anything ... bizarre about my way of speaking? ... I mean
> the words ... I use none but the simplest words, I hope, and yet I
> sometimes find my way of speaking very ... bizarre. (p. 8)

The archaic phrases have biblical overtones: 'the highways and byways' (p. 13); 'safe to haven' (p. 35).

The Koran is intimated in a reference to Miss Fitt's 'sacrifices' (p. 21) on her behalf. 'I am sorry for all this ramdam, Miss Fitt' (p. 23). She means, of course, Ramadan.[50] She is alluding to Miss Fitt's earlier disclosure about being distray, 'when I start eating my doily instead of the thin bread and butter' (p. 20). The benign malice of Maddy's repartee in her encounter with Miss Fitt heightens as they climb the steps, arm in arm...'This is worse than the Matterhorn, were you ever up the Matterhorn, Miss Fitt, great honeymoon resort....' (p. 22). But Mrs Rooney's language tends more towards self-pity than to sarcasm. 'Her lyric cadenced plaining'[51] contributes greatly to 'the play's enchantment, dependent as the enchantment is on language...'[52]

The second language section consists of Mr Rooney's 'frigid rhetoric'[53] and evasive short, sharp answers to her 'plaining', contrasting strongly with his wife's effusive candour. 'Chilling her lyricism',[54] from his first word 'Maddy' spoken in a tone of reproof, to his last command: 'Leave the boy alone, he knows nothing! Come on!' (p. 40), his language is charged with calculated cynicism.

He derides Maddy's language even as she uses it to comfort him:

> Never pause ... safe to haven ... Do you know, Maddy, sometimes
> one would think you were struggling with a dead language. (p. 35)

Maddy's simple reply underlines the sense of transience that pervades the play:[55]

Well, you know, it will be dead in time, just like our own poor dear
Gaelic, there is that to be said.

Mr Rooney's language also betrays symptoms of 'the troubled mind' (p. 36),
another subtle strain running through the play.[56] These indications develop
with the play, giving it the semblance of a plot; the mystery of a 'whodunit';
and the denouement 'which has most troubled critics'.[57]

Both of them regard Irish as a dead language.[58] Yet, Dan flaunts his
learning on it, as they trudge home from the station. It is an evasive tactic,
to divert Maddy's investigation of the train delay into linguistics.[59]

> Mrs Rooney: (*in great agitation*). No, I must know, we won't stir from
> here till you tell me. Fifteen minutes late! On a thirty minutes run! It's
> unheard of!

Dan's 'relation' (p. 32) of events on the train, and his long recitation about
retirement, literally left her cold. ('I feel very cold and faint', p. 34). When
the train halted somewhere on the line, Dan told her, he 'sat on, without
misgiving ... time flew by ...' (p. 35). A few seconds later he admitted having
acted 'like a caged beast' (p. 36).

> Mrs Rooney: That is a help sometimes.
>
> Mr Rooney: After what seemed an eternity we moved off. And the
> next thing was Barrell bawling the abhorred name. I got down and
> Jerry led me to the men's, or Fir as they call it now, from Vir Viris I
> suppose, the V becoming F, in accordance with Grimm's Law.
> (*Pause.*) The rest you know. (*Pause.*) You say nothing? (*Pause.*) Say
> something, Maddy. Say you believe me. (p. 36).

Whether she can believe his story about the train is the core of the enigma
of this play.[60] She and all of us, *cannot* accept his explanation of the
derivation of the Irish word, *Fir*.[61]

Fir (men), plural of *Fear* (man) is not of Latin origin. It belonged to the
Irish language centuries before Latin came in with christianity in the fifth
century. David Greene tells us: 'The first loanwords we can identify come
from the Latin of the first Christian missionaries ...' Thereafter the Irish
vocabulary was extended and influenced by the Latin language of the
Church in Ireland.[62] But, he states authoritatively:

> The basis of the vocabulary is, of course, Indo-European through
> Celtic: *dó* 'two', *deich* 'ten', *fear* (Latin *vir*) 'man', ... and hundreds of
> other words have unchallenged Indo-European etymologies, and
> certainly came to Ireland with the Celtic invaders.[63]

Fir is the only pure Irish word in the play ('gobstopper' (p. 27) is half
Irish and half English.) It is interesting that Beckett gives this key word[64]
and the linguistic exercise to Dan, to demonstrate that his 'scholarship'

is as unreliable as the narrative it adorns.

The third type of language used is Hiberno-English. Beckett seems to like this 'hybrid language',[65] and his extensive use of it accounts for an important part of the cultural atmosphere of this radio drama. Hiberno-English is so pervasive throughout the play that some of it merges into the dialogue like standard colloquial English.

The vocabulary of *All That Fall* is mainly standard modern English. There are a few dialect words, e.g. *cleg* — meaning horsefly — 'Cleg-tormented eyes' (p. 8); *stravaging* (p. 17). The *Oxford English Dictionary* gives 'stravaging' as a Scots and Northern dialect word for 'to wander about aimlessly'. In this sense Mr Barrell uses it.

There are extraneous words which Beckett often slips into any list of rhythmic activities in his plays.[66] Dan's long list of 'horrors of home life' (p. 34), include *waning* and *scuffling*: '... waxing, waning, washing,... scuffling, shovelling ....' 'Waning' is not a household task. It comes teeming out of his stream of consciousness after the word 'waxing', with its intimations of floor polish and chamois leather. Similarly, 'scuffling'[67] is, or should be, extraneous to the domestic scene.

Hiberno-English as the basic medium of the dialogue is illustrated in the play by: (a) Verbal usage; (b) Syntax; (c) Idiom.

(a) *Verbal Usage* The Irish language has two forms of the verb 'to be'. One form corresponds to English 'is, was' (Ir. *tá, bhí*), and the other, called the copula, has no equivalent in British English, but in Hiberno-English is converted into a range of non-standard constructions using clauses beginning with 'It is, It's', etc.[68]

Beckett uses the copula construction frequently in this radio play: 'Is it that you have no head for heights?' Maddy asks Christy (p. 8). British English — Have you no head for heights?

Miss Fitt: Is it my arm you want then? (*Pause. Impatiently*)

Is it my arm you want, Mrs Rooney, or what is it? (p. 21)

A non-Irish speaker would say, 'Do you want my arm then?'

Beckett's use of the 'Is it' construction based on the Irish copula shows the faculty which the Irish language has for emphasising one element in a clause over others. In other circumstances Miss Fitt could have said: 'Is it you (that) wants my arm?' In these examples the basic question is converted into a relative clause headed by the conjunction 'that' which is not written, but understood.

(b) *Syntax* The syntax of the Irish language also underlies the word-order of the Indirect Questions. In Irish an Indirect Question retains the order of the Direct Question, whereas in Standard English the position of the verb and subject are changed.[69] Beckett gives two illustrations of this construction:

> Mrs Rooney: Oh there is that Fitt woman, I wonder will she bow to me. (p. 19)
>
> Mr Barrell: (to Tommy) Nip up to the box now and see has Mr Case anything for me. (p. 24)

In both examples the Indirect Question retains the reversed word-order of the original question, as it does in Irish, whereas Standard English would be: 'I wonder if she will bow to me' and 'see if Mr Case has anything for me.'

The Irishness of Maddy's language is overshadowed by her 'bizarre'[70] way of speaking. Her biblical expressions sound archaic and quaint in the context of modern English.

> Mrs Rooney: (*brokenly*). In her forties now she'd be, ...girding up her lovely little loins ... (p. 12)

The reversed word-order, and the conditional mood of the verb 'to be' with 'It is' understood, show that it is Hiberno-English ('It is in her forties now she'd be') but the biblical quotation — from Luke 12: 35 — has a greater impact on the ear. In Standard English, one would say, 'She would be in her forties now'.[71]

(c) *Idiom* The Hiberno-English idiom includes such pious expressions as are common to the Irish language and have been carried over into English through the centuries.[72] They are compelling phrases, whether issued as a request or a command:

> Mrs Rooney: Wait, for God's sake, you'll have me beheaded. (p. 16)
>
> Mr Slocum: Do as you're asked, Tommy, for the love of God. (p. 16)
>
> Mr Barrell: Ah God forgive me, it's a hard life. (p. 17).

After the pious idioms comes 'Thought for the Day':[73] 'Mr Tyler: ...Divine day for the meeting.' (p. 10). Later he said bitterly to Mrs Rooney:

> ... Now therefore we are doubly late, trebly, quadrupedly late. Would I had shot by you without a word.
>
> Tommy: (to Mr Slocum) You wouldn't have something for the Ladies Plate, sir? I was given Flash Harry.

In *All That Fall*, since 'Beckett wants to offer the ear as much variety as possible'[74] he gives the Hiberno-English expressions to all the characters, including, as we have seen, Miss Fitt and Mrs Rooney. Vivian Mercier says: 'Another unusual feature is the Irish English spoken by the working-class characters'.[75] They all speak Irish English at some stage in the text. In similar vein Ruby Cohn writes:

The structural division of *All That Fall*, with its changing auditory textures, shows Beckett's customary mastery of the genre, but his major achievement is his control of speech.

In this first successful return to his narrative language since *Watt*, the Anglo-Irish is localised and faintly out-of-date.

Her selected examples of this are by no means 'out-of-date':

We find such Irish locutions as 'surely to goodness', 'destroyed with', 'with time to spare', 'stravaging down here', 'get on with you now', 'nip up to', 'will you get along with you'.[76]

Moreover she omitted quite a number of more typical Irishisms, e.g.:

Christy: I suppose you wouldn't be in need of a small load of dung? (p. 8)

....

... She's very fresh in herself today. [the hinny]

Mr Barrell: ... Tommy! Blast your bleeding body ... (p. 17)

Mrs Rooney: (fretting over her torn frock) What will Dan say when he sees me?

Mr Slocum: Has he then recovered his sight? (p. 15)

Mrs Rooney: (being lifted into Slocum's limousine) Suppose I do get up, will I ever get down?

Mr Slocum: (breathing hard) You'll get down, Mrs Rooney, you'll get down. We may not get you up, but I warrant you we'll get you down. (p. 14)

Beckett's linguistic homecoming in *All That Fall*, and the refreshing respite from the discipline of writing in French drew his own comment on the play: 'It is a text written to come out of the dark.'[77]

As Vivian Mercier points out in 'Thesis/Antithesis':[78] 'The dark has many connotations for Beckett.' They vary with each play, but he frequently presents the dark as a source of illumination or discovery. Its meaning in this play may be deduced from Beckett's letters to director Alan Simpson who sought permission to *stage* the play at the Pike Theatre, Dublin, in January 1958. The first letter was firm:

I have already refused right left and centre permission to 'dramatise' *All That Fall*. I can't bear the thought of the adjustments it would require...

Simpson replied, saying that what he had in mind was 'little more than' a reading of *All That Fall*, 'with a few "props" such as steps, motor seat, bike, etc.' and assumed this would be all right. On 28 January, Beckett assured him that it was *not* all right:

By a straight reading I mean no props or make up or action of any kind, simply the players standing reading the text. The ideal for me would be a stage in darkness with a spot picking out the faces as required. It is a text written to come out of the dark and I suppose that is the nearest one could get to that with a stage reading. There could be a preliminary presentation of the characters, with lights on, by a speaker, who would also read the indications given in the text with regard to sounds, movements, etc., many of which I think could be omitted. No sound effects ... All I want you to observe is the strict limits of a reading ...[79]

Beckett made it absolutely clear that he intended the characters in *All That Fall* to be heard and not seen.[80] 'It is a text written to come out of the dark' means that it is clearly a radio play: coming from the dark basements of Broadcasting House, where ever they chance to be.[81] It means that language and sound are the essentials, in this play. The inspiration too, came out of the dark to Beckett as he considered the offer from the BBC in July 1956. On July 5, 1956, he wrote to Nancy Cunard in Texas:

... Never thought about a radio play technique, but in the dead of t'other night got a nice gruesome idea full of cartwheels and dragging feet and puffing and panting which may or may not lead to something.

Quoting this letter, Deirdre Bair adds:

It was the genesis of *All That Fall*, and he worked sporadically on it during the summer, finishing the first draft in a burst of energy in September 1956.[82]

With dramatic ingenuity, and intimate local knowledge, his illumination 'in the dark of t'other night' reached fruition, in the play he could have subtitled: 'A Nice Gruesome Idea'!

Referring to the destructive forces that Beckett parodies, Webb writes:

The deepest problem of this world is a general failure ... to live on a level deeper than that of shallow conventionality. The kind of gentility that isolates people from one another ... the kind of religious life that is concerned more with appearance than with any reality, in general the kind of timidity that inhibits any impulse toward individual thought and experience — all of this is what reduces the life of Boghill to sterility.

Miss Fitt fits the description, he says ...

Probably the best example in the play of the deadening, perverting power of convention is Miss Fitt, the very embodiment of 'gentility and church-going.'[83]

Notwithstanding 'all of this' — shallow convention, class distinction, religious facade — common features of society everywhere — life in Boghill is certainly *not* reduced to sterility, as some critics say:

> Sterility, in fact, is something of an obsession with these Irish sub-
> urbanites. ... This all-pervasive note of sterility infects love itself,
> something in which Maddy struggles still to believe.[84]

In fact 'sterility' is an obsession with the foreign critics of the play, perhaps because they are remote from the scene, and read too much into symbols. Only once does the word 'sterile' occur in the text (p. 38).

> Maddy: You know, hinnies ... aren't they barren, or sterile, or
> whatever it is?

Life in Boghill, as depicted in *All That Fall*, is the very opposite of sterile. It is a throbbing, pulsating, convivial life under a healthy addiction to the sport of kings.[85] In our world today, there are less edifying pursuits than their excitement over a race meeting, and more barren pastimes than having a flutter on Flash Harry in the Ladies Plate (p. 17).

In 'the oldest phallic kind of comedy', (Cohn p. 165), the lambs and the laburnum, the language and the landscape[86] are a riot of colour. The background music is not only the 'Death of the Maiden', but the cooing of the ringdoves, (p. 12) the vociferate bustle on arrival and departure of a local train, and implicit in this pastoral scene, 'the music of the growing grass'.[87]

The eleven characters — a cross section of the community — are all individualists, with no trace of 'the kind of timidity that inhibits any impulse towards individual thought and experience', as Webb infers. This is evident even in the minor characters. Fletcher writes: 'The minor figures are minimally sketched but assume a natural and vivid identity ....' (p. 73).

To one of the minor figures, Jerry, Beckett entrusts the key to the *mystery* in the play. As usual there is early warning of this, and as usual in a seemingly inconsequential piece of dialogue. Mrs Rooney, frantically look-ing for her husband at the station, and not seeing him anywhere, in des-peration called:

> Tommy! ... Did you see the master?
> Tommy: He'll be along, Ma'am, Jerry is minding him.
> *Mr Rooney suddenly appears on platform, advancing on small boy Jerry's
> arm* .... (p. 26)

Dan greeted Maddy in 'a voice as cold as Stonehenge'.[88] Later:

> Mr Rooney: Why did you not cancel the boy? Now we shall have to
> give him a penny.
> Mrs Rooney: (*miserably*). I forgot! I had such a time getting here! Such
> horrid nasty people!

(*Pause. Pleading.*)

Be nice to me, Dan, be nice to me today!

Mr Rooney: Give the boy a penny.

Mrs Rooney: Here are two halfpennies, Jerry. Run along now and buy yourself a gobstopper.

Jerry: Yes, Ma'am. (p. 27)

Gobstopper is a key word as the play rises to a crescendo of unreal realism in a medley of verbal and variously mechanical sounds. (p. 26) *Gob* is the Irish word for beak, mouth, bill, snout, and also for the mouth or mouth-piece of various tools and instruments.[89] *Gobach* is talkative or gossipy. Gobstopper, intimating a kind of silencer for Jerry who is privy to information concerning Dan's homicidal character, marks the beginning of the final movement, 'with psychological analyses and a mysterious end'. (Fletcher, p. 75). Jerry, on Dan's admission, is in grave danger of his master's violence.. 'Many a time at night, in winter, on the black road home, I nearly attacked the boy. (*Pause.*) Poor Jerry!' (p. 31).

Jerry was 'minding' Dan in the crucial moments when he was missing while Maddy in a frenzy of excitement sought him on the platform. Dan was unable to give a credible account of the circumstances of the child's death, or of his guilt or innocence with regard to it. Webb writes:

> Whether Dan has actually murdered the child on the train or not —
> the circumstances are vague but sinister — he is obviously homi-
> cidal ... (p. 52)

Jerry helps supply the final enigma in the mysterious end — he ran after Dan to give him 'something' he had dropped .... 'a kind of ball ... yet it is not a ball.' Dan says 'It is a thing I carry about with me' (p. 40).

A clue to the enigma of the ball may be found in *The Unnamable*, a horrendous novel that haunted Beckett as he wrote the play.[90] In it he stated: '... It is a great smooth ball I carry on my shoulders, featureless, but for the eyes, of which only the sockets remain...'[91]

The novel is autobiographical. '*The Unnamable* came from the depths of his being'.[92] It describes the progressive disintegration of a being, calling himself The Unnamable, because he cannot find in himself an atom of identity. Beckett himself said of it:

> In my last book *L'Innommable*, there's complete disintegration. No
> 'I', no 'have', no 'being', no nominative, no accusative, no verb.
> There's no way to go on.[93]

The Unnamable goes on, however, *talking*: the novel 'is really about the obsessive-compulsive need for words'.[94] In the same passage as above he says:

> ... I'm a big talking ball, talking about things that do not exist, or that
> exist perhaps, impossible to know, beside the point.[95]

Beckett frequently uses material, metaphor and ideas from an earlier work,
in a current piece of writing.[96] Lines[97] from *The Unnamable* are echoed by
Mr Rooney:

> ... The loss of my sight was a great fillip. If I could go deaf and dumb
> I think I might pant on to be a hundred. Or have I done so?... (p. 32)

Blind Dan carries the symbolic ball about with him. He had proved himself
an inveterate talker in two long speeches: (*Narrative tone*). In one of them he
was 'talking about things that do not exist' (p. 34); in the other, 'that exist
perhaps, impossible to know'. His detailed explanation of how things were
on the train, he calls a 'composition'.

> Mr Rooney: Where was I in my composition?
>
> Mrs Rooney: At a standstill. (p. 35)

Beckett can create reams with one word. 'Something' or a 'thing' is a key
word, and mystery assumes the volume of its vagueness as rage fuels the
enigma of the ball.

> Mr Rooney: (*violently.*) It is a thing I carry about with me. (p. 40)

Beckett infers that Dan, like The Unnamable, is just 'a big talking ball', the
content, fact or fiction — 'beside the point'. 'For certainties, Beckett will
never cease to tell us, are largely conventions and bounded by a mystery.'[98]

Finally, Jerry is the innocent who brings about the 'trick ending' which
'has most troubled critics' (Fletcher, p. 75). Speaking against 'the master's'
insistence he gives the explanation Maddy had failed to elicit from Dan, as
to why the train was late.

> *Jerry:* It was a little child fell out of the carriage, Ma'am. (*Pause.*) On
> to the line, Ma'am. (*Pause.*) Under the wheels, Ma'am.
> *Silence. Jerry runs off. His steps die away. Tempest of wind and rain. It
> abates. They move on. Dragging steps, etc. They halt. Tempest of wind and
> rain.* (p. 41)

Jerry's stunning revelation, in three simple, staggered, sentences, beggars
human language; reverberating in *silence, standstill,* and the fundamental
sounds of cosmic symbols — *Tempest of wind and rain.*

Criticism of the surprise ending abounds and rebounds with varying
degrees of controlled irritation. Hugh Kenner writes:

> It comes as a brutal and shocking fact, rupturing the elegiac tone of
> the inimitably gentle grotesquerie by which we have been suffused
> for seventy-five minutes.
>
> Until now the indomitable language has absorbed every human
> shock.... But: 'Under the wheels, ma'am.' There is no reply. Not even

Mrs Rooney will be able to cope with this for several weeks. It is too
terrible for apothegm, epigram, cadence, or plaint.

The dead language with which she struggles and from which she
wrests the satisfactions of eloquence is suddenly defeated by something intransigently alive: a death.[99]

In his later book (1973) Kenner too, has absorbed the shock of the
denouement:

All That Fall ... ends ambiguously according to daytime logic but
logically according to the laws of a world where all reality is audi-
ble... Knowing how dependent we should be on words, Beckett in
his first radio script lavished all his resources of eloquence on
shaping the speeches; the work may have relieved him amid
Endgame's austerities.[100]

Fletcher and Spurling, have paid tribute to the wit and humour, and
declared *All That Fall* 'one of the most satisfying dramatic statements',
nevertheless express dissatisfaction with the surprise ending:

And the violent mystery of Jerry's closing words presents the hearer
with a problem not easily resolved — one perhaps more painful to
sustain than the blank stare of two men waiting at a roadside for a
saviour unable to keep an appointment; one certainly more pain-
fully concrete as the medium of wireless is baselessly immaterial, an
insubstantial pageant which leaves its enigmas entire.[101]

In his later book (1978), Fletcher too, has mellowed, being now familiar
with the Joycean element in Beckett's technique: 'Dissociated metaphor'.
He writes:

All through the play we are given ominous hints which are not so
evident on first reading or hearing as when one rereads with the
knowledge of the surprise ending. Not only is there an obsession
with death — Schubert's music, the various moribund relatives ....
but we also find specific hints about railway accidents such as the
unknown woman warning her little girl against being sucked under
the train. The whole thing is beautifully orchestrated until the last
few pages with its shock ending, and it is this which has most
troubled critics.[102]

Today we are more familiar with Beckett's 'all-pervasive dialectic',[103]
and can perceive the 'shock ending' as an integral part of his 'beautifully
orchestrated' dialogue, Schubert music and pastoral arias from the environs
of Foxrock. I see the 'trick ending' as a Beckettian stratagem to:

(a) Retract the biographical verities in the play. He wants to present
as yet another illusion,[104] the fact that in it he is 'creating with words
beings not himself, but perfecting his own identity in perfecting

their words'. He tries to extricate himself from the nostalgic sentiment that inspired the play.[105]

(b) As Kenner points out, ... 'the play is steeped in transience, a
transience more total because there is nothing whatever that we can
see, no tree onstage ....'[106] Beckett, the perfect dramatic tactician, is
very conscious of the transience of his medium — radio — and his
material — language/sound. He wants to salvage something from
'a purely aural landscape capitalising eerily on the fact that whatever falls silent disappears.' He gives a detective dimension to this
otherwise straight play with its mainly realistic, individualistic 'people', knowing where they are and why. Dan alone is saying: 'I dream
of other roads, in other lands. Of another home, another — (*he
hesitates*) — another home.' (pp. 32-3).

(c) The *impact* of the shock ending impels *involvement* in the play. It
is now the listener's or reader's chess game; their turn to begin
'plotting moves',[107] but in reverse, as they recall the scenario, and
reconstruct the scene. *All That Fall* now has a plot, as the title might
suggest. Casual words — 'mangling, ... banging and slamming. And
the brats, ... ' in Dan's narrative (p. 34); and a few pages earlier a
mother's caution to a child ... 'Mind yourself, Dolly!', and precaution
... 'Give me your hand and hold me tight, one can be sucked under.'
(p. 23) — must be reassessed in the light of: .... 'Under the wheels,
Ma'am.'

Mrs Rooney may not be able to cope with this for several weeks. But
Beckett makes sure that listeners may take years to collate the evidence
for or against Dan's responsibility for the child's death. However long it
takes, Beckett knows they will reach a 'standstill' (p. 34) (another checkmate!); with the ambivalent verdict 'Not Proven' the penny for their
'pains' (p. 40).

Meanwhile *All That Fall*, unlike Dan, gets a total reprieve. Like Time, its
very transience is the essence of its endurance. Such is the Beckett paradox!

NOTES

1 Quoted from Fletcher, et al., *A Student's Guide to the Plays of Samuel Beckett*, , p. 71.
2 Ibid.
3 Cohn, *Back to Beckett*, p. 158.
4 Bair, *Samuel Beckett*, p. 403.
5 The critics' acclaim came just at a time when his favourite play, *Fin de partie*, was

being rejected by all the Paris theatre managers who had refused *Godot*. See Bair, op. cit., pp. 402 - 405.

6   Fletcher, et al., *A Student's Guide to the Plays of Samuel Beckett*, pp. 71-3.

7   It is a combination of suburban, rural, and turf or racing country.

8   Quoted in Lyons, *Samuel Beckett*, p. 80.

9   Ibid., p. 82.

10 Fletcher, et al., *A Student's Guide to the Plays of Samuel Beckett*, pp. 72, 79.

11 O'Brien, *The Beckett Country*, p. 350, Note 48.

12 Metaphor hidden in the text. The term is used by Frank O'Connor to describe a metaphorical construction invented by James Joyce in *Ulysses*. Later it became a common element in Beckett's word coinage. See O'Connor, *A Short History of Irish Literature*, pp. 200 - 204.

13 Bellamy, D.J., 'The Wild Boglands' (pp. 15 - 21) and Piggott, C., 'Turf for the Family Fire' (pp. 29 - 35) in *Ireland of the Welcomes*, Vol. 36, No. 3, 1987.

14 See *Brewer's Dictionary of Phrase and Fable*, p. 917.

15 O'Brien, *The Beckett Country*, pp. 40, 350, Note 60.

16 Ibid., pp. 39 - 43.

17 *All That Fall*, p. 36. Mr Rooney's reference to Boghill in his 'story' about the late train.

18 O'Brien, Eoin, 'Beckett is of the World... but Irish', published in *A Supplement to 'The Irish Times'*, Saturday, April 12, 1986.

19 Mercier , *Beckett/Beckett*, p. 21.

20 Beckett sent the manuscript of *All That Fall* to John Morris at the BBC and included a note about the special kind of 'bruitage' (sound effects) that might be necessary. After much experimentation the various sounds needed were effectively produced. This led directly to the establishment of the BBC's Radiophonic Workshop. It is a monument to this unique play.

21 Bair, *Samuel Beckett*, pp. 31 - 34.

22 Jacobsen and Mueller *The Testament of Samuel Beckett*, p. 49.

23 Eoin O'Brien, writing on his decision 'to endow *The Beckett Country* with a visual perspective through the art of photography, rather than painting', says: 'The visual portrayal of that land could only be achieved by an artist willing to familiarise himself with the terrain, its people and its fickle sky and light'. The artist 'developed an empathy with the moods of the land and its Beckettian character.... often returning many times to a particular place to catch the moment when light, sky and object were in harmony with the Beckett spirit,.....' (From 'Beckett is of the World... but Irish').

24 Bair, *Samuel Beckett*, p. 20. His mother rode daily in a donkey-drawn cart. Christy's cart carried a load of manure. Beckett often saw this delivered at his home, for their large vegetable gardens. See p. 18.

25 In June 1926, he went alone to Tours, France, to begin a bicycle tour of the château country. A young American he met there joined him. Together they spent a

month cycling round the country. It marked the beginning of Beckett's fascination with France, (Bair, op. cit., p. 50).

26 'The bicycle is integral to Beckett's work;... it is perfectly appropriate that a bicycle should steal the scene at this point: it is the climax of the crisis... The pun seems to give the bicycle a personality, so that for a moment it is the centre of attention; yet it, too, disappears and is forgotten.' Quoted from Menzies, Janet, 'Beckett's Bicycles', *Journal of Beckett Studies*, Autumn 1980, No. 6, p. 98. The quotation refers to the bicycle in *Watt*, but it applies to *All That Fall*, too. The novel and the play have other features in common, including the setting.

27 Bair, *Samuel Beckett*, p. 52.

28 Bair, *Samuel Beckett*, pp. 52, 53.

29 O'Brien, *The Beckett Country*, p. 22. Connolly's Stores and public house, now called 'The Cornelscourt Arms', is pictured on p. 21.

30 Ibid., p. 349, note 32, which states that the Beckett family received their groceries daily from Mr Connolly's van.

31 Fletcher, et al., *A Student's Guide to the Plays of Samuel Beckett*, pp. 72, 73.

32 'The Slow and Easy' was the nickname bestowed by Samuel Beckett and his fellow pupils, on the local train of The Dublin and South Eastern Railway on which they travelled to and from the Earlsfort House School which was beside the Harcourt Street Station. The terminus and the train feature in many of Beckett's writings.

33 O'Brien, *The Beckett Country*, p. 32.

34 Ibid., p. 20.

35 Ibid., p. 40. Mr Fred Clarke is pictured sitting on the steps of the stand beside Beckett's father, William Beckett, at the Leopardstown Racecourse.

36 Ibid., p. 32. Mr Farrell is seen in his station-master's uniform. One of his Diplomas (1943) is also pictured here.

37 O'Brien, *The Beckett Country*, p. 350, Note 46. O'Brien writes: 'His grandfather had been station-master when the station was opened in the 1850's, and his father had been station-master before him. Thomas Farrell was appointed station-master in 1928.' Beckett would have known both Thomas Farrell and his father well. Mrs Rooney's profile of the father was very likely true.

38 Kenner, *A Reader's Guide to Samuel Beckett*, p. 161.

39 *Encyclopedia of Ireland*, p. 119.

40 Webb, *The Plays of Samuel Beckett*, pp. 52, 53.

41 Dinneen, *Irish-English Dictionary*, p. 358.

42 She does not call her *life* a manure-heap, but the trials of life, or tribulations that pile up and afflict her life with Dan; among them tyranny and frigidity. He wants her to count all the steps they climb. Maddy says she cannot count and guide him at the same time. He might fall and 'I would have that on my manure-heap on top of everything else', she says. (p. 29) He would scold her, and curse and blast. This he does at this point in any case: '*Painting, stumbling,*

ejaculations, curses, Silence.'

43 An irresistible urge to go on, to persevere, to continue. From *Molly*, p. 87.

44 Cohn, *Back to Beckett*, pp. 164, 165.

45 Beckett's own expression. See Jacobsen and Mueller, *The Testament of Samuel Beckett*, p. 162.

46 Isolation and alienation have *language* as their root cause there as elsewhere in the world.

47 Lyons, *Samuel Beckett*, p. 75.

48 Ibid., p. 78.

49 *All That Fall*, p. 18, the recipient is Mr Barrell; p. 22, Miss Fitt is Maddy's target.

50 Ramadan: The Mohammedan ninth month, the time of the annual fasting of thirty days; also, the fast.

51 Kenner, *A Reader's Guide to Samuel Beckett*, p. 161.

52 Ibid., p. 160.

53 Ibid.

54 Ibid., p. 161.

55 Kenner, *Samuel Beckett*, p. 169.

56 Note Dan's reaction to Maddy's line (p. 33): 'Something about your mind'.

57 Fletcher, et al., *A Student's Guide to the Plays of Samuel Beckett*, p. 75.

58 To paraphrase Mark Twain: Reports of its death are greatly exaggerated. According to the 1981 Census Irish speakers in Ireland (Republic) represented 31.6 per cent of the total population. See Appendix 1, *The Irish Language*.

59 Lyons, *Samuel Beckett*, p. 88.

60 Ibid. It is given no stronger credence than — 'possibly fictitious' here.

61 See Appendix I, *The Irish Language*.

62 Greene, David, *The Irish Language*, Dublin, 1966, pp. 17, 25.

63 Ibid., p. 25. The Celtic invaders came about 300 BC.

64 *Fir* or 'the men's' (Beckett writes it 'the men's, or Fir as they call it now,') or the gentlemen's toilet, is Dan's alibi in the 'detective story' element of this play.

65 Dolan, T.P., 'Samuel Beckett's Dramatic Use of Hiberno-English', *Irish University Review*, Spring 1984, p. 46.

66 *Waiting for Godot* has a litany of 'sports' in Lucky's speech, which brings in extraneous words, p. 43.

67 Scuffle v/i fight or struggle confusedly. Garmonsway, G.N., *The Penguin English Dictionary*, Penguin Books Ltd., 1965, p. 616.

68 Dolan, 'Samuel Beckett's Dramatic Use of Hiberno-English, p. 48.

69 Dolan, 'Samuel Beckett's Dramatic Use of Hiberno-English', p. 48.

70 *Bizarre* means eccentric, odd, strange, grotesque, quaint. (*The Penguin English Dictionary* p. 68.)

71 Dolan, 'Samuel Beckett's Dramatic Use of Hiberno-English', p. 49.

72 Rosenstock, Gabriel, 'Language and Grace', *Ireland of the Welcomes*, Vol. 31, No. 5, 1982, p. 31.

73 'Thought for the Day' was the title of a BBC early morning sermon of about five minutes duration. Beckett shows that the Godhead is enshrined in the idiom which they use unconsciously, but for them the real thought for the day concerns the race meeting, the punters and the tipsters.

74 Mercier, *Beckett/Beckett*, p. 148.

75 Ibid.

76 Cohn, *Back to Beckett*, p. 163.

77 Reid, *All I Can Manage, More Than I Could*, p. 68.

78 Mercier, *Beckett/Beckett*, p. 7.

79 Quoted in Murray, 'Beckett Productions in Ireland: A Survey', pp. 107-8.

80 He was unhappy with readings of the play in New York and with a stage presentation in Berlin in 1966.

81 Robert Pinger's translation of *All That Fall* (*Toux ceux qui tombent*) was broadcast in France in January 1963.

82 Bair, *Samuel Beckett*, p. 401.

83 Webb, *The Plays of Samuel Beckett*, pp. 47-8.

84 Fletcher and Spurling, *Beckett: A Study of His Plays*, pp. 85, 86.

85 Some facts about horse racing in Ireland from the *Encyclopedia of Ireland*, pp. 426, 427: 'Horse racing and breeding is a highly organised sport which plays a significant role in Ireland's social and economic life, providing large-scale employment, earning valuable foreign currency and returning more than a million pounds per annum in betting tax .... no comprehensive records prior to the 18th century. We do know that it formed an integral part of the entertainment at the celebrated games, the *Aonach Tailteann*, and that it has been carried on in the Curragh, Co. Kildare, for more than two thousand years. Indeed the name Curragh is derived from the Irish *Currach*, a race horse. ... More than 170 days' racing are held in the course of the year at ... 31 tracks ... The Curragh and Leopardstown each have 15 days racing.... ' Leopardstown, near Dublin, is the race course that figures in the play.

86 *All That Fall*, p. 23. Maddy describes 'The entire scene, the hills, the plain, the race-course....'

87 Kennelly, Brendan, 'A Tongue to a Stone', *Ireland of the Welcomes*, Vol. 30, No. 2, 1981, where he describes 'the music of the growing grass'.

88 Kenner, *A Reader's Guide to Samuel Beckett*, p. 161.

89 Dinneen, *Irish-English Dictionary*, p. 557.

90 *L'Innommable*, the third novel of the trilogy written in French between 1947 and 1949, was on Beckett's schedule for translation into English, in Summer 1956. Having to relive the torture of writing it 'was too terrible to contemplate'. Instead, he spent the summer on the first draft of the play.

91 *The Unnamable*, p. 307.

92 Bair, *Samuel Beckett*, p. 340.

93 Ibid., p. 338.

94 Ibid.

95 *The Unnamable*, p. 307.

96 Bair, *Samuel Beckett*, p. 339.

97 Lines from a passage ...'All those things have fallen ... with my eyes, my hair ... (p. 307).

98 Kenner, *Samuel Beckett*, p. 168.

99 Kenner, *Samuel Beckett, A Critical Study*, p. 174.

100 Kenner, *A Reader's Guide to Samuel Beckett*, pp. 159 - 160.

101 Fletcher and Spurling, *Beckett: A Study of his Plays*, p. 88.

102 Fletcher et al., *A Student's Guide to the Plays of Samuel Beckett*, p. 75.

103 Mercier, *Beckett/Beckett*, p. 11.

104 Kenner, *Samuel Beckett*, pp. 168 - 171.

105 Beckett was allowed to choose the subject: the play was commissioned by the BBC in 1956.

106 Kenner, *Samuel Beckett*, pp. 168-9.

107 Chess is the symbol he exploited when writing the two previous plays: *Godot* and *Endgame*. Bair, *Samuel Beckett*, p. 323.

Chapter Six

KRAPP'S LAST TAPE

When Beckett wrote *Krapp's Last Tape* in 1958, he had never seen a tape recorder. He had heard about a new machine which could store away for future use any song or story voiced in its presence, with every inflection and nuance irrevocably registered. He had also heard a radio broadcast of the Irish actor, Patrick Magee, reading extracts from *Molloy, Malone Dies*, and *From an Abandoned Work*, on the Third Programme of the BBC. The idea of the new machine recording Magee's voice was his inspiration for this play. He wrote the play for one actor, and utilising the device of the tape recorder to highlight the solitary figure image, and 'as a stage metaphor for time past',[1] he 'enables present to confront past and past to confront present'.[2]

This new play with new techniques further exploring his old theme — Time — is acclaimed by the critics as a brilliant dramatisation of the ideas contained in his essay on Proust (1931), concerning *Time* and *Habit*. In it Beckett stated his conviction that men

> ... are victims of this predominating condition and circumstance — Time ... victims and prisoners. ... There is no escape from yesterday because yesterday has deformed us, or been deformed by us. ...

and that

> Life is habit. Or rather life is a succession of habits, since the individual is a succession of individuals; the world being a projec-

tion of the individual's consciousness ... the pact must be continually renewed.[3]

Superficially it is a dramatisation of the Proustian ideas, written when Beckett's ambitious exuberance matched that of young Krapp ... 'Shadows of the opus ... magnum...' (p. 13), derided by K-39, with, 'Hard to believe I was ever that young whelp. The voice! Jesus! And the aspirations!' (p. 13)

Looking at the play in depth, it has little in common with *Proust*. The critics' interpretation would remove all guilt for his actions from Krapp, and place it on abstractions: Time and Habit. In fact, Krapp's free will renders him accountable for his actions; and *his* free will prevails throughout the play.

If Krapp — Beckett himself — is the victim of *Time*, it is that it elicits a confession of his indolence, sleezy diversions from sloth, and a belated admission that his way of life has obscured the meaning of life: '... Perhaps my best years are gone. When there was a chance of happiness.' (p. 20)

The 'chance of happiness' was the love he rejected for the chance of fame in the beckoning shadows of the opus magnum.[4] Nor is he the prisoner of Time: he is his own prisoner. 'Beckett has devised his own prison. He was thrust into it at an early age to serve a life sentence of solitary confinement, and what is merely a metaphor for others is a daily reality for him.'[5] Not Time but alienation is his goaler.

'*Krapp's Last Tape* projects a sense of time as a series of endings.'[6] The *endings* of relationships result in, or from, an acute sense of alienation.

The typical Beckettian paradox is that this self-willed alienation requires for its realisation the presence of others. He seeks company in order to enjoy his alienation.[7] The gregarious instinct remains intact, while all his other instincts conspire to destroy it. It is an exercise in the pursuit of personal 'freedom'.

In Beckett's first finished play, *Eleuthéria*,[8] Greek for 'freedom', written in French in 1947, the hero, Victor Krap, makes that kind of freedom his life's goal. Krap explains:

> D'abord j'étais prisonnier des autres. Alors je les ai quittés. Puis j'étais prisonnier du moi. C'était pire. Alors je me suis quitté.[9]
>
> First I was a prisoner of the others. Then I left them. Then I was a prisoner of myself. That was worse. Then I left myself.

Victor Krap was forced to admit in the end:

> I will never be free. (*Pause.*) But I will ceaselessly feel myself becoming free. (*Pause.*) I'll tell you how I'll live my life away: rubbing my chains against one another. From morning to night, and from night

to morning. That faint vain noise will be my life.[10]
We hear 'that faint vain noise' of Beckett's chains in his play of a decade later, *Krapp's Last Tape*.

Both Krap and Krapp are engaged in 'the search for self'.[11]

Habit, in its psychological meaning, 'automatic response to specific situations',[12] is an essential adjunct in the structure and credibility of the play. The snatches or fragments of his life-story recorded on tapes, while rich in detail, do not form a coherent narrative. Habit connects the three phases in Krapp's life, marking points of identification between the young man in his twenties, K-39, and K-69.

Stages in his development are held together in the play by habits and routines that grow on and with him over a period of forty years. Tendencies, e.g. his drinking, womanising, intellectual arrogance, and cynicism revealed in the young Krapp segment of tape, (pp. 12, 13), have become habit in the K-39 recording, despite 'the resolutions' quoted in the earlier tape. At 69, habit is so much part of his personality and way of life that for the obligatory birthday recording he has 'Nothing to say, not a squeak.' (p. 18). Yet, he has a squeak left for a few small mercies: '... Getting known ... Fanny ... booze ... Be again ...' (19).

Krapp's instant 'retrospect' on his 'last' tape:- 'this drivel' (p. 19), recalls Beckett's PM[13] on his essay on Proust, written in his own handwriting on the title page of a copy found in a second-hand bookshop in Dublin, some years ago. It read: 'I have written my book in a cheap flashy philosophical jargon'.[14] That cannot be said of *Krapp's Last Tape*.

Synopsis

Time: *A Late evening in the future.*

Home tape recording began in the middle 1950's, and as Krapp's archives span more than forty years of tapes,[15] the time of the play is put forward to 'a late evening in the future'.

Scene: *Krapp's den*. The word 'den' has many meanings in English. Figuratively, most of them fit Krapp's sanctum: 'cage for captive animal; hiding place of thieves; small private room; / small squalid room; a lair; cavern'.[16] The *Oxford Dictionary* gives as its colloquial meaning 'a small, comfortable study or workshop where a person may be alone and undisturbed'.[17] All of them have overtones of isolation, refuge, or self imprisonment. These images are recalled in comments by Eugene Webb: ' ... the key element in his character is moral isolation. He is a person who, through various choices at different times, has made his life into a prison and who is driven in old age to the realisation that he is about to die without having ever really lived.'[18] Hugh Kenner refers to Krapp in his den as a 'refugee from some vaudeville'[19] — the clown stereotype. C.R. Lyons says, 'he clearly sees his den as a refuge.'[20]

Productions and Reception

The play, which 'was early recognised as a minor dramatic masterpiece',[21] was performed and acclaimed internationally within two years of publication.[22] The one-man cast puts the onus of success or failure on the actor, and Beckett allows him a margin of freedom from the rigid specifications of the text, to enhance his interpretation of the character.[23] Wherever the play is realised the actor shares the laurels with the author, who, in later productions, is often its director as well.

Krapp's Last Tape was first performed at the Royal Court Theatre, London, on October 28, 1958: Patrick Magee played Krapp. The original manuscript of the play is titled 'Magee Monologue',[24] and his performance justified this distinction. Tending towards the indigenous understatement, a critic wrote '... the soliloquy has found, for the first and probably the last time, a form which combines the immobile mask and the mobile face, mime and speech, monologue and dialogue, and offers all their various resources to one performer'. (Roy Walker, *Twentieth Century*, December 1958).[25]

Performed in New York in January 1960, it was assessed as Beckett's 'best dramatic poem about the old age of the world', flawless and economical, haunting and harrowing. (Robert Brustein, *New Republic*, 22 February 1960).[26]

The first production in France was at the Théâtre Récamier, Paris, on March 22, 1960. A French actor, R.J. Chauffard, played Krapp. It was seen as 'a kind of lyrical poem of solitude' (Robert Kanters, *L'Express*, 31 March 1960), and there was general critical acclaim.[27]

The play was performed at the Empire Theatre, Belfast, on June 14, 1960. The veteran Irish actor, Cyril Cusack, was in his element as Krapp. Implicit in enthusiastic reviews of Cusack's interpretation of the character was praise for the play. One critic called it 'a gem of acting' (The *Northern Whig*, 15 June, 1960). Another described it as 'altogether miraculous... This was an experience of life, explored to the last ounce of weariness, lechery, disillusion and fantasy' (Ray Rosenfeld, *Plays and Players*, August 1960).[28]

The performance at the Queen's Theatre, Dublin, a week later, left the actor's laurels intact, but the play was considered 'too sordid'. A reviewer wrote: 'only an artist of Cusack's brilliance could make it tolerable' (M.C. in *The Evening Press*, 21 June, 1960).[29] The following weeks saw perform-ances of *Krapp's Last Tape* (on a double bill with *Arms and the Man*), by the Irish touring company founded by Cyril Cusack, in Rotterdam, Amster-dam, The Hague, Antwerp and Paris. The plays were presented at the Sarah Bernhardt theatre, for the International Festival of Theatre in Paris, on July 8, 1960. For his portrayal of Krapp, Cyril Cusack won the best actor award at the Paris International Festival that year.

In 1969 Beckett directed a German translation of *Krapp's Last Tape* in the Berlin Schiller-Theatre Werkstatt. Martin Held played Krapp. For this first performance Beckett gave new stage directions, and simplified the stage picture. Krapp was depicted as a solitary, broken old man rather than as a clown-alcoholic. The purple nose is discarded, but he added rheumatic fingers for fumbling; and 'stressing the worn rather than the farcical quality of Krapp's clothes'[30] for the actor, Beckett gave a new dimension to the interpretation of the play. It is not only Krapp's last tape, but virtually his last gasp, with an eerie presence of the reality of death: his death this time.[31] The new directions included Krapp's turning round anxiously once or twice, as if, Beckett told Martin Held, 'Old Nick' were there: 'Death is standing behind him, and unconsciously he's looking for it, it's the end ... he's through with his work, with love and with religion.'[32]

'The definitive performance ... has been that of Martin Held in a produc-tion directed by Beckett himself for the Berlin Schiller-Theatre Werkstatt which has been universally acknowledged as outstanding'.[33]

Thereafter, international interest in the play intensified: Dublin became the venue for new productions. *Krapp's Last Tape* was presented at the Focus Theatre, Dublin, on June 28, 1973. The play was directed by Peter O'Shaugh-nessy, an Australian professor, who also played Krapp 'to the life', accord-ing to drama critic Kane Archer of *The Irish Times* (30 June 1973).

In May 1980, Beckett directed the San Quentin Drama Workshop Pro-duction, presented by the Goodman Theatre, Chicago, at the Peacock Theatre, Dublin. This new presentation of *Krapp's Last Tape* (in a double bill with *Endgame*) gave Dublin audiences a unique opportunity 'of coming to an understanding of Beckett's own ways of interpreting his plays practi-cally'.

Beckett's 'several new ideas on the play' were executed exactly in Rick Cluchey's performance of Krapp. But the new ideas seemed as close to Holy

Writ as the original stage directions, deemed rigid and restrictive. These were productions 'for the truly committed, and for the academic readers of Beckett'. 'The Dublin critics did not warm to them... probably because of their strictness and exactitude.'[34] Still, the Beckett-directed versions of *Krapp* and *Endgame* were, said one truly committed academic, 'classic, in that they embody modifications by Beckett of his own concerns'.[35] They are classic, too, in that they portray Krapp's *alter ego*, at seventy-four, 'embarking on a new ... retrospect.' (p. 13)

Location

Krapp's long tape — Spool five — recounts three moving, momentous experiences in his life; though not in chronological order. The location of each event is set at the edge of water: the weir of the Grand Canal, Dublin; the jetty of Dun Laoghaire Harbour; and the edge of a lake near Germany's Baltic coast.[36] Other landmarks that gild the narrative — the Nursing Home, lighthouse, 'the pines and dunes' of a Baltic landscape — link the imagery of *endings* evoked by the water's edge with visions of serenity, sanctuary, and seclusion.

Krapp's last tape — the one he discarded, that gives the play its title — edits Spool five, and adds new nostalgic details which include points of location on the Wicklow Mountains, where he rambled with his dog: 'Be again on Croghan on a Sunday morning, in the haze, with the bitch, stop and listen to the bells.' (p. 19).

A few lines earlier he recalls an evening service in Church: 'Went to Vespers once, like when I was in short trousers.... Went to sleep and fell off the pew.' (pp. 18-19). The Beckett family worshipped in the Church of Ireland parish church of Tullow, built in 1864, and a mere five minutes walk from Cooldrinagh.[37] The Becketts' pew was near the pulpit.[38]

The first location, the weir of the Grand Canal by Huband Bridge,[39] recalls the bitter memory of his mother's death. There, in the early evening of August 25, 1950, he sat on a bench, watching the window of a room in The Merrion Nursing Home, where his mother lay dying.[40] He does not name the Nursing Home, but says simply, 'the house on the canal where mother lay a-dying, in the early autumn, after her long viduity ...' (p. 14).

The second location, the jetty of Dun Laoghaire Harbour, marks the scene of a happier circumstance that profoundly influenced Beckett's professional life. This setting, at a particular time — the spring equinox — has an aura of metaphysical strands woven into an experience that Beckett describes as 'the miracle that ...' (p. 16) changed his life.[41]

Dun Laoghaire Harbour, cherished 'gateway' to Ireland, is on the southern shore of Dublin Bay, seven miles from Dublin city. The name Dun Laoghaire (pronounced *Doon Laye-reh*), meaning Leary's Fort, derives from the fortress built there by Laoghaire, a fifth-century king of Ireland. Built between 1817 and 1859, of stone from the granite quarries of nearby Dalkey, the harbour has two fine granite piers that afford a spacious terminus for the mail-boat and car-ferry services from Holyhead, North Wales.[42] It figures frequently in the wanderings of various Beckett characters.[43] Within the harbour area, enclosed by the East Pier 3,500 feet and the West Pier 4,950 feet in length, a small wooden jetty, the Carlyle pier, was built to berth the mail-boat.

This wooden jetty is the symbolic and authentic setting for the epiphany, the 'memorable equinox' (p. 11) bestowed on Beckett's battered spirit.[44] The mighty twin granite piers that at once embrace and repulse the sea, could emit healing force,[45] and 'the fire that set it (the vision) alight' (p. 16). This revelation,[46] of the depth of his talent, is portrayed vividly, almost mystically, in the play. At the sea-end of the East Pier the lighthouse 'flings its brilliant beam of light across the bay' every thirty seconds. About 600 feet from the lighthouse, the spinning wind-gauge mounted on top of a granite structure of Greco-Egyptian style has recorded wind speed and direction since its erection in 1852, as one of the first of its kind in the world.[47]

The third location, scene of 'Farewell to love', can be gleaned from Krapp's last tape: his intimations of *Effi Briest*[48] and the bleak Baltic landscape ...

> ... Scalded the eyes out of me reading *Effie* again, a page a day, with tears again. Effie.... (*Pause.*) Could have been happy with her, up there on the Baltic, and the pines, and the dunes. (*Pause.*) Could I? (*Pause.*) And she? (*Pause.*) Pah! (*Pause.*) ... (p. 18)

The tape, eventually wrenched off the machine, is replaced by the old tape — Spool five. This is wound forward to the passage where Krapp, in the last minutes of his sixty-ninth birthday, relives the boat love scene in the sweet sad strains of evocation .... 'We drifted in among the flags and stuck. The way they went down, sighing, before the stem! (*Pause.*)(p. 19).

Evocation

Krapp's Last Tape is an authentic recording of three fragments from Beckett's personal life. His biographer writes:

> For the subject matter of *Krapp*, Beckett turned away from the arid

intellectualism of *Fin de partie* and returned to his own life. It is one of the most openly autobiographical of his writings, and one which he worked over with painstaking precision in an attempt to disguise these traces.[49]

The traces Beckett tried vainly to disguise[50] merely reveal the surge of evocation, unwittingly tapped by Magee, 'an Irishman fond of whiskey and a good story, with a boisterous personality and mellifluous voice that enthralled him'.[51] Beckett told Magee that he was amazed when he first heard him speak because Magee's voice was the one heard inside his mind when the play was calling for a 'character'. 'Almost every sentence recalls some parts of his life, yet reality never intrudes upon the artistic integrity of the play.'[52]

Evocation overwhelmed him and he wrote for the first time, and with apparent detachment, about his mother's death. Details of the ledger entry for Spool five — 'Mother at rest at last. ... H. ... The black ball ...' (p. 11) — are given under *Location*; and the impact of the recording is amplified in *Language*. But a fact relevant to the painful episode he recounts is not included in either: Beckett nursed his mother during her last illness.[53] Eoin O'Brien recalls: 'Beckett told me that he spent three days, waiting up throughout the nights, with his mother during her last illness.'[54]

His mother died in the early evening of 25 August 1950. Deirdre Bair writes:

> All day long Beckett had sat beside her bed, watching her laboured breathing, until he could stand it no more. Then he went for a walk along the Grand Canal and then he returned to the nursing home, sat outside for a while on the bench, shivering in the evening wind. When he looked up at her window, he saw the shade go down, the signal that she had died.[55]

In his immortal record of that poignant scene, the words, 'wishing she were gone', and 'All over and done with, at last'[56] (pp. 14, 15) do not intimate sardonic or studied indifference, but a resigned serenity, born of her suffering and his.

Evocation has another spiritual dimension in the Jetty scene, that follows a resigned — 'Ah well ...' (p. 15) at the end of the 'weir' episode on the tape. The mystical experience recalled is conveyed with words uncommon to Beckett — 'vision', 'miracle', 'fire'. However, the background to this 'turning-point'[57] was quite common for him. He calls it his 'old weakness'.[58] His biographer explains:

> The excessive drunkenness was ... a refuge from the reality of his

writing. To relieve some of the tension these self-confrontations induced, he resumed his old habit of walking nonstop for miles. On one of his late-night prowls, when he had been drinking just enough to make his thought processes churn, he found himself out on the end of a jetty in Dublin harbour, buffeted by a winter storm. Suddenly the vision occurred which was to result in the voluminous production in the next few years, the kind of writing that has come to be defined as 'Beckettian'.[59]

Beckett wrote four drafts of *Krapp's Last Tape*.[60] The description of the 'vision' in the final text has been pared down to the barest minimum. A few fragmentary sentences recount the 'revelation'[61] that had a profound influence on his creative sensibility.

The outer reality of the jetty episode depicts the permanent and passing forces of Nature playing on his senses. The backdrop of darkness -- except for the lighthouse beaming across the Bay -- matches the dejection that drove him there on 'that memorable night in March'[62] 1946. He heard 'the howling wind, never to be forgotten ...' (p. 15) He saw 'great granite rocks the foam flying up in the lighthouse and the wind-gauge spinning like a propeller,...' (p. 16) He saw and felt the force of the stormy sea battering the granite bulk of the East Pier. He watched the foam rise and glisten in the lighthouse beam, then sink back into the turmoil of the sea. He felt Nature's ordered turmoil reflected elements within his own nature, that had to be fought and conquered, released and harnessed, if his vision as a writer would ever see that 'stain upon the silence'.[63]

> ... clear to me at last that the dark I have always struggled to keep under is in reality my most — ... unshatterable association until my dissolution of storm and night with the light of the understanding and the fire — ... (p. 16)

The inner reality[64] of the jetty experience became apparent when 'the vision', 'the miracle', and 'the fire that set it alight' coalesced into Beckett's lightning conversion — his acknowledged revelation. Charlton Lake has written of it thus:

> Like Saul on the road to Damascus, like Paul Valéry during his *nuit de Gênes*, Beckett had his blinding revelation one stormy postwar night as he wandered around the Dublin harbour area. He suddenly realised he had one subject — himself — and henceforward he would tell that story, with all its dark side, directly, through a narrator whose voice would always be his own. What he had recorded over the years, he would now play back.[65]

Patrick Wakeling writes of that moment:

At that moment he faced his deepest feelings, he knew for the first time that it was possible to express them from the pulpit of his craft, and that he would not be overwhelmed by the loneliness and the turmoil. ... It flashed upon him that he must use precisely what he feared most; rather than concealing his bitterness, his self-reproach beneath the intellectual apparatus of learned scorn.[66]

Deirdre Bair says: 'The first person narrator speaks from this point on in Beckett's fiction.'[67]

From now on Beckett had one subject — himself; one technique — monologue; and one story — that of all mankind. The 'dark' he had always struggled to keep under became his light, his company and his sanctuary.

With all this darkness round me I feel less alone ... I love to get up and move about in it, then back to ... me ... Krapp. (p. 12)

The third ledger entry in his clinical filing system: 'Farewell to -- (*he turns page*) — love (p. 11) is Krapp's final play-back on his sixty-ninth birthday. The strains of evocation from 'Farewell to love' have a poignant ring for the old man. Beckett records 'moments' of the boat scene in great detail, but typically, leaves the main story untold. In giving us the background to the love story behind it, Deirdre Bair gives cohesion to the fragments vouchsafed on the tape.[68]

Old Krapp plays the tape, and savours its contents even more than the 'Memorable equinox', rarefied though that is. ...

— Upper lake, with punt, bathed off the bank, then pushed out into the stream and drifted. She lay stretched out on the floorboards with her hands under her head and her eyes closed. Sun blazing down, bit of a breeze, water nice and lively ...[69]

Old Krapp plays the tape through, broods, drinks, records a cynical reply, with nostalgic yearnings — not at all amorous —

Be again in the dingle on a Christmas Eve, gathering holly, the red-berried. (*Pause.*) Be again on Croghan ... listen to the bells. (*Pause.*)... Be again, be again. (*Pause.*) ... (p. 19)

— rips it off the machine, and replays once more the farewell to love. (p. 19-20)

TAPE:— gooseberries, she said, I said again I thought it was hopeless and no good going on and she agreed, without opening her eyes. (*Pause.*) I asked her to look at me and after a few moments — (*Pause.*) — after a few moments she did, but the eyes just slits, because of the glare. I bent over her to get them in the shadow and they opened. (*Pause. Low.*) Let me in. (*Pause.*) We drifted in among the flags and stuck. The way they went down sighing, before the stem! (*Pause.*) I

lay down across her with my face on her breasts and my hand on her. We lay there without moving. But under us all moved, and moved us, gently, up and down, and from side to side.
(*Pause.* Krapp's *lips move. No sound.*)
Past midnight. Never knew such silence. The earth might be uninhabited.
(*Pause.*)
Here I end this reel. Box — (*Pause.*) — three, spool — (*Pause.*) — five. (*Pause.*) Perhaps my best years are gone. When there was a chance of happiness. But I wouldn't want them back. Not with the fire in me now. No, I wouldn't want them back.
(Krapp *motionless staring before him. The tape runs on in silence.*)

Language

Language is considered under three aspects: Vocabulary, Idiom, and Rhythm or sound patterns.

Vocabulary

The vocabulary in this play is standard English, but Beckett 'does show a writer's enjoyment of words and sensitivity to them'.[70] Old Krapp revels in the word 'Spooool', and symbolically breathes life into it with, 'the little rascal!' and 'the little scoundrel!' (pp. 10, 11)

The light and dark of the stage setting are reflected in the words and imagery of the canal scene — the 'dark young beauty ... all white and starch ... black hooded perambulator ... little white dog ... black ... rubber ball' (pp. 14, 15).

On the word colour palette, the 'rusty black' of old Krapp's clownish costume shades into the 'dirty brown' roller blind that signalled his mother's death (pp. 9, 15). Evergreen memories of the dingle holly[71] match the memory of 'a shabby green coat'.[72]

Idiom

The idiom in *Krapp's Last Tape* illustrates the time-span between the K-39 tape, and the K-69 recording, which he himself called 'drivel' (p. 19). Referring to the author's 'sensitivity' to words, Fletcher remarks:

> Beckett uses this ... characteristic as a means of distinguishing between the Krapp that we see and the one that we hear on the tape. The language of Krapp the younger is more learned and even precious compared with Krapp senior's; note the latter's irritation at the former's pompous, pedantic style and his stopping in the tape whenever the younger Krapp begins to declaim.[73]

Krapp-at-39 uses the standard idiom with simile and metaphor; as if 'shadows of the opus ... magnum' (p. 13) still linger, with 'perhaps a glint of the old eye to come',[74] haunting his ambition.

Alec Reid highlights the time-lapse thus:

> We *hear* Krapp-at-39, 'sound as a bell', as the tape claims, and 'intellectually at the crest of the wave — or thereabouts'; but at the same time we *see* the old man on the stage, short-sighted, shuffling, coughing, no longer able to remember what the tape was about. In that moment Krapp's words are immaterial; sight and sound combine to make us know in one brief second the flight of thirty years.[75]

The idiom old Krapp employs is trite, colloquial, and occasionally coarse. In the last tape there are expressions such as: ...'that stupid bastard'... (p. 17) — Krapp-at-39 ...'on this old muckball'.. (p. 18) — on Earth 'Take his mind off his homework!' (p. 18) In the context, 'homework' is a slang word for girl. (He had just paid tribute to — 'The eyes she had!') 'The sour cud and the iron stool.' (p. 18) This sentence can mean, as Fletcher notes 'Indigestion and constipation respectively.'[76] But it means something more than that in this play.[77] The idiom — chew the cud (fig.) reflect[78] — is also shimmering through the text of this recording. 'The sour cud ...' in the context, indicates remorse, regret, ambition turned sour.

Old Krapp has food for thought and much reflection in the K-39 tape he has just heard. His response recognises rejected opportunity:

> (*Pause. Weary.*) Ah well, maybe he was right. (Pause.) Maybe he was right. (p. 18)

The flight of thirty years is implied in his question: 'What's a year now? The sour cud and the iron stool.' (p. 18) The 'iron stool' refers to the Stool of Repentance,[79] intimating that his guilt is purged publicly, year after year, by the meagre sales of the masterpiece[80] for which he said farewell to love.[81]

> Seventeen copies sold, of which eleven at trade price to free circulating libraries beyond the seas. Getting known (*Pause.*) One pound six and something, eight I have no doubt. (*Pause.*) (p. 18)

In the sterling currency then (1958) in use, the price he quotes — one pound six shillings and eight pence, or £1. 6s. 8d., was the average cost of such a book.

Colloquial expressions: 'scalded the eyes out of me'; 'finish your booze'; 'Once wasn't enough for you' (pp. 18, 19); and his lewd description of Fanny (p. 18), put old Krapp's sensitivity to language among the 'shadows' reflected in his song:

> Now the day is over,

Night is drawing nigh-igh,
Shadows — (*coughing, then almost inaudible*) —
of the evening
Steal across the sky.[82]

Rhythm

The rhythm or sound patterns of this 'lyrical poem of solitude'[83] are deliberately written into the speeches, Alec Reid points out 'through the words he has chosen, the way he has arranged them, and the pauses which he has put down to separate them.' As the voice on the tape vividly recounts three distinctly different experiences, each laden with life's ironies, we become conscious of three distinct sound patterns.

> Gradually we distinguish an even-paced measure for narrative speech, a slower, long-drawn-out lyrical tempo, and a brisker, harsh, sardonic tone, and we notice the periods of silence marking the change from one rhythm to the next. From the interplay of these rhythms we gradually realise that Krapp-at-39 is torn by two radically opposed elements in his character, and that the conflict still racks the old man sitting at the table in front of us.[84]

The narrative, lyrical, and sardonic tones ensure that the emotional authenticity of the experience is 'created',[85] and 'interpretation' is 'not left to the insight of the actor'.[86] In short, the built-in rhythm of the language here reserves for Beckett the sole right of interpretation.

Alec Reid describes its dramatic impact, saying, 'We must hear the passage if we are to feel the texture of the whole experience.'[87]

TAPE: — bench by the weir from where I could see her window.	Detail of sensation. Narrative.
There I sat, in the biting wind, wishing she were gone. (*Pause.*)	Lyrical. Mood changes.
Hardly a soul, just a few regulars, nursemaids, infants, old men, dogs, I got to know them quite well — oh by appearance of course I mean!	Quickening to narrative. Sardonic.
One dark young beauty I recollect particularly, all white and starch, incomparable bosom, with a big black hooded perambulator, most funereal thing. Whenever I looked in	Lyrical. Attention to colour. Quickening through narrative

her direction she had her eyes
on me. And yet when I was bold
enough to speak to her —
not having been introduced —
she threatened to call a policeman.
As if I had designs on her virtue!
(*Laugh. Pause.*)
The face she had! The eyes! Like
.... (*hesitates*) .... chrysolite!

to sardonic.

The sound of the laugh
marks climax of the sardonic
movement. The pause is essential
for the change to lyrical. Note how
much is achieved from the laugh
to the resumption of the narrative —
only ten words are used.

(*Pause.*) Ah well .... (*Pause.*)
(pp. 14, 15)

Krapp recognises rejected opportunity.

I was there when — (Krapp
*switches off, broods, switches on
again.*) — the blind went down,
one of those dirty brown roller
affairs, throwing a ball for a
little white dog as chance would
have it. I happened to look up
and there it was, all over and
done with, at last. I sat on for
a few moments with the ball
in my hand and the dog yelping
and pawing at me. (*Pause.*)
Moments. Her moments, my
moments. (*Pause.*) The dog's
moments. (*Pause.*) In the end I
held it out to him and he took
it in his mouth, gently, gently, A
small, old, black, hard, solid,
rubber ball.

Back to narrative.

Note precision of detail, especially
colour making the scene vivid and
urgent.

Change to lyrical with the pause.
Note the repetition of 'moments'.
Emotion evoked through sound.
Back to narrative.
Repetition evokes emotion. Precise
 detail, hammering the moment
 home to us.

(*Pause.*) I shall feel it, in my hand
until my dying day. (*Pause.*) I
might have kept it. (*Pause.*) But I
gave it to the dog.
(*Pause.*)
Ah well....

Back to lyrical.

(*Pause.*)

Krapp recognises rejected opportunity.

Spiritually a year of profound gloom and indigence, until that memorable night in March, at the	Back to narrative.
end of the jetty, in the howling wind, never to be forgotten, when	Lyrical.
suddenly I saw the whole thing. The vision at last. This I fancy is	Narrative.[88]
what I have chiefly to record this evening.... (p. 15)	

The same rhythm flows subtly through the rest of the tape. The lyrical cadences of the last lines, thrice played from the old 'Spooool', soothe Krapp like a lullaby. ... 'We lay without moving. ...'

Language in *Krapp's Last Tape* is the essence of the play. The vocabulary creates the visual imagery of the scenes recalled. The idioms, like clichés, anchor the text in ordinary everyday life. The sound patterns afford insight into the soul of the lonely old man — a spent force — trying desperately, from fragments of his life story, to establish what in fact that force was. Alec Reid thinks it an inevitable, universal finale: 'Time was, time is; to this favour must we all come.'[89]

The Text and the Technique

An assessment of the text and the technique is given briefly by the drama critics, following productions of *Krapp's Last Tape* in various European capitals. Critics, like the rest of the audience, receive or judge the play, as spectators in the auditorium. Directors of the play view and review the text and the technique from a closer and more practical standpoint.

Director Ben Barnes records his close-up view of author and play:[90]

> The author, in spite of a popular perception of his work for the stage as something abstruse and rarefied, is in fact one of the most physical and theatrical of playwrights who uses the medium as the message and who, with consummate stagecraft, integrates the text and the visual and technical matters with a sureness of touch which suffers no alteration or embellishment.

Ben Barnes, who has 'complete faith in Beckett's theatre and his vision', and has directed many of his plays, recalls *Krapp's Last Tape* thus:

> Krapp will always be for me an old spider in the web of his memories. It wasn't from the wind I got the image — the environment is described as 'a den', the gait as 'a laborious walk' and the colour and shape of the costume further confirms the image: Rusty black narrow trousers too short for him. Rusty black sleeveless

waistcoat, four capacious pockets. Heavy silver watch and chain. Grimy white shirt open at neck, no collar. Surprising pair of dirty white boots, size ten at least, very narrow and pointed. (p. 9)

Director Barnes continues ...

More potently however Krapp elaborating and reviewing the threads of his web is brilliantly captured in the stage image of the reel-to-reel tapes, the 'Spooool' of the monologue. This central imagery would be made redundant in Krapp's Last Video-tape.[91]

Beckett had refused permission to a Dublin theatre interested in mounting a production of the play using video instead of a reel-to-reel tape recorder. He will not permit his works to be adapted to media other than the ones they were originally written for.[92] However, Beckett allowed *Krapp's Last Tape* to be made into a musical, by his friend Marcel Mihalovici. The composer chose *La Dernière Bande* — the French translation by Beckett and Pierre Leyris published in March 1959 — because, he said,

the melancholy poetry which it releases, as well as its violent eruptions, offered me wonderful opportunities for musical contrast.[93]

Mihalovici set the complete French text to music which fills the numerous pauses in the monologue as well as accompanying the words.

The opera, called in French, *Krapp ou La Dernière Bande*, in English simply, *The Last Tape*, and in German, *Das letzte Band*,[94] was published in Paris in 1961. Beckett supervised the musical composition, as he is wont to do with stage productions of the play.

Mihalovici asked Beckett to explain the text to him, and Beckett agreed to go through it line by line while Roger Blin acted it and Mihalovici took careful notes on the cadence of the text, its rhythm and length.

It took Mihalovici fourteen months to turn the ten pages of Beckett's text into a musical score of two hundred and sixty pages; yet the performance took only fifteen minutes longer than that of the original play.

When the work was finished, Beckett thought it very good, and Mihalovici was pleased that none of the original poetry of the play had been lost in the transposition to music.[95]

The passion and poetry throbbing through the combined human and technical creation of *Krapp's Last Tape*, transposed into music, might well be called -- The Song of Samuel Beckett! It is also the song of life on Earth, till the last tape 'runs on in silence' (p. 20). Meanwhile, we hear the soothing strains of Dryden's song —

'What passion cannot Music raise and quell'[96]

NOTES

1 Cohn, *Back to Beckett*, p. 165.

2 Fletcher and Spurling, *Beckett: A Study of his Plays*, p. 91.

3 *Proust*, pp. 2 - 3, 8.

4 Bair, *Samuel Beckett*, pp. 112, 113.

5 Wakeling, *Irish University Review*, Spring 1984, Special Issue, p. 7.

6 Lyons, *Samuel Beckett*, p. 99.

7 See Bair, *Samuel Beckett*, p. 118 for evidence of Beckett's 'eccentric behaviour' in literary circles in Dublin, and how, by choice, he 'remained on the fringe of this sedate literary atmosphere', until he was barred from the homes of friends, where the gatherings took place.

8 *Human Wishes*, an unfinished play intended to tell the story of Dr Samuel Johnson and Mrs Thrale, was abandoned before the first scene was completed. He was only co-author of *Le Kid* (1931), written in French, as a parody of Corneille's *Le Cid*.

9 *Journal of Beckett Studies*, Number 9, (1984), p. 64.

10 Quoted in Cohn, *Back to Beckett*, p. 126. *Eleuthéria* is still unpublished and unproduced as a play.

11 Ibid., p. 127.

12 Garmonsway, *The Penguin English Dictionary*, p. 325.

13 Post-mortem (fig.) discussion of something after it has ended. *The Penguin English Dictionary*, p. 532.

14 See Bair, *Samuel Beckett*, p. 100, and p. 554 (note 56), for the name of the present owner of that copy of *Proust*.

15 Reid, *All I Can Manage, More Than I Could*, p. 77.

16 Garmonsway, *The Penguin English Dictionary*, p. 193.

17 *The Advanced Learner's Dictionary of Current English*, p. 309.

18 Webb, *The Plays of Samuel Beckett*, pp. 66.

19 Kenner, *A Reader's Guide to Samuel Beckett*, p. 129.

20 Lyons, *Samuel Beckett*, p. 101.

21 Fletcher et al., *A Student's Guide to the Plays of Samuel Beckett*, p. 114.

22 *Irish University Review*, Spring 1984, pp. 109 - 111.

23 Ibid., p. 120.

24 Lyons, *Samuel Beckett*, p. 92.

25 Quoted in Fletcher et. al., *A Student's Guide to the Plays of Samuel Beckett*, p. 114.

26 Ibid., p. 115.

27 Fletcher et. al., *A Student's Guide to the Plays of Samuel Beckett*, p. 115.

28 *Irish University Review*, Spring 1984, p. 111.

29 Quoted in Murray, 'Beckett Productions in Ireland: A Survey', p. 111.

30 Cohn, *Back to Beckett*, p. 171.

31 Lyons, *Samuel Beckett*, p. 102.

32 Fletcher et. al., *A Student's Guide to the Plays of Samuel Beckett*, p. 115.

33 Ibid., p. 115.

34 Murray, 'Beckett's Productions in Ireland: A Survey', p. 120.

35 Ibid. Quotation from J.C.C. Mays, JOBS (No. 8, Autumn 1982).

36 Beckett does not name the lake, but implies that there are other lakes nearby ... '
— upper lake, with the punt, bathed off the bank ...' (p. 16). It must be one of the
string of lakes flanking Germany's Baltic coast.

37 The name of Beckett's family home in Foxrock. 'Cooldrinagh' is the anglicised
form of the Gaelic — *Cúl Draigheanach*, which means 'back of the blackthorn
hedge'. See O'Brien, *The Beckett Country*, p. 347, Note 6.

38 O'Brien, *The Beckett Country*, p. 23.

39 Ibid., pp. 196-7.

40 Bair, *Samuel Beckett*, p. 343.

41 Wakeling, 'Looking at Beckett: The Man and the Writer', pp. 5-6.

42 The entrance is 850 feet wide and with its massive piers encompasses an area of
250 acres of water.

43 O'Brien, *The Beckett Country*, pp. 80 - 88.

44 Bair, *Samuel Beckett*, pp. 297 - 299.

45 See Appendix II, 'Stone in the Mythology of Ireland'.

46 Wakeling, 'Looking at Beckett: The Man and the Writer', pp. 5, 6.

47 O'Brien, *The Beckett Country*, p. 355.

48 Theodor Fontane's famous novel *Effi Briest* (1895), is one of Beckett's favourites
in German literature. *All That Fall* has a reference to it, indicating that Dan
Rooney, too, was moved by Effie's love story, p. 29. Effi Briest, the young victim
of an arranged marriage to an older man in the Prussian Civil Service, falls in
love with a young Army Officer stationed on the Baltic coast; and takes to
meeting him in the sand dunes. Her tragic end has strands of Fate in common
with the love story submerged in *Krapp's Last Tape*.

49 Bair, *Samuel Beckett*, p. 415.

50 O'Brien, *The Beckett Country*, p. 83. Bair, op. cit., p. 591, Note 3. Typescripts of
Krapp's Last Tape are in the Humanities Research Centre in Austin, Texas.
Beckett's letter to Jake Schwartz, 15 March 1958, is also there. In it he said he had
'4 stages, in typescript with copious and dirty corrections, of a short stage
monologue I have just written (in English) for Pat Magee.'

51 Bair, op. cit., p. 415.

52 Ibid.

53 O'Brien, *The Beckett Country*, p. 197.

54 Ibid., p. 368, Note 3.

55 Bair, *Samuel Beckett*, p. 343.

56 Kenner, *A Reader's Guide to Samuel Beckett*, pp. 130 - 132.

57 The word 'turning-point' ('The turning-point at last'), is used in an earlier draft
version of the play. See O'Brien, *The Beckett Country*, p. 83.

58 His drinking habit, the subject of a resolution — 'To drink less, in particular'

recorded by Krapp-at-27. K-39 is 'sound as a bell, apart from my old weakness ...' pp. 13, 11.

59 Bair, *Samuel Beckett*, pp. 297, 298.

60 One version is quoted in O'Brien, *The Beckett Country*, p. 83, another draft version is quoted by Bair, op. cit., p. 298.

61 The word 'revelation' is not in the text; it was used by Beckett himself in a discussion about a film documentary by Radio Telefis Eireann. He told Seán O'Mórdha that what occurred on the pier on that memorable night was 'a revelation'. See O'Brien, *The Beckett Country*, p. 355, Note 17.

62 There is a stronger, clearer reference to the jetty 'turning-point' in the story 'La Fin' (*The End*), which he finished after his return to Paris in May 1946. See Wakeling, 'Looking at Beckett: The Man and his Work', pp. 5 - 7.

63 Beckett said 'I could not have gone on through the awful wretched mess of life without having left a stain upon the silence.' Quoted in Bair, *Samuel Beckett*, p. 539.

64 Its influence on his future writings.

65 O'Brien, *The Beckett Country*, pp. 81, 83, 355, Note 16.

66 Wakeling, 'Looking at Beckett — The man and his Work', p. 6.

67 Bair, *Samuel Beckett*, p. 298.

68 Bair, *Samuel Beckett*, pp. 57-60, 70-72, 81-83. The girl in the boat, Peggy Sinclair, was Beckett's first cousin, and for a few years the love of his young life. Her mother, Cissie (Fanny) Beckett, was his father's only sister. Her father, Boss Sinclair, an art dealer, moved from Dublin, with his wife and four daughters, to Kassel, Germany, just after the end of World War I. From 1927 to 1930, Beckett spent part of his long official holidays with the Sinclairs, in Kassel.

69 *Krapp's Last Tape*, p. 16. The event he describes took place in the summer of 1929. Beckett was with the Sinclairs 'for their annual holiday in one of the smaller resort towns along the Baltic Sea'. (Bair, op. cit., p. 81) Both his parents and hers disapproved of the romance between the two cousins, though for different reasons. Hence the word 'hopeless' in the text of the boat scene. See Bair, *op. cit.*, p. 71.

70 Fletcher et al., *A Student's Guide to the Plays of Samuel Beckett*, p. 118.

71 *Krapp's Last Tape*, p. 19 (Recorded on Krapp's 69th birthday.)

72 Ibid., p. 13 (Recorded on his 39th birthday, but refers to young Krapp's 'girl in a shabby green coat', ten or twelve years earlier). Recollections of the girl and the holly-gathering are dismissed as 'all that misery' and 'All that old misery' respectively, by Krapp (pp. 13, 19).

73 Fletcher et al., *A Student's Guide to the Plays of Samuel Beckett*, p. 118.

74 *Krapp's Last Tape*, p. 14. A glint of the old eye means a gleam of the old vision of the opus magnum. He wants to be a writer, and produce at least one masterpiece. *Gleam* means (fig.) flash of feeling or comprehension, i.e. inspiration for the opus magnum (*The Penguin English Dictionary*, p. 311).

75 Reid, *All I Can Manage, More Than I Can*, p. 21.

76 Fletcher et al., *A Student's Guide to the Plays of Samuel Beckett*, p. 123.

77 In *Waiting for Godot*, Beckett uses the expression — 'The Hard Stool' (p. 40), in the same figurative sense.

78 *The Penguin English Dictionary*, p. 176.

79 *Brewer's Dictionary of Phrase and Fable*, p. 861. The Stool of Repentance as a low stool left in front of the pulpit in Scottish churches. People who had broken church laws sat on the stool during divine service, after which the penitent had to stand on the stool and receive the minister's rebuke.

80 *Murphy* (1938), his first novel, on which he had set high hopes which did not materialise. Bair, *Samuel Beckett*, pp. 242, 243.

81 Ibid., pp. 112, 113.

82 *Krapp's Last Tape*, the verse is from the hymn by S Baring-Gould (1834 - 1924), who also wrote the popular hymn 'Onward, Christian soldiers'.

83 The words of a drama critic in Paris, written when *Krapp* premièred there in March 1960.

84 Reid, *All I Can Manage, More Than I Could*, pp. 21, 22.

85 Ibid., p. 19. A play is 'created' when it is performed publicly, according to Beckett.

86 Kenner, *A Reader's Guide to Samuel Beckett*, p. 131.

87 Reid, *All I Can Manage, More Than I Could*, p. 22.

88 Reid, op. cit., p. 23.

89 Reid, op. cit., p. 21.

90 Barnes, 'Aspects of Directing Beckett', p. 69.

91 Barnes, op. cit., p. 69.

92 Ibid.

93 Quoted in Mercier, *Beckett/Beckett*, p. 152.

94 Elmar Tophoven, who translated other works by Beckett, translated the play, and spoke it aloud for the musical composition.

95 Bair, *Samuel Beckett*, p. 427.

96 John Dryden (1631-1700), this line is a kind of refrain in 'A Song for St Cecilia's Day, 1687'. Quiller-Couch, Sir A. (ed.), *The Oxford Book of English Verse*, 1900, Reprinted 1948, p. 479.

Chapter Seven

EH JOE

Eh Joe (1966) was Beckett's first television play. He wrote it in English in April-May 1965 for the Irish actor, Jack McGowran,[1] whose portrayal of Vladimir in *Waiting for Godot* won him the award of British Television Actor of the Year in 1961. The character was first called J, then Jack, and finally Joe.[2] Although it premièred on German television with a German actor, the play was first broadcast on BBC 2 (T.V.), on July 4, 1966. Beckett himself helped direct it. McGowran played Joe.

Both critics and public were less than enthusiastic about the work. They found it excessively gloomy. A 'lugubrious experience',[3] observed one critic. 'Dreary and very dull to watch' was the audience consensus.[4] Beckett's plays frequently improve on acquaintance, and *Eh Joe* has improved its rating considerably. The critics admit that:

> Since then, however, most people have congratulated Beckett on his success, at first attempt, in exploiting the medium to the full.[5]

Literary critics assess the play on other criteria, e.g. credibility, and the absence of symbols and enigmas. One writes:

> Perhaps the relative weakness of *Eh Joe* within the canon is simply that it is *too* simple. Beckett's drama thrives on symbols of unassignable value ...[6]

Eh Joe too, has symbols — the sea, the moon, stones — and their 'unassignable value' lend a transcendent dimension to the play. Beckett reserves these symbols for the final enigma. *Eh Joe* is apparently a sequel to *Krapp's Last Tape*. Links between the two plays include, apart from the autobiographical factor and the theme — (love and loneliness), the symbols. In *Eh Joe* they have a sinister connotation in keeping with the atmosphere of the play.

> Sea — The association of might, madness, engulfing tidal flow follows 'Faint lap of sea ...' (p. 20)
>
> Moon — unshatterable association with love and lunacy. It was a full moon.
>
> Stones — small enough to fondle, could be Cursing Stones. 'The *solitaire*' (p. 21), has ambivalent symbolism.

He is now 'embarking on a new ... retrospect';[7] but 'less and less is allowed to stand between the narrator and the tale'.[8]

Krapp's fragmented past returns at his bidding via the tapes, whereas Joe's memories are boxed up in his brain, and against his will rear up to haunt him. On his thirty-ninth birthday, Krapp 'sat before the fire with closed eyes, separating the grain from the husks'. (pp. 11, 12). About twenty years later, Joe, 'sitting on edge of bed, ... eyes closed' (p. 15), (Whatever happened to the grain?) has the husks blown back at him by a voice sounding within his consciousness.

The obvious symbols — camera and voice — are part of Beckett's stock-in-trade for his later plays whose protagonists are *listeners*. The symbolism of the camera in this play has been variously interpreted as:' ... the camera in this play seems to represent the protagonist's self-perception ...'[9] '... the scrutinising and inquisitorial camera represents the woman, it is also indicative of Joe's own introspection ...'[10] 'The camera ... as representing Joe's masochism as well as his self-perception.'[11] The camera in itself does not symbolise anything in this play. It is one of Beckett's props, as the tape recorder is in *Krapp's Last Tape*. The camera simply records the scene and registers Joe's reaction as the spool of conscience uncoils in a preview of Judgement Day.

Scene: Joe's room. It could be called his 'den', for Joe 'is another man in flight'.[12] A man in his late fifties, grey hair, wearing an old dressing-gown and carpet slippers, he is sitting on the edge of his bed, his back to the camera. He gets up and proceeds to secure his sanctum against a possible attack from without, or even from within. 'Standing intent' after each security check; window, door and cupboard are locked; their hangings carefully drawn. He even looks under the bed, and satisfied that there is nothing to fear there he sits on the edge of the bed, facing the camera, and begins to relax. 'Joe ... relaxed, eyes closed.' But not for long.

An assailant is about to laugh at his precautions. The assailant is a *Voice*: its owner one of the many women who once loved Joe, and has been discarded by him with a parting promise — 'The best's to come'. (16)

We *see* Joe and study his face — 'Practically motionless throughout, eyes unblinking during paragraphs, impassive except in so far as it reflects mounting tension of *listening*.'

We *hear* the *Voice* — 'Low, distinct, remote, little colour, absolutely steady rhythm, slightly slower than normal', which seems to emanate from Joe himself, who looks as though he is listening to an inner voice.

We build up a portrait of Joe as the Voice and camera 'start in on' him in nine slight moves towards the face and peel off the masks which had concealed him from himself and others.[13] Each move of the camera is stopped by the Mocking voice resuming her portrayal of 'that lifelong adorer', (17) who resembles Krapp in his inability to love. The last move of the camera is the final stroke in the portrait of Beckett himself, as etched by his biographer:

> His relationship with women, then, is probably best described as fleeting and therapeutic; unable to relate to anyone, he was most certainly unable to put aside thoughts of himself long enough to feel any emotion for another. For him, romantic love was something to snicker at, and he reserved his most sarcastic comments for it.[14]

Location

The events recalled in Move 4 took place in Dublin — St Stephen's Green, a public park at the top of Grafton Street. It covers twenty-two acres; and among its many attractions is an artificial lake inhabited by numerous wild fowl. Sitting 'watching the ducks' is a restful pastime enjoyed by many visitors to 'the Green' (p. 18).

For move 9 the scene moves farther south to — Killiney Bay, south of Dublin Bay; a picturesque sweep of coastline between Dalkey and Bray. Viewed from the summit of Killiney Hill (512 feet), this crescent-shaped expanse of blue water backed by the green heights of Bray Head and the purple quartzite mass of the Wicklow Mountains, presents a panorama said to rival the Bay of Naples. It has a fine beach two miles long. The *White Rock Strand* ('the Rock', p. 21), a favoured bathing place, has deep water even when the tide is out.

Killiney is a paradise for the 'rockhounds', 'always looking for the beautiful or unusual', in smooth, sea-groomed stones. Seven varieties of these have been identified among the pebbles on the beach. An assessment of the stone boon may clarify the significance of *stones* (p. 21), in the moving episode of the climactic close ... 'Lips on a *stone* ...' of Move 9:

> ... Near Dublin is Killiney Strand. Here is a good variety — iron-stained quartz, translucent quartz, milky quartz, pale-pink chalced-ony (pronounced kalsedonny), flints and their near-relations cherts in various hues of greys and browns, sometimes with white patches. ... Occasionally green and pink granites can be found washed down from the Western Isles of Scotland.[15]

Evocation

Evocation, thrust upon him, constitutes the entire text. Beckett is remembering episodes of his life in Dublin, and still more, those which inspired his escape from it to Paris or Kassel.[16] As a freelance writer in Dublin in the early thirties, he seems to have spent a good deal of his free time trying — often unsuccessfully — to attract or elude particular women of his acquaintance.[17] He satirised all of them in the hastily-written novel, *Dream of Fair to Middling Women*, and in a later book, *More Pricks than Kicks* (1934), into which he incorporated much of the unpublished *Dream*.[18] He modelled many of his less worthy characters in both books on some of the women he ostensibly loved.[19]

Of particular relevance to *Eh Joe* is Beckett's cruel betrayal of 'The green one' (Move 7), whom he called 'The Smeraldina' (sometimes Smerry). Bair tells us,

> He even inserted verbatim a letter from the sadly ailing Peggy, who wrote English phonetically as she spoke it with her heavy German accent. Not only did he incorporate her letter into *Dream*, but he later retained it as 'The Smeraldina's Billet Doux' in *More Pricks*.[20]

Beckett's unflattering self-portrait in *Eh Joe* reveals a sense of guilt. One point on which all critics agree is that the Woman's Voice is ...

> ... the voice of conscience, reproaching Joe for what he did, not to the owner of the voice but to another, more vulnerable woman: The green one ...[21]

On Beckett's relationship with Lucia Joyce, who loved him literally to the point of madness, Bair writes:

> Passivity in many forms has been the distinguishing characteristic of all Beckett's relationships with women throughout his life, and he carried it to the extreme with Lucia.[22]

As a psychiatrist, Wakeling adds:

> I would go further and say that most of Beckett's dealings with the world display the same trait simply because passivity is the best way

for one of his schizoid make-up ... to remain ungot at, intact. In a word, safe.

Explaining the term 'schizoid' he gives Laing's view:

> It refers, he says, 'to an individual, the totality of whose experience is split in two ways: in the first place, there is a rent in his relation with his world and, in the second, there is a disruption of his relationship with himself. Such a person is not able to experience himself 'together with' others or 'at home in' the world, but, on the contrary, he experiences himself in despairing aloofness and isolation; moreover, he does not experience himself as a complete person but rather as split in certain ways, perhaps as a mind more or less tenuously linked to a body, as two or more selves, and so on. ... Further, the most basic division within the schizoid person lies between the so-called true-self and the false-self. The true-self is that part guarded from the outside world which is experienced as less real.[23]

Laing's further explanation of a schizoid make-up is borne out in Beckett's behaviour, as recorded by his biographer; and in his one-man plays, particularly, *Krapp's Last Tape* and *Eh Joe*.

> Such a schizoid individual in one sense is trying to be omnipotent by enclosing within his own being, without recourse to a creative relationship with others, modes of relationship that require the effective presence to him of other people and of the outer world. He would appear to be, in an unreal, impossible way, all persons and things to himself. The imagined advantages are safety for the true self, isolation, and hence freedom from others, self sufficiency and control.

The disadvantages are these:

> ... that this project is impossible and, being a false hope, leads on to persistent despair; secondly, a persistent haunting sense of futility ... since the hidden shut-up self, in disowning participation ... in the quasi-autonomous activities of the false-self systems, is living only 'mentally'. Moreover, this shut-up self, being isolated, is unable to be enriched by outer experience and so the whole inner whole comes to be more and more impoverished, until the individual may come to feel he is merely a vacuum.[24]

In *Eh Joe*, is borne out, too, the oft-quoted dictum of C.G. Jung: 'Therefore you can read a writer's mind when you study the characters he creates.'[25]

Language

The language is terse, almost telegrammatic prose, since each verbal taunt means a jab of self-perception for Joe. Beckett told a writer in 1970, '... self perception is the most frightening of all human observations ... when man faces himself he is looking into the abyss.'[26] The vocabulary is modern standard English, except for:

> *dollop n* (coll) large shapeless lump.[27] Dollop also has shades of meaning: dose, surfeit, excess. In the context it means, a dose or a surfeit of silence. (Move 8).
>
> *His Nibs* (slang) smart gentleman.[28] The capital letters indicate God in the context. (Move 8).
>
> *thug, thuggee*; words of Hindustani origin: *thug n.* One of an organisation of religious assassins in India. Hence, any cutthroat or ruffian. (Hind. *thag,* thug) — thuggee, *n.* The system of secret assassination practised by thugs.[29]

Beckett coined the phrase *mental thuggee* as a neat metaphor for Joe's 'Throttling the dead in his head' (Move 2). The Voice challenges Joe '... Put your thugs on that ...' (Move 5), i.e. assassinate His voice, if you can. Ruby Cohn writes, 'mental thuggee' is the arresting phrase for the murder of those who loved him.'[30]

The Irishness of the language is conveyed by numerous examples of Hiberno-English in its various forms.

Verbal usage. In Irish every sentence begins with the verb. The Voice frequently begins with the verb when emphasis or/and imagery enhance the narrative, and expose Joe's guilt ...

'Hurrying me into my coat ...' (p. 16).

'Throttling the dead in his head ...' (p. 17).

'Bundling her into her Avoca sack ...'[31] (p. 19).

'Trailing her feet in the water like a child ...' (p. 21).

'Clawing at the shingle now ...' (p. 21).

'Scoops a little cup for her face in the stones.' (p. 21).

The copula form of the verb, with its advantage of emphasising one element of a clause over others, the 'is it' construction, is clear in 'Is it that you want?' (p. 17). Normally, an English-speaking person would say, Is that what you want? The difference may seem slight, but the copula is distinctively Irish.[32]

Syntax. Use of the reflexive pronoun: 'I was strong myself when I started ... In on you ...' (p. 18), and the phrase, 'Started in on you ...' (p. 17), are common in current Hiberno-English. Beckett uses the construction in other plays.[33]

The reversed word order peculiar to this hybrid language is seen in: 'Powerful grasp of language you had ...' (p. 18). 'Very fair health for a man of your years.' (p. 19).

Expressions like -- 'Otherwise he'd be plaguing you *yet*' (still) (p. 17);

'Before they *go*' (die) (p. 21); and 'What are they *at*?' (doing) (p. 21) are given a sense of immediacy by the short words common in the Irish language idiom. The Irish idiom is also seen in the sentence: 'No Joe ... Not for the likes of us ...' (p. 17).

The phrase 'the likes' is a translation of the original, leithéid (pl. leithéidí). Beckett uses it in other plays,[34] particularly when he translates them from the original French.

Language in *Eh Joe* also reflects the socio-cultural atmosphere of the Irish scene. Christian symbols of hope: 'On Mary's beads we plead her needs and in the Holy Mass ...' (Move 8) juxtapose pagan symbols of worship — sea, moon, stones — playing on despair (Move 9). The frequent references to God (Move 5), His justice (Move 8), and His love (Move 9), tend to opt for hope rather than despair, in a play on the thorny theme of self-perception. Its last line: 'Compared to Him ...' (Move 9), is hope itself.

The Text and the Technique

In the opening lines the tone is set, and a pattern of thesis/antithesis that pervades the play is made obvious.[35] His false-self defences are breached. A *heart* he kept 'ungot at, intact'[36] is declared 'dry rotten ...'

> Woman's Voice:
>
> Thought of everything? ... Forgotten nothing? ... You're all right now, eh? ... No one can see you now ... No one can get at you now ... Why don't you put out that light? ... There might be a louse watching you ... Why don't you go to bed? ... Or is the heart already? ... Crumbles when you lie down in the dark ... Dry rotten at last ... Eh Joe? (p. 16).

Move 1

The false-self sheds its first mask — deception. The Voice taunts him with his suave, standard farewell to the women he loved and left ...

> The best's to come, you said that last time ... Hurrying me into my coat ... Say it you now, Joe, no one'll hear you ... Come on, Joe, no one can say it like you, say it again now and listen to yourself ... The best's to come ... You were right for once ... In the end.

Move 2

The second mask — self-deception — is removed by painful, personal truths. His *mind*, bent systematically to serve the false-self, is now just a 'penny farthing hell' unable to distinguish fact from fantasy. Joe 'is living only "mentally".'[37] He has 'always managed to escape his voices by persuading himself that they were *merely* mental and consequently could be dismissed.'[38] He strangled voices from the past. 'Mental thuggee' he called the exercise.

> You know that penny farthing hell you call your mind ... That's where you think this is coming from, don't you? ... That's where you heard your father ...[39] Started in on you one June night and went on for years ... On and off ... That's how you were able to throttle him in the end ... Mental thuggee you called it ... One of your happiest fancies ... Mental thuggee ... Otherwise he'd be plaguing you yet ... Then your mother when her hour came ...[40] Weaker and weaker till you laid her too ... Others ... All the others ... Such love he got ... God knows why ... And look at him now ... Throttling the dead in his head. (p. 17)

Move 3

The third mask — self-isolation — is scorned as a self-defeating tactic. Webb speaks of 'the self-centred isolation to which his way of life has brought him',[41] intimating that isolation is the *result* of his actions; whereas Laing sees it as the *cause* of such conduct.[42] The 'despairing aloofness and isolation' of the schizoid make-up mark Beckett's relationships from early childhood.[43] The Voice could well ask ...

> Anyone living love you now, Joe? ... Anyone living sorry for you now? ... Watch yourself you don't run short, Joe ... Ever think of that? ... What it'd be if you ran out of us ... Not another soul to still ...

She reminds him that the 'voices' are preferable to the vacuum of silence that will follow ... 'the silence of the grave' without the peace of the grave.[44]

> ... That old paradise you were always harping on ... No Joe ... Not for the likes of us. (p. 17).

Move 4

The fourth mask — ambivalence — is a trait of Beckett's character reflected in many of his plays.[45] The Voice, softened by nostalgia, reproaches him for destroying the things he loved: her voice and her love. Joe's ambivalence is unveiled in the text, by *contrast* of location, evocation, and language.

Location: Love's young dream, in a romantic Dublin setting, is recalled in a lonely, loveless limbo,[46] where he is 'straining to hear' the voice he is trying to strangle:

> I was strong myself when I started ... In on you ... Normal strength ... Like those summer evenings in the Green ... In the early days ... Of our idyll ... When we sat watching the ducks ... Holding hands exchanging vows ... How you admired my elocution! ... Among other charms ... Voice like flint glass ... Powerful grasp of language

you had ... Flint glass ... You could have listened to it for ever ... And
now this ... Squeezed down to this ... (p. 18).

Evocation: The voice that was near, clear, and charming in the idyllic
setting of St Stephen's Green, is now remote, low, and colourless, according to
the stage directions. It will soon fade into a whisper. 'The whisper' is the
definitive expression of his ambivalence, his 'love and hate of the same
object'.[47]

> ...How much longer would you say? ... Till the whisper ... When you
> can't hear the words ... Just the odd one here and there ... That's the
> worst ... Isn't that what you told me ... Before we expire ... The odd
> word ... Straining to hear ... Why must you do that? ... When you're
> nearly home ... What matter then ... What we mean ... It should be
> the best ... Another stilled ... And it's the worst ... Isn't that what you
> said? ...

Language: Joe's 'powerful grasp of language' is seen in the double-edged
metaphor used to express his great admiration of her elocution ... 'Voice like
flint glass'. Flint glass[48] — a symbolic metaphor for strength and clarity; it
was meant as a compliment, 'in the early days' of their idyll. 'And now this'
... Its strength and clarity reduced to the point where Joe is 'straining to hear
... the odd word', flint glass is an ironic metaphor for a voice that is hard,
heavy, low, slow and colourless. This metaphor fits Beckett's stage directions for the Voice.

Mental thuggee recoils on Joe. 'Another stilled' (p. 18) means his voice
of conscience stilled. She predicts that he will be his own last victim.[49] 'You
stop in the end ...'. When he has silenced the whisper in his head he has
severed the last tenuous link with language. He has destroyed his first and
last love — language.[50] 'Till you join us ...' (p. 18)

Move 5

The fifth mask — presumption — is pierced by a sharp reminder that God
is not mocked. Joe, being 'all persons and things to himself'[51], only talks to
God. When he has throttled all the dead in his head, God will talk to him,
she warns him.

> How's your Lord these days? ... Still worth having? ... Wait till He
> starts talking to you ... When you're done with yourself ... All your
> dead dead ... (p. 18)

A reference to Joe's health corresponds to facts with regard to Beckett's
medical history.[52] It implies even if he could free his afflicted mind from
the past, bodily afflictions cannot be willed away.

> Very fair health for a man of your years ... Just that lump in your

bubo[53] ... Silence of the grave without the maggots ... to crown your
labours ... (p. 19)

The only difference, she says, between his mind devoid of memories,
communication, love, and his (eventually) dead body, is the latter's unsa-
voury attraction for maggots. No more echoes from 'all the dead voices'.[54]
Dead silence is Joe's elixir.

... Till one
night ... 'Thou fool they soul' ... Put your thugs on that ... Eh Joe? ...
Ever think of that? ... When He starts in on you ... When you're done
with yourself ... If you ever are.

Move 6

Self-revelation is the purpose of this short paragraph, with factual depth,
and insight into Beckett's character, hidden in simple, single words. Recall-
ing her own 'great love God knows why' for Joe, she tells him she 'found a
better' (p. 19). Preferable in all respects ... Kinder[55] ... Stronger[56] ... More
intelligent[57] ... Better looking[58] ... Cleaner[59] ... Truthful[60] ... Faithful[61] ...
Sane[62] ... Yes ... I did all right.

Move 7

Joe's duplicity is unmasked. Beginning with the seventh camera move she
talks about another woman who loved Joe: one who was less fortunate than
herself, for she 'did all right' afterwards.

But there was one who didn't ... You know the one I mean, Joe ...
The green one[63] ... The narrow one[64] ... Always pale[65] ... The pale
eyes ... Spirit made light[66] ... To borrow your expression ... The way
they opened after ... Unique ... There was love for you...[67]

Joe loved this woman too, and parted, or departed, with practised
gallantry, and a suave farewell.

The best's to come, you said ... Bundling her into her Avoca sack ...
Her fingers fumbling with the big horn buttons ... Ticket in your
pocket for the first morning flight[68] ... You've had her, haven't you?[69]
... She went young ... No more lip from her.[70]

Move 8

Move eight unmasks his egomania.

Ever know what happened? ... She didn't say? ...[71] Just the an-
nouncement in the *Independent*[72] ... Will I tell you? ... Not interested?
Well I will just the same ... I think you should know ...

Joe does not want to know details of something as casual as death.[73] And
he wants 'no more old lip from her' either.

... That's right, Joe, squeeze away ... I'll soon be gone ... the last of them ... Unless that slut loves you ... Then yourself ... That old bonfire[74] ... Years of that stink[75] ... Then the silence ... A dollop of that ... To crown all.

As in Move 5, she warns Joe that silencing the voice of conscience does not erase its guilt. *Silence*, the 'crown' he seeks for his labour of self love, will not appease his Lord. It will make His indictment all the more distinct.

.... Till His Nibs ... One dirty winter night ... 'Mud thou art.'[76]

Move 9

The last mask falls. The Voice, feigning to 'cut a long story short' (p. 20), in fact, makes a short story long, as Beckett unmasks his own morbid preoccupation with suicide.[77] 'There's love for you' is the motif.

A romantic setting, Killiney Bay, near his home, is the scene of a quasi-ritual suicide — the sea, moon, and stones project their primeval power to exact sacrifice on to the power and passion of love. The sacrifice — self-destruction — is given the aura of an epiphany.

Beckett uses the three symbols, acting and interacting on three senses: seeing, hearing, feeling, in a lurid description of three attempts at suicide. The transcendent dimension develops from this fusion of symbols and senses; till the 'green one', driven by love and drawn by the intangible lure of sea, moon, and stones, drifts into madness.[78]

Strains of eerie ritual pervade the text, creating powerful imagery of colour, tone and touch: from the festive *lavender* silk slip, the pale *green* eyes, the beaten *silver* of the moon, to the *grey* hue of the cold stones engulfed by the cruel sea. Darkness is intimated too; and the ephemeral intensity of the senses pitted against the abiding influence of the symbols:

Seeing	Hearing	Feeling
1. Full moon ...	Faint lap of the sea ...	Lips on a *stone* ...
2. Moon going off the shore behind the hill ...	*Voice drops to a whisper*	*Breasts* in the stones ...
3. Light gone ...	No sound ...	And the *hands* ... In the stones ... Till they go ... (pp. 20, 21)

The text opens with an image of peace and contentment:

All right ... Warm summer night ... All sleeping ...

Like a fanfare of muffled drums signalling the start of a druidic rite,[79] comes the rhythmic call of the sea:

Faint lap of the sea through open window ... (p. 20) Gets up in the

end and slips out as she is ... Moon ... Stock[80] ... Down the garden
and under the viaduct ... Sees from the seaweed the tide is flowing
... Goes on down to the edge and lies down with her face in the wash
... Cut a long story short doesn't work ...

His description of her second attempt at suicide borders on the melodra-
matic. ...

... Gets out the Gillette... ... Back down the garden and under the
viaduct ... ... Cut another long story short doesn't work either ...
You know how she always dreaded pain ...

Her third (and successful) attempt at self-destruction is drawn-out, but
dramatic intensity increases as the Voice pitch decreases, and vivid imagery
sharpens when *Voice drops to a whisper* (p. 21), and Joe is straining to hear
words in italics, straining to exact his remorse. Symbols dominate the final
scene. The impact of sea, moon and stones on her diminishing perception
is drawing her inexorably to the ultimate sacrifice.

Subtly the symbols play on her love-lorn sensibility. Beckett portrays this
sequence in the poetry of intimation:

Unconscionable[81] hour by now ... Moon going off the shore behind
the hill ... Stands a bit looking at the beaten silver ... Then starts along
the edge to a place further down near the Rock[82] ... Imagine what in
her mind to make her do that ... Imagine ... Trailing her feet in the
water like a child ... ... Lies down in the end with her face a few
feet from the tide ... (p. 21)

The dramatic emphasis is now on stones -- symbols of 'unassignable
value'[83] perhaps, but which provide Beckett with a conveniently enigmatic
ending to a poignant episode.

... Scoops a little cup for her face in the stones ... The green one ...
The narrow one ...[84] ... ...
Voice drops to a whisper, almost inaudible except words in italics.
Lips on a *stone* ... Taking Joe with her ... Light gone ... 'Joe Joe' ... No
sound ... To the *stones* ... ... *Imagine* the hands ... The *solitaire* ...
Against a *stone* ... Imagine the *eyes* ... *Breasts* on the stones ... And the
hands ... Before they go ... *Imagine* the hands ... What are they at? ...
In the *stones* ...
Image fades, voice as before.

The Voice continues, expanding the image and the enigma of '*hands* ...
What are they at? ... In the *stones* ...':

What are they fondling? ... Till they go ... *There's love for you* ... Isn't
it Joe? ... Wasn't it Joe? *Eh Joe?* ... Wouldn't you say? ... Compared to
us ... Compared to Him ... *Eh Joe?*
Voice and image out. End

Many associations, pagan and christian, mingle in the dramatic impact of the italicised words whispered with relentless censure, up to the last ironic taunt about Joe's pretensions to omnipotence: 'Compared to Him'.[85]

The words in italics intimate mythological, cosmic, and sociological realities commonplace in Ireland, but which Beckett keeps below the surface of the text.

Mythological: The stones she was 'fondling' were small stones as indicated in an earlier line: 'Scoops a little cup for her face in the stones ...' She could be using the small, water-rounded stones as 'Cursing Stones' or even as 'Praying Stones', both being old Irish customs, frequently the one shading into the other. On this ancient practice, Patrick Power writes:

> Perhaps the most interesting rituals in maledictory practices were those in which stones were used. Stones, such as gems, are used so often as talismans, that one might expect to have them utilised for cursing and bringing down ill-luck.[86]

The ritual varied according to the size and location of the 'cursing stones'.[87] Often the 'stone was turned anti-clockwise by the curser while the imprecation was uttered'. The small, coloured or speckled stones available at 'the Rock', she appears to be *fondling* : a euphemism to accord with the motif *There's love for you*. (p. 21)

Cosmic: Stones were used for cursing because of 'the hardness, coldness and lifelessness which seems part of a stone'.[88] Hence the saying, 'a heart of stone' — a pitiless heart. It is a fact that certain stones give off energy and emit a healing force.[89] The dichotomy of the sensory and cosmic evaluation of stones extends to the sense, in the context, of the word 'fondling'. Fondling the stones — turning them anti-clockwise — could mean using them as 'cursing stones' or 'praying stones'; probably the latter, intimated earlier: 'On Mary's beads (also turned anti-clockwise) we plead her needs ...' (Move 8, p. 19). It would indicate her forgiveness for Joe's deception, thereby putting her love on a higher plane than theirs, and nearer to divine love. The motif 'There's love for you' ... Compared to us ... Compared to Him ...' shatters Joe's 'omnipotence'.

The last italicised *Eh Joe?* (p. 21), a loaded question[90] posed ten times by the persistent Voice seeking an admission of guilt, received a symbolic reply from silenced Joe.[91] Clas Zilliacus recounts that, in the Stuttgart Sud Deutsche Rundfunk production, directed by Beckett himself:

> a little sneer appeared on Joe's face, and it remained there for the fade-out. In this way, perhaps, the author created an opportunity to

repudiate the undeniable sentimentality of his drama by insisting on the incurability of the old lecher....[92]

Beckett ought to know. But it also means that Joe has the (unspoken) last word. The 'little sneer', albeit an afterthought by the author-director,[93] illustrates how in fact, simply by being himself, 'Beckett's drama thrives on symbols of unassignable value'.[94]

I do not agree that *Eh Joe* is either sentimental, or 'too simple'.[95] As one of Beckett's periodic public confessions, it represents the pricks and kicks of conscience, played back by a narrator in other Beckett writings.[96] This way of purging guilt collected in the subconscious over the years is an imperative, and a portrayal of the Puritan conscience.[97]

Hugh Kenner expands on the historical background, development, and expression of this trait, and concludes:

> The Beckett books and plays are repeatedly public confessions by men who have cut themselves off and have nothing left but the language to fondle, old language, new language. Keeping going, that's their job now.[98]

Joe's grin means, then, On! On![99]

NOTES

1 He died in 1973 having won universal acclaim for 'his superlative interpretation of everything that Beckett wrote' up to then (*Irish Times* 1.2.1973).

2 Cohn, *Back to Beckett*, p. 209.

3 Fletcher et al., *A Student's Guide to the Plays of Samuel Beckett*, p. 186.

4 Ibid.

5 Ibid.

6 Fletcher and Spurling, *Beckett: A Study of his Plays*, p. 99.

7 *Krapp's Last Tape*, p. 13.

8 Wakeling, 'Looking at Beckett: The Man and the Writer', p. 6.

9 Webb, *The Plays of Samuel Beckett*, p. 127.

10 Fletcher et al., *A Student's Guide to the Plays of Samuel Beckett*, p. 187.

11 Ibid.

12 Webb, *The Plays of Samuel Beckett*, p. 127.

13 Webb, *The Plays of Samuel Beckett*, p. 129: '... the voices are masks that a deeper level of his mind uses to try to call attention to certain truths about himself that are tied up with the memories they represent.'

14 Bair, *Samuel Beckett*, p. 205.

15 Peche, George, 'Rockhounds', *Ireland of the Welcomes*, Vol. 34, No. 1, 1985, p. 14.

16 Bair, *Samuel Beckett*, pp. 104, 110, 112.

17 Ibid., p. 205.

18 Ibid., pp. 129, 130.

19 Ibid., p. 205.

20 Ibid., p. 130. As Peggy was dead then (1934), her parents were horrified and cut him off from 'the one haven left in his life', their home. He complained about this, but had 'little remorse' for his deeds.

21 Mercier, *Beckett/Beckett*, p. 133.

22 Bair, *Samuel Beckett*, pp. 86, 89, 92, 93.

23 Wakeling, 'Looking at Beckett: The Man and the Writer', p. 9.

24 Quoted, in Wakeling, 'Looking at Beckett: The Man and the Writer', pp. 9, 10.

25 Jung, C.G., *Analytical Psychology: Its Theory and Practice. The Tavistock Lectures*, London, Routledge and Kegan Paul, 1968, p. 81.

26 Mercier, *Beckett/Beckett*, p. 4.

27 *The Penguin English Dictionary*, p. 218.

28 Ibid., p. 470.

29 *The Practical Standard Dictionary*, Funk & Wagnalls Company, New York, 1939, p. 1171.

30 Cohn, *Back to Beckett*, p. 210.

31 A tweed cape or loose coat. *Avoca Weavers* is a firm making Avoca tweeds (loosely woven tweed), formerly based at Wooden Bridge in the Vale of Avoca, Co. Wicklow, and now at Glencormac, near Bray, Co. Wicklow. The Avoca river, famed in song and story, evokes imagery of water and scenic beauty that anticipate Move 9.

32 Dolan, 'Samuel Beckett's Dramatic Use of Hiberno-English', p. 48.

33 *All That Fall*, p. 19.

34 Dolan, op. cit., p. 50.

35 Here, the opposition Thought/Forgotten; everything/nothing; light/dark; are examples. This aspect of Beckett's technique is explained fully by Mercier in *Beckett/Beckett* (1977), Chapter I.

36 Wakeling, 'Looking at Beckett: The Man and the Writer', p. 9.

37 See Laing's description of the schizoid personality, *Irish University Review*, Spring 1984, p. 10.

38 Webb, *The Plays of Samuel Beckett*, p. 128.

39 Beckett's father died on June 26, 1933, at the age of 61. There was a strong bond of affection between father and son, and Sam sat at his father's bedside for days before his death. Afterwards, he could only remember how his father had joked during his illness, and his last words, 'fight, fight, fight' (see Bair, *Samuel Beckett*, pp. 147-8).

40 His mother died on August 25, 1950. His memories of her were short-lived, due to 'the feelings of dependency, guilt and neglect that haunted his relationship

with her.' (Bair, op. cit., p. 340).

41 Webb, *The Plays of Samuel Beckett*, p. 129.

42 A schizoid individual, being 'all persons and things to himself ... the imagined advantages are safety for the true self, isolation, and hence freedom from others, self sufficiency and control'. (Laing, p. 78).

43 See Bair, *Samuel Beckett*, pp. 22, 23, 140, 141, 156.

44 The woman's prediction about Joe finally 'hearing himself ... till not a gasp left there either ...' fits in with Laing's statement: '... this shut-up self, being isolated, is unable to be enriched by outer experience, and so the whole inner whole comes to be more and more impoverished, until the individual may come to feel he is merely a vacuum.' (Laing, p. 78).

45 Bair, *Samuel Beckett*, p. 132.

46 The word *limbo* is used in its figurative meaning: 'place for unwanted or forgotten people and things'. *The Penguin English Dictionary*, p. 420.

47 Ibid., Definition of *ambivalence*, p. 20.

48 Flint glass: variety of brilliant glass containing lead silicate. *The Penguin English Dictionary*, p. 283 — 'silicate: salt of silicic acid; rock chiefly composed of the silicate of a metal'. Ibid., p. 637; 'silica: hard white or colourless mineral with a high melting point'. Ibid.

49 He will be 'alone with the sole object of his worship, himself ... to endure the punishment of getting precisely what he asked for ...' Webb, *The Plays of Samuel Beckett*, p. 129.

50 Joe loved language more than he loved any or all of the women he deceived with its subtleties and ambiguity. In the play ... Move 1 and Move 7 reveal the light and shade of Joe's 'powerful grasp of language'. Also, see Webb, op. cit., p. 128.

51 Laing, R.D., *The Divided Self: A Study of Sanity and Madness*, London, Tavistock Publications, 1960, p. 78.

52 Bair, *Samuel Beckett*, pp. 140, 141.

53 Beckett's psychosomatic illnesses included bursitis, boils, cysts, among others.

54 *Godot*, p. 62. See *Irish University Review*, 1984, p. 92.

55 That was not difficult. See Bair, *Samuel Beckett*, pp. 140 - 142. In *Dream of Fair to Middling Women* (1932), he 'viciously satirises many people who have remained lifelong, steadfast friends'. (Bair, op. cit., p. 129).

56 Beckett was prone to all kinds of illnesses from his early 20's. 'By December 1930, Beckett was ... beginning to fall prey to unusual physical ailments that accompanied his most severe mental depressions. ... As his solitude deepened, his illness multiplied.' (Bair, op. cit., pp. 111, 140).

57 *More* is the operative word here. Beckett liked to compare and categorise young writers, using himself as the yardstick. At 27, lonely, bored, and unable to capture his muse 'he began mentally to divide creative persons into two labels: those who (like himself), kept their own counsel and waited for their muse, and those who did not, for whom he had great contempt and whom he subsequently called

noncreative writing machines'. (Bair, op. cit., p. 141).

58 At 24, Beckett was a 'very handsome young man', in the eyes of his female students (Bair, op. cit., p. 110). At 27, no longer an Adonis, his fair to middling good looks were not improved by his Bohemian way of life, as 'he drifted aimlessly in an alcoholic fog'. He lost interest in his personal appearance, and 'began to lead a solitary existence'. (Bair, op. cit., p. 140).

59 Beckett's unkempt appearance at that time (1931) embarrassed his relatives and many of his friends. In January 1931, 'his desperate physical appearance' induced his family to let him 'flee to Kassel' (where 'The green one' awaited him). When he got there, he found a continuous party circuit too demanding on his physical and mental state. A crisis in their love affair was looming. (Bair, op. cit., p. 112).

60 Beckett was 'absolutely truthful' to one friend only — Thomas McGreevy — to whom he 'poured out all the agony, anger and uncertainty of his existence ... to whom he told his innermost, deeply secret thoughts'. (Bair, op. cit., p. 140).

61 The play is based on his infidelity to women. For the many examples of this, see Bair, op. cit., pp. 92, 112, 118, 119.

62 References to Beckett's sanity — or doubts about it — as expressed by family and friends, are recounted by Bair, op. cit., pp. 64, 134 - 145, 156, 167, 168.

63 Cross-reference to *Krapp's Last Tape*, p. 18. It is the same girl -- Peggy Sinclair, the green-eyed cousin.

64 Reference to the boat scene, *Krapp's Last Tape*, p. 17 ... 'but the eyes just slits, because of the glare ...'

65 Peggy's pallor is mentioned by Bair, op. cit., p. 123. It was a symptom of tuberculosis. Beckett was staying with the Sinclairs in Kassel at the time (early 1932).

66 Shorter version of the lines in *Krapp's Last Tape*: 'The eyes she had! ... all the light and dark ... (p. 18)

67 Krapp admitted that he loved and lost against his will. He had an ambiguous attitude towards love and women, as well as towards himself.

68 The ticket was for the boat. The word 'flight' is meant as kind of escape. He was running away from Kassel, his relatives, and particularly from Peggy.

69 'His infatuation with Peggy's green eyes and disarming manner had quieted. He decided to bow out to her German suitor ...' Bair, op. cit., pp. 112, 113.

70 Lip (coll): impudence. See Bair, op. cit., p. 112 for evidence of the autobiographical basis of this text.

71 The question is ironic and scornful. She could not say; and he promptly silenced her voice or memories of her: 'No more old lip from her' (Move 7).

72 *Irish Independent*, one of Ireland's national newspapers.

73 'Beckett treats death with casual irony'. (Bair, op. cit., p. 145).

74 Reference to *Krapp's Last Tape*, p. 20. Krapp did not want to live his 'best years' again...'Not with the fire in me now'. The 'slut' here is 'Fanny ... Bony old ghost ...' in that play.

75 The sense of smell in an unpleasant form will replace the sense of hearing when he has killed off 'the last of them'. That 'stink' can also be Joe himself in his 'foul old wrapper' (Move 5).

76 'His Nibs' (God) will not say 'Dust thou art' but as 'One dirty winter night' is meant as morally, i.e. sexually 'dirty', He will say, 'Mud thou art.' The figurative meaning of the word *mud* is something despicable. *The Penguin English Dictionary*, p. 461.

77 His biographer makes numerous references to this: 'Suicide as an intellectual exercise had first intrigued Beckett at Trinity ...' i.e. in 1923. This being his main conversational theme, he bored and alienated friends at TCD and later in Paris. In 1928, Richard Ardlington (who later judged the prize-winning poem *Whoroscope*), described Beckett as 'the splendidly mad Irishman — who wanted to commit suicide ...' A recurring topic of conversation initiated by him was, 'suicide and all its aspects', whenever he met his circle of intellectuals in the famous cafés of Montparnasse, The Dôme and the Coupole. (Bair, op. cit., pp. 64-65).

Of particular relevance to *Eh Joe* is his reaction to the developing mental breakdown of Lucia Joyce, in 1929, when he was close to the Joyce family. Bair (op. cit., p. 79) describes how Beckett watched Lucia drift into madness (almost wholly due to unrequited love for him). 'He thought Lucia was becoming insane ... He speculated excitedly whether her madness would lead to suicide. He thought Lucia's reckless intelligence might veer too far one day and self-destruction became the only possible resolution of the conflict within her tortured mind. The possible manifestations of her behaviour fascinated him.'

78 As in *Krapp's Last Tape*, the sea represents 'the threat of madness, the sheer terror of life, the impossibility of going on'. (Wakeling, 'Looking at Beckett: The Man and the Writer'). Krapp, however, transcended that threat, even turned it to good account. (Bair, op. cit., p. 298). The 'green one' succumbed to the threat that Beckett associated with the sea, probably because her driving passion is love, whereas his is ambition. (Bair, op. cit., p. 112).

79 The Druids celebrated the summer solstice. 'Month of June' is mentioned later on in Move 9. There are overtones of pagan beliefs and customs elsewhere in the text, e.g. the closing lines and imagery they present (p. 21).

80 In the text it means fixed or standing still. In the context of the overtones referred to, it underlines the pagan symbolism, since 'To worship stocks and stones is to worship idols, *stock* here being taken as a type of motionless, fixed thing, like a treestump.' (*Brewer's Dictionary of Phrase and Fable*.)

81 Not governed by sense or prudence. Not only was it late at night, but at an hour when her powers of judgement were weak.

82 The White Rock Strand has deep water even when the tide is out.

83 Fletcher and Spurling, *Beckett: A Study of his Plays*, p. 99.

84 Lines from *Krapp's Last Tape*, already quoted in Move 7.

85 Move 5.

86 Power, *The Book of Irish Curses*, p. 29.

87 There are many famous cursing stones throughout the country. For the exact locations, see Power, *The Book of Irish Curses*, pp. 29 - 33.

88 Ibid., p. 33.

89 Callahan, Philip S., 'Butterfly Rock', *Ireland of the Welcomes*, Vol. 34, No. 1, pp. 44, 45.

90 It is the provocative question that gave the play its title. The word 'loaded' (fig) containing a hidden danger or trap. *Penguin English Dictionary*, p. 424.

91 The vacuum of silence threatened in Move 3 must now engulf Joe, since the last voice is stilled.

92 Zilliacus, Clas, *Beckett and Broadcasting: A Study of the Works of Samuel Beckett for and in Radio and Television*, Abo Akademi, 1976, p. 190.

93 It is not included in the stage directions, as for instance, in *That Time*, a 'smile, toothless for preference' is stipulated for Listener.

94 Fletcher and Spurling, *Beckett: A Study of his Plays*, p. 99.

95 Opinion expressed by Fletcher and Spurling in *Beckett: A Study of his Plays*, p. 99.

96 *More Pricks Than Kicks* (1934); *First Love* (1972); *The Unnamable* (1958); *Krapp's Last Tape* (1958).

97 Kiberd, Declan, 'Samuel Beckett and the Protestant Ethic' in Martin, A. (ed.), *The Genius of Irish Prose*, Mercier Press, Dublin 1985, pp. 127 - 130.

98 Kenner, *A Reader's Guide to Samuel Beckett*, pp. 134-5.

99 For Beckett's 'imperatives' on keeping going, see *Molloy: Malone Dies: The Unnamable*, pp. 86, 87.

Chapter Eight

THAT TIME

Further exploiting the benefits of modern technology for theatrical innovation, Beckett wrote the stereo radio drama piece, *That Time*, in the
summer of 1974. He classified the play as 'of the *Not I* family'.[1]

First published in 1976 by Grove Press, New York, it was first performed
at the Royal Court Theatre, London, on May 20, 1976, for the Beckett Festival
celebrating the author's seventieth birthday. Patrick Magee, for whom he
wrote the play, performed the rôle of *Listener*. *That Time* was part of a triple
bill with *Footfalls* (1976) and *Play* (1963).

Criticism of three totally different plays inevitably drew comparisons
and contrasts: *That Time* emerged with few compliments for the author or
the play, from that première. Once again Beckett had puzzled and disturbed
the audience,[2] and the critics voiced a general groan, particularly against
the two new scripts. A review in the *Sunday Times*, 23 May 1976, entitled
'The Heart of Darkness', deduced from these that Beckett 'has become a
Jansenist. He now believes in utter damnation. No soul can be saved by
good works.' The reviewer, Harold Hobson, concluded, 'They may have to
be fought for as *Waiting for Godot* ... had to be fought for,' and called them
'poems of strange and terrible beauty.'[3]

The triple bill was performed at the Arena Theatre, Washington, D.C., in
December 1976, with an American cast directed by the late Alan Schneider.
The reaction to the new plays was patient;[4] the reviews positive. Drama

critic, Mel Gussow, in the *New York Times* described them as 'strange, hypnotic, and exquisite'.[5]

That Time had its Irish première at the Peacock Theatre, in April 1978, in a bill with *Act Without Words I* (1958), and *Come and Go* (1965). Directed by Paul Brennan, John Molloy played Listener; the designer was Eddie Doyle. The next production in Dublin, at the Players' Theatre, TCD, on August 18 1981, was directed by Alan Gilsenan. Brendan Ellis, who portrayed Listener, was also the designer.

In the 'family' of Beckett plays where the 'character',[6] having no body, is represented by an enormous, rapidly-talking Mouth, or a suspended, breathing Head, the role of director, actor, or designer has no artistic priority in a successful realisation of the play. The director's applied art is that 'of convincing the actor to forfeit the notion of character in the service of poetic stage images ...' For his part 'the actor must accept this de-personalisation before any progress can be made.'[7] The designer of the stage images must create, according to the letter of Beckett's specifications, the vision of a poet striving to probe the mystery of identity.

In this pursuit, Beckett presents his character as an illuminated Head, in which memories revolve and recoil in a pattern of repetitive narratives linking three phases of a life-time. They are: childhood, youth, and old age, recalled in voices A B C.

The décor is symbolic. The stage is in darkness: the head of an old man, Listener, suspended in the black void 'about ten feet above stage level midstage off centre'. The audience sees an 'Old white face, long flaring white hair as if seen from above outspread.' The only *live* sounds made by Listener during the twenty-five minute performance are the 'slow and regular' sounds of breathing that break the 10 seconds-silence at three points indicated in the text. In this brief interval the eyes open; and close again when the voice resumes.

Listener hears three separate recorded narratives, each coming from a different loudspeaker, but each spoken in his own voice, addressing him as 'you'. The pronoun 'you' concedes a consciousness of roots and relationships absent in *Not I*.[8] A search for the missing pieces of a viable identity is the odyssey unfolded in *That Time*.

The play has similarities to *Krapp's Last Tape*. One of them, noted by Vivian Mercier in the Epilogue of his book, is: 'That Time ... uses a variation of the same technical means to create a unique mood.'[9] A fundamental element in the creation of this 'unique mood' is *location*.

Location

C.R. Lyons writes: 'Beckett eliminates the sense of a location in the scene of *That Time*. The play does not take *place* in any literal sense.'

He amplifies the statement, and concludes:

> ... the division of voice and face, establishing an arbitrary relation-ship between the consciousness that hears and the words that it speaks, forms an image of mental function not of space.[10]

Here he is exploring a metaphysical[11] aspect of the play. I am concerned with the physical location of the landmarks that excite this mental function, however feebly.

The reality is, that the play does take place, and in the literal sense Beckett deemed it should, namely, that the audience becomes a collective *Listener*, too. The essence of this dramatic experience is the aural impact of the play 'where the trappings of the theatre are shed and the emphasis is on language accompanied by a single stage image'.[12]

Location is more specific in *That Time* than in any of the four plays preceding it in this study. It is basic to the play, evoking the nostalgia that pervades the text. The old man, piecing together fragments from the flotsam of his life, is desperately trying to clutch at some thing or place that will anchor him in time, establish him as 'somebody', renew his sense of belonging somewhere. The strands of memory are frail, but the corner-stones of his reminiscences are fixed and firm.

Each of the three voices locates Listener on a stone —

> A: the flat stone in the ruin where he hid as a child;
>
> B: the long low stone where the young lovers sat;
>
> C: the marble slab seat in the Portrait Gallery.

Foley's Folly, the 'bit of a tower still standing' (p. 10), object of his sentimental journey recorded in the A passages, has been identified by Beckett himself as *Barrington's Tower*,[13] still standing in the foothills of the Dublin Mountains, about a mile from his home.[14]

The Tower *ruin* provided a childhood retreat in a way the intact structure could not : it had a flat stone where he sat with his imaginary companions; or 'with the light coming in where the wall had crumbled away poring on his book well on into the night ...' (p. 14) Eoin O'Brien describes its other attractions for young Beckett:

> From the hideout in Foley's Folly, Beckett had a commanding view of the Wicklow mountains, and, to the east, the sea coast of Killiney; on a clear day Wales could be sighted ....

Moreover:

> The blue of sea and sky, viewed from Foley's Folly, are ever chang-
> ing in hue and shade, and, at the end of the day, continued to enthral
> the errant youth committed to an early bed, no doubt as a punish-
> ment for his lengthy wandering.[15]

In Beckett's childhood memories, Foley's Folly is ringed by a vicious
circle of refuge from, and reluctant homecoming to, parental discipline.
Though this is more clearly stated in his other writings,[16] in *That Time*, it is
recognised that :

> The picture portrayed is one of a defiant child at peace with his
> picture book in the moonlit ruin overlooking Dublin Bay, not dis-
> pleased by the anxiety that he may be causing his concerned par-
> ents.[17]

> ... and they all out on the roads looking for him.[18]

The wharf (pp. 10, 16), of his arrival and departure on the same day, is
Dun Laoghaire Quay, scene of the 'miracle' described in *Krapp's Last Tape*.
Foxrock is about three kilometres inland from Dun Laoghaire Harbour.

The road from the Quay to the High Street, Dun Laoghaire, has a marked
incline: the gradient is reflected in the old man's posture as he hurried

> straight off the ferry and up the rise to the high street to catch the
> eleven ... head down press on up the rise to the top ... (p. 12)

There he waited for the number eleven tram, 'till the truth began to dawn'.[19]
There was now

> no getting out to it that way so what next ... foot it up in the end to
> the station bowed half double get out to it that way ... (p. 13)

He found the station deserted and derelict: trains no longer ran from the
city to Foxrock.[20] Harcourt Street station, city terminus of the Dublin and
Southeastern Railway, where suburban trains arrived from and departed
to Foxrock, was

> all closed down and boarded up Doric terminus of the Great South-
> ern and Eastern all closed down ... so what next. (p. 13)

The way back to his childhood refuge physically barred, he still lingered on
the sunless steps of the Doric terminus ...

> ... gave up and sat down on the steps in the pale morning sun no
> those steps got no sun ... (p. 13)

Three times he 'gave up and off somewhere else'[21] to find a stone location
in the sun; then squatted

> down on a step in the pale sun a doorstep say someone's doorstep
> for it to be time to get on the night ferry and out to hell out of there ...
> (p. 13)

The movement recorded in the A passage is circular. Listener went straight from the wharf of Dun Laoghaire Harbour with 'only one thought' in his head (p. 12), to get out to Foxrock and the ruin refuge of his childhood, 'to hide in again till it was night and time to go' (p. 15). In the event, when 'that time came' (p. 15), he went

> back down to the wharf with the nightbag and the old green greatcoat your father left you trailing on the ground ... not a thought in your head only get back on board and away to hell out of it ... (p. 16).

In contrast to the circular motion, motivated by one thought, is the static image of the old man 'huddled on the doorstep' (p. 14), 'drooling away out loud' (p. 15), countless thoughts ('making it all up on the doorstep... for the millionth time', p. 15), that revolve round the romance[22] of childhood '... there was childhood for you ...' (p. 15).

The B passages are set in an idyllic landscape befitting their romantic content. The long low stone 'at the edge of the little wood' (p. 9); fields of ripening wheat stretching as far as the eye could see (p. 11); the streams, the towpath (p. 12); and the sand (strand) are all part of Beckett country and the environs of Foxrock.[23]

The C passages have a city location. They revolve round three public institutions: the Portrait Gallery; the Public Library; and the Post Office, in Dublin city.

The Portrait Gallery — *The National Gallery of Ireland*[24] situated in Leinster Lawn, Merrion Square West is near Trinity College Park, and not far from St Stephen's Green, where lovers sat 'exchanging vows' in *Eh Joe* (p. 18). The Portrait Gallery provides an interesting survey of Irish historical personalities over the last three centuries. In the thirties, Beckett found 'solace and refuge' there.[25]

The Public Library — *The National Library of Ireland*[26] in Kildare Street, is the State Library and the largest public library in the country. Founded in 1887, it now contains over half a million books, besides maps, prints and MSS, including some of the illuminated manuscripts produced in the monastic libraries from the sixth century.

The Post Office 'with all the forms and pens on their chains' (p. 14), is *The General Post Office* in O'Connell Street. This historic[27] city landmark features in *Murphy* (1938). There is an associative link between *That Time* and *Murphy*, whose characters are drawn from Beckett's circle of acquaintances. One of them, Neary, was ejected from the main hall of the General Post

Office, having clearly no warrant in the place at the time.[28]

Listener went in out of the cold and rain, as he had done in the Portrait Gallery and the Public Library; but, unlike these two havens of peace, he felt uneasy in the Post Office ... 'taking a look round for a change before drowsing away' (p. 14). Fear foiled his routine cat-nap. ...

> perhaps fear of ejection having clearly no warrant in the place to say
> nothing of the loathsome appearance ... (p. 15).

With the General Post Office as a common location, his fear of ejection, 'perhaps' stems from the factual ejection described at length in the novel forty years before.[29]

As in voice A and B, voice C draws from 'the old scenes the old names' (p. 12) a cluster of memories with an authentic ring of evocation.

Evocation

Evocation, and Listener's own reaction to it, make up the entire text. 'He returned to his own life to write this play'. When in 1974, poetry failed 'to start some creative impulse', to help ward off depression, and brooding on his own mortality, Beckett forced himself to write this play.[30] His creative impulse was, then, 'to keep the void out' (p. 11), just as in the play, he admits to:

> making up to keep the void out just another of those old tales to keep
> the void from pouring in on top of you the shroud (p. 11).

However, Beckett is remembering, rather than making up, fragments from his childhood, youth, and adult life, recalled by voices A B C. The narratives sketch the portrait of the artist, drawn with consummate accuracy in 'Looking at Beckett: The Man and the Writer'.[31]

'Writing *That Time* seemed to release an autobiographical swell that he had kept under control for many years',[32] his biographer tells us. This is the first and only play that touches on his early childhood. Voice A evokes memories of a tower ruin where he hid and played as a child. What was he hiding from? From his mother's ire and 'ferocious beatings' when he played his daring games at home.[33]

The selective glimpses of his childhood presented in the A narrative give the impression of a docile boy, presumably passing the time with his picture book, before coming of age for school on his sixth birthday. The truth is:

> He seemed to set out deliberately to provoke his mother's anger, as
> if to test the supremacy of her will or his, as he invited her beatings
> by inventing one foolhardy scheme after another, earning him the
> lifelong nickname of the 'Family Jonah'.[34]

The scenes from his childhood depict him as a loner by choice, seeking to avoid the physical presence of others:

> ... slip off when no one was looking and hide there all day long on
> a stone among the nettles with your picture book (p. 10).

Sitting on the stone 'where none ever came' (p. 10) he would carry on 'loud imaginary conversation' with himself, creating his own company 'being together that way' (p. 14):

> ten or eleven on a stone among the giant nettles making it up now
> one voice now another till you were hoarse and they all sounded
> the same well on into the night ... (p. 11).

Evocation is now turning the pages of Beckett's real picture book of life. The 'ten or eleven on a stone' were his *dramatis personae* for a childhood venture into the Theatre of the Absurd. In that childhood imagination were the tender roots of histrionic intuition that flowered in the desert of post-war disillusionment with conventional art forms, and received ideas.[35]

In the second A passage he mentions his mother, in the context of his childhood refuge and his thwarted effort 'to look was it still there to hide in again' (p. 15).

> when was that was your mother ah for God's sake all gone long ago
> that time you went back that last time to look was the ruin still there
> where you hid as a child someone's folly (p. 10).

The reference is, of course, to Foley's Folly, but the inference is to his mother's folly in striving to mould him into her 'model' boy. According to his biographer:

> From the very beginning of Beckett's development as a rational
> human being, May was determined to conquer his stubborn refusal
> to be reached, his unwillingness to show all the ordinary emotions,
> from fear to affection. And he was just as determined to maintain
> his independence from her domination. The battle of wills between
> mother and son began when Samuel Beckett was little more than
> three years old, and it continued, through periods of rage and
> depression, for the length of May's lifetime.[36]

Apart from the childhood scene the images in the A narrative are of institutions, structures, relationships and sentiments crumbling: not yet obliterated, as their traces are still there:

> not a tram left in the place only the old rails (p. 9);
> not a wire to be seen only the old rails all rust (p. 10);
> Doric terminus ... the colonnade crumbling away (p. 13);
> all the homes gone ... that kip on the front where you no she was
> with you then still with you then (p. 10);

not a curse for the old scenes the old names not a thought in your
head only get back on board and away to hell out of it and never
come back (p.1 6).

Voice A and voice C recall the famous overcoat Beckett inherited from
his father : 'the inheritance shared by many of Beckett's old men.'[37] The 'old
green greatcoat' decked the bedraggled figure 'huddled on the doorstep'
(p. 14), near the Doric terminus;[38] or 'huddled up on the slab' in the empty
Portrait Gallery (p. 10). The 'old green greatcoat your father left you' stroked
the ground, as Listener strode back down to the wharf to 'get back on board'
the emigration boat. (p. 16). In *That Time*, where all the other objects of
evocation are disintegrating, 'the old green holeproof coat[39] your father left
you' (p. 14), as the seamless mantle of his identity, appears indestructible.

All three strands of memory reflect the variable Irish climate. The A
narrative atmosphere is: a grey day; pale morning sun; and later just pale
sun. The B passages concern young love, and have bright sun and blue skies.
The C narrative tells of an endless winter, always raining, and very cold.

Voice B recollects love scenes from Listener's early youth. The rhythmic
simplicity of language recaptures the first stirrings of romantic love that
quicken the rhythm of life.[40] Vivian Mercier remarks, Voice B evokes a scene
virtually without parallel in Beckett:

> on the stone together in the sun on the stone at the edge of the little
> wood and as far as eye could see the wheat turning yellow vowing
> every now and then you loved each other just a murmur not touching
> or anything of that nature you one end of the stone she the other ....[41]

In *That Time*, or any other time, Beckett could not leave this idealistic and
tender passage as a stain upon his *oeuvre*. The love vows renewed, in slightly
different phrasing, three times, he then reveals that the B passages evoke a
wonderland of reverie rather than reality. Fancies formed in the emotional
'daze' (p. 10) of adolescence became fantastic love scenes set in the well-trod
Beckett country. Thus, back to reality for Beckett, in B passage four:

> hard to believe harder and harder to believe you ever told anyone
> you loved them or anyone you till just one of those things you kept
> making up to keep the void out ... (p. 11).

The B passages recount dreams and not memories. Scenes 'float up' from
certain romantic points of location; then gradually 'sink and vanish' (p. 13),
in the sultry stillness of a summer noon. The visions return in other settings,
but fade out in the usual symbolic finish,[42] 'great shroud billowing in all
over you on top of you ...'[43] (p. 16) when the idyll is over, and Listener has
'no words left' to keep the void at bay.

The figures in the dream — a youth and a girl — are seen as two silhouettes sitting on a stone at the edge of a wood, gazing at fields of ripening wheat, but never regarding each other:

> no sight of the face or any other part ... never turned to each other
> just blurs on the fringes of the field ... no better than shades no worse
> if it wasn't for the vows (p. 12).

The 'vows' sustain the profile, while the silhouettes vary the locale, but keep a place in the sun, 'always together somewhere in the sun' (p. 12).

In the second image the silent couple stand on the towpath, facing downstream into the sun, watching the river flow down to the sea.[44] The third image places them by the sea, still strangers: 'stretched out parallel in the sand in the sun' (p. 13).

Then comes a turning-point ('always having turning-points', p. 12). All the images fade out gradually.

> stock still side by side in the sun then sink and vanish ... (p. 13).

First the lady vanishes, only his silhouette remains on the familiar landscape:

> or alone in the same scenes making it up that way to keep it going
> ... alone ... and no vows to break the peace ... (pp. 14, 15).

But that very peace recalls the vision of the girl: dream and reality merge in desire and doubt:

> and every now and then in the great peace like a whisper so faint
> she loved you hard to believe you even you made up that bit till the
> time came in the end.... (p. 15).

Finally, the scenes themselves fade away, as 'alone on the towpath' he remembers:

> 'the sun going down till it went down and you vanished all vanished' (p. 14).

Now, for the first time, 'the dark' enters into the B narrative.

> that time in the end ... by the window in the dark and the owl flown
> to hoot at someone else ... hour after hour not a sound ... no words
> left to keep it out so you gave it up there by the window in the dark
> or moonlight ... (p. 16).

This is 'the recurrent motif of the inexorable in Beckett: refuge is in darkness, hell is in light'.[45] He stood by the window in the dark, unable to recall the scenes:

> you tried and tried and couldn't any more no words left — gave up
> for good and let it in —'

At this point he is overwhelmed by the emptiness ('void') he has tried to ward off for so long:[46]

a great shroud billowing in all over you on top of you ... (p. 16).

This last stage of the dream now reveals its significance. The dream was an expression of an adolescent yearning for love, reassurance, and companionship. It was also an attempt to keep out the 'void' of loneliness, and avoid the vacuum of silence. But, 'that time in the end' when he is alone by the window in the dark and silent night —

hour after hour hour after hour not a sound —

and the great emptiness eventually overwhelms him, Listener admits to feeling ...

little or nothing the worse little or nothing (p. 16).

He has now crossed the threshold of adulthood, and into the reality of its adventures.

Voice C records three memorable adventures Listener encountered in adult life. They appear as 'metaphysical adventures',[47] or moments of inner enlightenment he experienced in the Portrait Gallery, the Post Office, and the Public Library. These institutions afford the C passages autobiographical authenticity; and Beckett the adventure of exploring the notion of identity in relation to the Berkeleyian principle : *Esse est percipi aut percipere* (To be is to be perceived or to perceive).[48]

Listener starts out as a non-person: the unnamable, restless loner, wandering 'all over the parish' (p. 13), muttering to himself about himself ...

when you started not knowing who you were from Adam ... no
notion who it was saying what you were saying whose skull you
were clapped up in whose moan had you the way you were ... (p. 12)

While inwardly preoccupied with himself, Listener made 'the old rounds' of the parish

crawling about year after year sunk in your lifelong mess muttering
to yourself who else... (p. 11).

Three external factors remained constant :

always winter then always raining always slipping in somewhere
when no one would be looking in off the street out of the cold and
rain ... places you hadn't to pay to get in... (pp. 13, 14)

Eoin O'Brien confirms the autobiographical content of these lines:

For Beckett, impecunious and lost in uncertainty, the National
Gallery in Dublin provided sanctuary on lonely wet days, as did the
National Portrait Gallery in London in later years.[49]

Listener's first adventure is in the Portrait Gallery. After his customary cat-nap his awareness returns:

till you hoisted your head and there before your eyes when they
opened a vast oil black with age and dirt someone famous in his

time some famous man or woman or even child ... behind the glass
where gradually as you peered trying to make it out gradually of all
things a face appeared had you swivel on the slab to see who it was
there at your elbow. (p. 11)

Of all things a *face* appeared! Listener was not only nameless but faceless.
A 'face' is a sign of identity. Listener had no identity. ...

did you ever say I to yourself in your life come on now (*eyes close*)
could you ever say I to yourself in your life (p. 11)

He perceived the reflection of a face in the glass, but it was only a reflection,
another 'Not I' for 'I' does not exist for Listener.

His moment of inner enlightenment comes when *he* is 'perceived' in the
Portrait Gallery as a person.

not knowing who you were from Adam ... there alone with the
portraits of the dead black with dirt and antiquity ... not believing it
could be you till they put you out in the rain at closing-time (p. 12)

Listener can 'never the same after this', for three philosophical questions
now accompany him on his 'rounds':[50]

1. What is identity and how can one express it?
2. Who are you in actual fact?
3. What does it mean, 'to exist'?

These questions remain unsolved until the end, when, like the love scenes
in the B narrative, they fade away and cease to occupy him, for he has no
words left to keep them going ...

till the words dried up and the head dried up and the legs dried up
whosoever they were or it gave up whoever it was (p. 13)

Listener's second metaphysical adventure takes place in the Post Office.
This time the revelation concerns co-existence with other living people. He
'perceives' the people occupied and preoccupied with the 'Christmas bustle', and anticipates their hostility:

so this look round for once at your fellow bastards thanking God for
once bad and all as you were you were not as they till it dawned that
for all the loathing you were getting you might as well not have been
there at all the eyes passing over you and through you like so much
thin air ... (p. 15)

He perceives his fellow human beings but he is not perceived by them, for
they are too busy to notice him. His moment of inner enlightenment here,
means that the moment he turns his attention to other people, he finds he
has rank and relationship with them. He ranked himself higher than his
'fellow bastards', but that shows he is developing self-awareness in society
instead of in solitude. He infers that there are other people even less

fortunate than he. The 'loathing' he always feels he awakens in others, now disappears into the 'thin air' he describes. Much of the loner-syndrome goes with it. The next adventure finds him in the company of others sharing an experience with them.

Finally, the third and last metaphysical adventure is set in the Public Library. As usual he slipped into the Library unperceived. He perceives an assembly of older people sitting round a table, and he joins them

> sitting at a big round table with a bevy of old ones poring on the page and not a sound (p. 16)

But there are in fact three symbolic sounds to be heard through the 'silence' of the Library ...[51]

> not a sound only the old breath and the leaves turning and then suddenly this dust ... when you opened your eyes from floor to ceiling nothing only dust and not a sound only what was it it said come and gone ... something like that come and gone come and gone no one come and gone in no time gone in no time (p. 16).

Language

Comparison with that of *Krapp's Last Tape* is inevitable, since Krapp and Listener are Beckett himself, striving 'before embarking on a new ... retro-spect'[52] to name the unnamable. Fletcher and co-authors' comment on Language in *That Time* is, simply: 'This reflects a return to the oral beauty which marked plays of an earlier period, *Krapp's Last Tape* in particular.'[53]

Three distinct sound-patterns in Krapp's recordings[54] parallel the three-fold sound pitch stipulated for Listener.[55] Vivian Mercier sees more Irish-ness in the A passages of the play than in the B and C narrative. 'Voice A, the most immediately Irish in rhythm and syntax, is concerned with "that time you went back that last time to look was the ruin still there where you hid as a child ... "'[56]

Rhythm conveys the sense of nostalgia that permeates the play: 'that last time ...' (p. 9) indicates that Listener's pilgrimage was the last of a series of such visits to Foley's Folly. His repeated homecoming is likewise intimated in the final A passage: 'or was that another time all that another time ...' (p. 16). Rhythm in effect amplifies the statement, and clarifies the situation, in the B passages the end of the adolescent love dream is announced with poetic diction contrived by the rhythm and repetition of simple words ...

> on the stone alone on the end of the stone with the wheat and blue or the towpath alone on the towpath with the ghosts of the mules

the drowned rat or bird or whatever it was floating off into the sunset ...
(p. 14).

In one C passage, rhythm flowing from alliterative lines carries the narrative to the climax of the *dust* scene in the Library:

> The Library that was another place another time that time you slipped in off the street out of the cold and rain when no one was looking ... something to do with dust something the dust said sitting at the big round table with a bevy of old ones poring on the page and not a sound (p. 16).

In all three strands — A B C — rhythm is a form of punctuation, as there is no formal punctuation in the text. Since the impact of *That Time* is exclusively aural, the rhythmic flow of Listener's phrases,[57] with his selective repetition in slightly different word-order,[58] contributes greatly to the interpretation and understanding of the play.

Syntax includes a few examples of Hiberno-English construction and idiom: Voice A ... 'to look was the ruin still there...' (p. 9), illustrates the copula form (the non-English form) of the verb 'to be', already explained within the Language section of *All That Fall*. The expression in British English would be: 'to see if the ruin was still there.' To *look* and to *see* are not the same; and Beckett instils more poignancy into the mission by indicating the earnestness of it. Thus, 'to look was the ruin still there' shows total concern for this monument of childhood memory; and a desire to recapture the magic of the solitude it provided ('to hide in again', p. 15). Standard English: 'to see if, or whether, the ruin was still there' has no sense of urgency, but suggests casual curiosity without sentimental attachment. Stressing his single-minded intent, 'to look was the ruin still there' is repeated six times in the A narrative.

The phrase 'where none ever came' occurs four times in the context of the tower ruin he occupied alone with his picture book. This poetic expression almost gives him a claim to the right of ownership of Foley's Folly.[59] In standard English it would read: 'where nobody ever came'. Anyone outside his tower is not spoken of as a person, but referred to as 'they' ('and they all out on the road looking for you', p. 11). 'None (of them) ever came' to his throne on the stone.

The Hiberno-English idiom, 'For God's sake' and 'Thank God', familiar from *All That Fall*, occurs four times in the course of this play. Each time it marks a 'turning-point'[60] in Listener's consciousness. Reality has shattered his illusions about 'the old scenes the old names':[61] reorientation involves a return to a definite point in time and awareness. For Beckett that point in time is his mother's death — in 1950. Other casualties of time are assessed in relation to it, as seen in the A passage:

> ... not a wire to be seen only the old rails all rust when was that was your mother ah for God's sake all gone long ago ... (p. 10).

Voice C recalls a visit to the Portrait Gallery that proved a turning-point; and he tries to place it in time:

> was your mother ah for God's sake all gone long ago all dust the lot you the last huddled up on the slab ... (p. 10).

After the revelation in the Portrait Gallery, the C voice declares ...

> never the same but the same as what for God's sake did you ever say I to yourself in your life (p. 11).

Occasionally, one word can encompass in symbolism, or association, the experiences of a life-time: *Rust* is the operative word in the A narrative: 'the old rails all rust' (p. 10). The 'old rails' were not only the tram and train rails, but also the old ways and way of life Listener knew — and returned to for spiritual renewal. Rust symbolises the ravages of time, disuse, neglect, and forgetfulness. In the same ('rust') passage he has forgotten the name of the Folly he came to visit:[62] 'where you hid as a child someone's folly Foley was it Foley's Folly bit of a tower ...' (p. 10).

Millstone[63] is a telling metaphor in the B narrative. The lovers sat on a stone, vowing mutual love: 'you one end of the stone she the other long low stone like millstone ...' (p. 9). This oblique reference to the agony and the ecstasy of love is renewed in a later passage ...

> on the stone in the sun ... vowing every now and then you loved each other just a murmur tears without fail till they dried up altogether ... (p. 11).

Dust[64] is a symbolic word in the C narrative. It is first mentioned once, in the Portrait Gallery, with reference to his family: 'all gone long ago all dust the lot you the last' (p. 10). The word dust occurs twice in a later passage, introducing the phenomena in the Public Library: 'something to do with dust something the dust said' (p. 16). Finally, in the last passage dust is reiterated three times, as the eerie scene unfolds, to reveal what in fact the dust said .... three words: ... 'come and gone' ... (p. 16).

The Text and the Technique

The play divides naturally[65] into three parts separated by two pauses each lasting ten seconds. Beckett's directions read:

> (*Silence 10 seconds. Breath audible. After 3 seconds eyes open.*)

When the play ends the final stage directions call for another 10-second silence, and the curtain smile from Listener:

> (*Silence 10 seconds. Breath audible. After 3 seconds eyes open. After 5
> seconds smile, toothless for preference. Hold 5 seconds till fade out and
> curtain.*)

The performance of *That Time* takes about twenty-five minutes.

In each of the three parts twelve statements are made, four by each voice
A B C, arranged so that a different voice precedes each pause:

> I ACB ACB ACB CAB
> (*Silence 10 seconds ...*)
> II CBA CBA CBA BCA
> (*Silence 10 seconds ...*)
> III BAC BAC BAC BAC
> (*Silence 10 seconds ...*)
> (*... smile ... curtain*)

The 10-second silences follow moments in which each of the voices intimates doubt, spatial, temporal or psychological confusion.[66]

Part I

Voice B confesses the possibility that his love story is a figment of the
imagination:

> just one of those things you kept making up to keep the void out
> just another of those old tales to keep the void from pouring in on
> top of you the shroud (p. 11)
> (*Silence 10 seconds ...*).

Part II

Voice A speaks of spatial, temporal and also mental confusion:

> huddled on the doorstep ... not knowing where you were or when
> you were or what for ... like that time on the stone the child on the
> stone where none ever came (p. 14)
> (*Silence 10 seconds ...*).

Part III

Voice C recalls an occasion of psychological bewilderment: an experience
in the Public Library that puzzled and disturbed him so deeply that he was
'never the same after never again after something to do with dust':

> whole place suddenly full of dust ... from floor to ceiling nothing
> only dust and not a sound only what was it it said come and gone
> was that it something like that come and gone ... gone in no time (p.
> 16)
> (*Silence 10 seconds ... Curtain*).

Commenting on the structure of *That Time*, Fletcher and co-authors write:

'Apart from his characteristic concern for combinations, variations and symmetries, Beckett does not appear to have any particular kind of sequence ... in mind.'

Beckett's own comment to the authors was, they say,

> that the control is stylistic through the technique of association; he wished, he said, to make each passage verbally interesting and to provide it with some associative connection with the next.[67]

In short, Beckett relies on language to give cohesion to the fragments of a life-story relayed by voice A B C 'without solution of continuity'.[68]

But since the play is autobiographical — a fact they do not mention — it is clear that the life-cycle is the sequence Beckett has in mind. The child seeking seclusion in the old ruin; the idealistic youth seeking communication with the opposite sex; the old man battered by a friendless world returning to his childhood sanctuary seeking peace, seclusion and strands of an identity, is the natural sequence that comes over in the play.

An 'associative connection' is made principally by the chronological sequence of voice A B C. The pauses that divide *That Time* into Part I, II, and III, are part of Beckett's technique to complicate the piece, as the life it depicts is complicated, contradictory and cussed.

NOTES

1 Bair, *Samuel Beckett*, p. 536.

2 The previous occasion was in 1973, when *Not I* premièred at the Royal Court Theatre, London. The impact on the audience is discussed by Lyons, *Samuel Beckett*, pp. 154 - 159.

3 Quoted in Bair, op. cit., p. 537.

4 They accepted 'that these plays signified a new movement and direction, still undefined, in Beckett's writing' (Bair, op. cit., p. 538).

5 Quoted in Bair, op. cit., p. 537.

6 Lyons, *Samuel Beckett*, pp. 160 - 165.

7 Quoted in Barnes, 'Aspects of Directing Beckett' pp. 86 - 87.

8 The 'imaginary conversations' (p. 11) presuppose an acquaintance, real or desired, with others. The same passage, A, states ... 'and they all out on the road looking for you ...', intimating a home and people who cared for him.

9 Mercier, *Beckett/Beckett*, p. 234.

10 Lyons, *Samuel Beckett*, p. 161.

11 Metaphysical in the sense of: 'Dealing with abstractions' apart from, or opposed

to, the practical'. *The Practical Standard Dictionary of the English Language*, Funk and Wagnalls.

12 Quoted in Barnes, 'Aspects of Directing Beckett, p. 86.

13 Beckett supplied this fact to Dr Eoin O'Brien for his book, *The Beckett Country*. See ibid., Note 43, p. 350. The Tower was built in 1818 by John Barrington. It figures under different names in many of Beckett's writings. O'Brien notes (Note 43): 'In the first manuscript of *That Time* (Reading University Library, MS No. 1477/1) the name "Barrington's Tower", though erased, is clearly visible; this later became "Maguire's" and finally "Foley's Folly".'

14 O'Brien, *The Beckett Country*, p. 27.

15 O'Brien, *The Beckett Country*, p. 29.

16 *Company*, a prose piece composed between May 1977 and August 1979, recalls scenes from the past that show how he loved his father and feared his mother. As in *That Time*, Beckett speaks of himself in the second person singular ...

> You slip away at break of day and climb to your hiding place on the hillside ... Back home at nightfall supperless to bed. You lie in the dark and are back in that light. (*Company*, pp. 32, 33).

17 O'Brien, *The Beckett Country*, p. 30.

18 *That Time*, p. 14.

19 Dublin city trams were phased out about 1947, and replaced by the double-decker buses.

20 The Dublin and Southeastern Railway was one of many uneconomic railway lines closed down by the Department of Transport, between 1958 and 1964. The railway tracks have been removed. Harcourt Street and Foxrock were among the 218 redundant railway stations in the country. Foxrock station is now a private home.

21 This sets the pattern for his wanderings in search of a place or base with which he could identify: a location to which he had some right or association, that would obviate the phrase 'no warrant' in the place, that occurs twice on page 15, in the text of Voice A and Voice C.

22 The tendency in retrospect to idealise childhood or exaggerate its adventures was very strong in this lonely old man.

23 O'Brien, *The Beckett Country*, pp. 5, 19, 75.

24 Ibid., pp. 138 - 155.

25 Bair, *Samuel Beckett*, p. 208.

26 There are about twenty pubic libraries in the city and suburbs. The tradition of library provision in Ireland dates from c. 600 A.D. *Encyclopedia of Ireland*, pp. 370, 371.

27 The Proclamation of the Irish Republic was made from the General Post Office on Easter Monday, 24th April 1916. In the central hall a bronze statue of the dying Cuchulain (legendary Irish hero of pre-Christian times), was erected as a memorial to the seven signatories to the Proclamation who were executed in 1916. Cuchulain also figures in *Murphy*.

28 *Murphy*, pp. 33 - 35.

29 Beckett wrote *Murphy* between 1934 and 1936. Bair, *Samuel Beckett*, pp. 190 - 198.

30 Bair, *Samuel Beckett*, pp. 534, 536.

31 Wakeling, 'Looking at Beckett: The Man and the Writer', pp. 5 - 17.

32 Bair, op. cit., p. 536.

33 Ibid., op. cit., p. 23.

34 Bair, *Samuel Beckett*, p. 23.

35 Esslin, *The Theatre of the Absurd*, p. 23.

36 Bair, *Samuel Beckett*, p. 23.

37 Lyons, *Samuel Beckett*, p. 164.

38 The city terminus, as familiar to Beckett and his father as Foxrock station, is mentioned wistfully in *Texts for Nothing* VII (1967) '... there I am far again from that terminus and its pretty neo-Doric colonnade ...'

39 The word 'holeproof' stresses the durability of the material, and symbolically, the nature and strength of family ties that form the basis of identity.

40 This phase of growing-up emotionally is relatively short in duration, as the narrative indicates later on (p. 16).

41 Mercier, *Beckett/Beckett*, p. 235.

42 A great billowing cloud is the cinematic symbolism for a dream.

43 Beckett calls it 'a great billowing shroud' to indicate, not only the dawn of reality, but the end of a phase — adolescence — that nurtured the day-dreams.

44 The line 'facing downstream into the sun sinking' (p. 12), is an oblique reference to the romantic beauty of sunset on the Liffey, described in many of Beckett's writings. See *Malone Dies* (1956), p. 230.

45 Barnes, 'Aspects of Directing Beckett', p. 70.

46 This is mentioned earlier in Part I in the series CAB.

47 Libera, Antoni, 'Structure and Pattern in *That Time*', *Journal of Beckett Studies*, Autumn 1980, Number 6, pp. 83 - 85.

48 George Berkeley's famous axiom that Beckett literally plays with in *Film* (1964). From *The Treatise concerning the Principles of Human Knowledge* (1710).

49 O'Brien, *The Beckett Country*, p. 139.

50 Libera, Antoni, 'Structure and Pattern in *That Time*', p. 83.

51 As is frequently the case in Beckett's writings, the qualification of the statement is more important and relevant than the statement itself.

52 *Krapp's Last Tape*, p. 13.

53 Fletcher et al., *A Student's Guide to the Plays of Samuel Beckett*, p. 204.

54 Reid, *All I Can Manage, More Than I Could*, pp. 21-2.

55 See Beckett's Note, p. 8.

56 Mercier, *Beckett/Beckett*, p. 234.

57 In the last A passage (p. 16) the rhythm of the narrative marks time with the march of the native determined to 'foot it' (p. 13):

> back down to the wharf with the nightbag and the old green greatcoat
> your father left you trailing on the ground ...

58 This is particularly and deliberately marked in the final C passage (p. 16).

59 Foley's Folly has now been rebuilt, and people live in it. It is a square tower, large enough for occupancy. See O'Brien, *The Beckett Country*, p. 350, Note 43, for details of present ownership.

60 *That Time*, C passage, pp. 11, 12.

61 Ibid., p. 10.

62 O'Brien, *The Beckett Country*, p. 29.

63 The word is used in its figurative meaning: burden or encumbrance. 'Millstone *n* one of two circular stones for grinding corn'; (*fig*) encumbrance'. *The Penguin English Dictionary*, p. 450.

64 For the many old idioms symbolising the word *dust* see *Brewer's Dictionary of Phrase and Fable*, p. 311. *Dust* has been slang for money for more than 300 years. Jonathan Swift (1667 - 1754), used 'dust' in this sense in a charity sermon. Swift repeated his text, 'He who giveth to the poor, lendeth to the Lord,' three times, then added: 'Now, brethren, if you like the security, *down with your dust*.' That ended the sermon. Ibid.

65 'Naturally' means theatrically — according to Beckett's plan to subtly depict the ravages of time on mind and body.

66 Lyons, *Samuel Beckett*, p. 162.

67 Fletcher et al., *A Student's Guide to the Plays of Samuel Beckett*, p. 203.

68 *That Time*, Note p. 8.

CONCLUSION

In the particular is contained the universal.[1]

James Joyce

Samuel Beckett did not find that elusive quarry — identity — or resolve 'the question of being' in any of the five plays. But he made his point — identity, like time is never static. Identity is ephemeral, ethereal, mysterious, as Esslin writes:

> ... because the self is a mystery, ever elusive ... at each point in time our self is a distinct and different entity ...[2]

To the question of being, solemnly posed in *Godot*: 'What are we doing here, *that* is the question', Vladimir answers himself: 'We are waiting for Godot to come' (p. 80). The five plays form a kind of Russian doll capsulated in time. All five probe the mystery of the relativity of time.

Waiting for Godot is a drama about time:

> Time past — Gogo and Didi were fifty years together.
> Time present — They are waiting for Godot.
> Future Time — They will go on waiting. (*They do not move.*)

All That Fall, a play about time, encompasses:

> Past time — Minnie's death forty years before. (p. 9)
> Present — Dan's birthday and its repercussions.
> Future — Dan reveals his plans for the future. (p. 33)

Krapp's Last Tape is all about time :

> Past time — recorded in the tapes. (pp. 11 - 17)
> Present time — Krapp records his Last Tape. (pp. 17 - 19)
> Future time, however short, is not ruled out. (p. 20)

Eh Joe is also a play about time.

> Past time — Voice recalls past events for Joe.
> Present time — Joe listens reluctantly to the Voice.
> Future time — Joe's expectation of 'Thou fool thy soul' (p. 19).

That Time, by definition a play about time, is a microcosm of *Waiting for Godot*. Listener finally settles in the Public Library, where 'with a bevy of old ones' he reads in silence. In the Library, holding dusty records of human activity, history, and unfinished business from centuries past, there are three symbolic sounds:

... 'the old breath' — life

... 'the leaves turning' — time passing

... the dust saying 'come and gone ...' (p. 16).

That Time reiterates lines in *Waiting for Godot* uttered in anguish by blind Pozzo ... (p. 89)

They give birth astride of a grave, the light gleams an instant, then

it's night once more.

In *That Time*, the dust speaks for that 'instant'... 'come and gone in no time' (p. 16). Between 'one come' and 'gone in no time' (p. 16) we are waiting for Godot — *Go deo* — all mankind ... waiting till ... 'the old breath' fades into the long breath of Eternity... 'was there ever any other time but that time' (p. 16). The end is in the beginning of *Murphy*:

'The sun shone, having no alternative, on the nothing new.'[3]

NOTES

1 Bair, *Samuel Beckett*, p. 130.

2 Esslin, *The Theatre of the Absurd*, p. 90.

3 *Murphy*, London, Calder & Boyars, 1970, p. 5.

BIBLIOGRAPHY

1 *Sources/Editions Used*

BECKETT, Samuel: *Waiting for Godot*, London: Faber and Faber, 1965.
　　　　All That Fall, London: Faber and Faber, 1969.
　　　　Krapp's Last Tape and Embers, London: Faber and Faber, 1970.
　　　　Eh Joe and Other Writings, London: Faber and Faber, 1967.
　　　　That Time, London: Faber and Faber, 1976.

Other Works by Samuel Beckett

　　　　'Dante... Bruno. Vici.. Joyce', in *Our Exagmination Round his Factification for Incamination of Work in Progress*, Paris, 1929, London: Faber and Faber, 1972.
　　　　Whoroscope, Paris: The Hours Press, 1930.
　　　　Proust, Three Dialogues, London : Calder, 1965.
　　　　More Pricks Than Kicks, London : Chatto and Windus, 1934.
　　　　Murphy, London: Calder and Boyars, 1970.
　　　　Watt, Paris: Olympia Press, 1958.
　　　　Endgame, London: Faber and Faber, 1958.
　　　　From an Abandoned Work, London : Faber and Faber, 1957.
　　　　Texts for Nothing VII, London: Faber and Faber, 1967.
　　　　Eleuthéria — A three-act play written in French in 1947: Neither published nor performed to date.
　　　　Three Novels Molloy: Malone Dies: The Unnamable, London: Calder and Boyars, 1959.
　　　　Film, New York: Grove Press, 1969.
　　　　Breath and Other Short Stories, London: Faber and Faber, 1971.
　　　　Poems in English, London: Faber and Faber, 1971.
　　　　Not I, London: Faber and Faber, 1973.
　　　　For To End Yet Again, London: Faber and Faber, 1976.
　　　　Company, London: John Calder, 1980.
　　　　Stirrings Still, New York: Blue Moon Books, 1989, and London: John Calder, 1989.
　　　　what is the word — Comment dire, London: John Calder, 1989.

II. *Books, Essays, and Articles on Samuel Beckett*

ALVAREZ, A., *Beckett*, London: Fontana/Collins, 1973.

BAIR, Deirdre, *Samuel Beckett: A Biography*, London: Picador edition, Pan Books, 1980.

BARNES, Ben, 'Aspects of Directing Beckett', in *Irish University Review*, Vol. 14, No. 1, Spring 1984. Dublin: Wolfhound Press.

CALDER, John, (ed.) *A Samuel Beckett Reader*, London: Calder and Boyars, 1967.

COHN, Ruby, *Back To Beckett*, Princeton, New Jersey : Princeton University Press, 1976.

DEANE, Seamus, 'Joyce and Beckett', *Irish University Review*, Vol. 14, No. 1, Spring 1984. Dublin: Wolfhound Press.

DOLAN, T.P. 'Samuel Beckett's Dramatic Use of Hiberno-English', *Irish University Review*, Vol. 14, No. 1, Spring 1984, Dublin: Wolfhound Press.

ELLMANN, Richard, *Four Dubliners Oscar Wilde James Joyce W.B. Yeats Samuel Beckett*, London: Hamish Hamilton, 1987.

ESSLIN, Martin, 'Samuel Beckett: The search for self', *The Theatre of the Absurd*, London: Pelican Books, 1982.

----------: *Meditations : Essays on Brecht, Beckett, and the Media*, London: Eyre-Methuen, 1980.

FLETCHER, John and SPURLING, John, *Beckett. A Study of his Plays*, London: Eyre Methuen, 1972.

FLETCHER, John; FLETCHER, Beryl S., SMITH, Barry, BACHEM, Walter, *A Student's Guide to the Plays of Samuel Beckett*, London : Faber and Faber, 1978.

HESLA, David H., *The Shape of Chaos : An Interpretation of the Art of Samuel Beckett*, Minneapolis : University of Minnesota Press, 1971.

HIGGINS, Aidan, 'Foundering in Reality: Godot, Papa, Hamlet and Three Bashes at Festschrift', *Irish University Review*, Vol, 14, No. 1, Spring 1984.

JACOBSEN, Josephine, MUELLER, William R., *The Testament of Samuel Beckett*, London: Faber and Faber, 1966.

KEARNEY, Richard, 'Beckett: The Demythologising Intellect', in *The Irish Mind: Exploring Intellectual Traditions*, Ed. Richard Kearney, Dublin: Wolfhound Press, 1985.

KENNER, Hugh, *Samuel Beckett, A Critical Study*, London: Calder, 1962.

--------------------: *A Reader's Guide to Samuel Beckett*, London: Thames and Hudson, 1973.

KIBERD, Declan, 'Samuel Beckett and the Protestant Ethic', in *The Genius of Irish Prose*, Ed. Augustine Martin, Dublin: The Mercier Press, 1985.

LIBERA, Antoni, 'Structure and Pattern in *That Time*', *Journal of Beckett* Studies, Autumn 1980, Number 6, London: Calder, 1981.

LYONS, Charles R., *Samuel Beckett*, London : The Macmillan Press, 1983.

MAYS, J.C.C., 'Young Beckett's Irish Roots', *Irish University Review*, Vol. 14, No. 1, Spring 1984, Dublin : Wolfhound Press.

MAHON, Derek, 'A Noise Like Wings : Beckett's Poetry', *Irish University Review*, Vol. 14, No. 1, Spring 1984. Dublin: Wolfhound Press.

MERCIER, Vivian, *Beckett/Beckett*, New York: Oxford University Press, 1979.

-----------------------: *The Irish Comic Tradition*, New York: Oxford University Press,

1969.

MURRAY, Patrick, *The Tragic Comedian: A Study of Samuel Beckett*, Cork: The Mercier Press, 1970.

MURRAY, Christopher, 'Beckett's Productions in Ireland: A Survey', *Irish University Review*, Vol. 14, No. 1, Spring 1984, Dublin: Wolfhound Press.

O'BRIEN, Eoin, *The Beckett Country*. Samuel Beckett's Ireland, Dublin: The Black Cat Press in association with London: Faber and Faber.

REID, Alec, *All I Can Manage, More Than I Could*: An Approach to the Plays of Samuel Beckett. Dublin: The Dolmen Press, 1968.

REID, Alec, 'Impact and parable in Beckett', in *HERMATHENA A Trinity College Dublin Review*, No. CXLI. Winter 1986. This issue is devoted entirely to Beckett — 'Beckett At Eighty : A Trinity Tribute', Ed. Terence Brown and Nicholas Grene.

WAKELING, Patrick, 'Looking at Beckett — The Man and the Writer', *Irish University Review*, Vol. 14, No. 1, Spring 1984. Dublin: Wolfhound Press.

WEBB, Eugene, *The Plays of Samuel Beckett*, London: Peter Owen Ltd., 1972.

ZILLIACUS, Clas, *Beckett and Broadcasting : A Study of the Works of Samuel Beckett for and in Radio and Television*, Abo: Abo Akademi, 1976.

III. *Other Works/Books, Literary and Cultural Publications, quoted or consulted*

BELLAMY, David J., 'The Wild Boglands', *Ireland of the Welcomes*, Vol. 36, No. 3, May - June 1987.

CALLAHAN, Philip S., 'Butterfly Rock', *Ireland of the Welcomes*, Vol. 34, No. 1, Jan. - Feb. 1985.

CURTAYNE, Alice, *The Irish Story : A Survey of Irish History and Culture*, Dublin: Clonmore and Reynolds, 1962.

DOWLING, P.J., *The Hedge Schools of Ireland*, Cork: The Mercier Press, 1968.

DRYDEN, John, 'A Song for St Cecilia's Day, 1687', *The Oxford Book of English Verse*, Oxford (New Edition), 1948.

GAILEY, Alan, *Irish Folk Drama*, Cork: The Mercier Press, 1969.

GREENE, David, *The Irish Language*, Dublin: The Three Candles, 1966.

HARBISON, Peter, 'The Turoe Stone', *Ireland of the Welcomes*, Vol. 34, No. 1, Jan. - Feb. 1985.

HERRIES Davies, G.L., 'The Making of Ireland', *Ireland of the Welcomes*, Vol. 34, No. 1, Jan. - Feb. 1985.

HUGHES, Kathleen, 'The Golden Age of Early Christian Ireland (7th and 8th Centuries)', *The Course of Irish History*, Ed. T.W. Moody and F.X. Martin, Cork: The Mercier Press, 1967.

JEFFARES, Norman A., Foreword to *HERMATHENA— A Trinity College Dublin Review*, 'Beckett at Eighty: A Trinity Tribute', No. CXLI. Winter 1986, University of Dublin.

JOYCE, James, *A Portrait of the Artist As a Young Man*, New York: New American

Library, reprinted by Viking Press, 1949.

----------------: *Ulysses*, London: The Bodley Head, 1960.

----------------: *Finnegan's Wake*, London: Faber and Faber, 1975.

JUNG, C.G., *Analytical Psychology: Its Theory and Practice, The Tavistock Lectures*, London: Routledge and Kegan Paul, 1968.

KENNELLY, Brendan, Introduction to *The Penguin Book of Irish Verse*, also edited by Professor Brendan Kennelly, London: Penguin Books, 1970.

--------------------------: 'Mythology' and 'Irish Thought', in *Encyclopedia of Ireland*, Dublin: Allen Figgis, 1968.

--------------------------: 'A Tongue to a Stone', in *Ireland of the Welcomes*, Vol. 30, No. 2, March - April 1981.

LAING, R.D., *The Divided Self : A Study of Sanity and Madness*, London: Tavistock Publications, 1960.

LUCY, Seán, 'What is Anglo-Irish Poetry?', in *Irish Poets in English*, Ed. Seán Lucy. Dublin: The Mercier Press, 1973.

LYDON, J.F., 'The Medieval English Colony' , in *The Course of Irish History*, Ed. T.W. Moody and F.X. Martin, Cork: The Mercier Press, 1967.

Mac AIRT, Seán, 'The Development of Early Modern Irish Prose', in *Seven Centuries of Irish Learning*, Ed. Brian O Cuív, Radio Eireann: Thomas Davis Lectures. Broadcast in 1958, under the general title — 'Irish Literature from Clontarf to the Boyne'. Published for Radio Eireann by The Stationary Office, Dublin.

MAC INTYRE, Tom, 'Sentinels of Secret Places', *Ireland of the Welcomes*, Vol. 34, No. 1, Jan. - Feb. 1985.

MILTON, John, *Paradise Lost*, Book IV. New York: The New American Library of World Literature, Inc., 1961.

O'FARRELL, Padraic, *How the Irish speak English*, Cork: The Mercier Press, 1980.

O'CONNOR, Frank, *A Short History of Irish Literature*, New York: Capricorn Books.

O'CUIV, Brian, 'An Era of Upheavel', in *Seven Centuries of Irish Learning*, Ed. Brian O'Cuiv.

O'TUAMA, Seán, 'The New Poetry'. Ibid.

PECHE, George, 'Rockhounds', in *Stone: Ireland of the Welcomes*, Vol. 34, No. 1, Jan. - Feb. 1985.

PFEIFFER, Walter, 'Aspects of Ireland': *Ireland of the Welcomes*, Vol. 30, No. 6, Nov. - Dec. 1981.

PIGGOTT, Charlie, 'Turf for the family fire': *Ireland of the Welcomes*, Vol. 36, No. 3, May - June 1987.

POWER, Patrick C., *A Literary History of Ireland*, Cork: The Mercier Press, 1969.

------------------------: *The Book of Irish Curses*, Dublin: The Mercier Press, 1974.

PURCELL, Brendan, 'In Search of Newgrange: Long Night's Journey Into Day' in *The Irish Mind*, Ed. R. Kearney, Dublin: Wolfhound Press, 1985.

ROBINSON, Tim, *Setting Foot on the Shores of Connemara*, Mullingar: The Lilliput

Press, 1984.

ROSENSTOCK, Gabriel, 'Language and Grace': *Ireland of the Welcomes*, Vol. 31, No. 5, Sept. - Oct 1982.

RYNNE, Stephen, 'Shapes' in *Stone, Ireland of the Welcomes*, Vol, 34, No. 1, Jan. - Feb. 1985.

SEVERIN, Tim, *The Brendan Voyage*, London: Hutchinson, 1978.

TUNNEY, Paddy, 'The Stone Fiddle': *Ireland of the Welcomes*, Vol 34, No. 1, Jan. - Feb. 1985.

WILDE, Oscar, 'The Truth of Masks': *Complete Works of Oscar Wilde*, Introduced by Vyvyan Holland, London: Collins, 1981.

WINTER, Dana, *Stone — a poem, Ireland of the Welcomes*, Vol. 34, No. 1, Jan. - Feb. 1985.

YEATS, W.B., *The Land of Heart's Desire* (1894).

----------------: *The Only Jealousy of Emer* (1919), The Collected Plays of W.B. Yeats, London: Macmillan.

Dictionaries and Encyclopedia

DINNEEN, Rev. Patrich S., *An Irish-English Dictionary*, Compiled and edited by Rev. P. Dinneen, (New Edition), Dublin: The Educational Company of Ireland, Ltd., 1970.

DE BHALDRAITHE, Tómas, *English-Irish Dictionary*, Dublin: Stationary Office, 1959.

GARMONSWAY, G.N. with SIMPSON, Jacqueline, *The Penguin English Dictionary*, Harmondsworth, Middlesex: Penguin Books Ltd., 1965.

VIZETELLY, Frank H., *The Practical Standard Dictionary of the English Language*, New York: Funk and Wagnalls Company, 1939.

BREWER, Rev. E.C., *Brewer's Dictionary of Phrase and Fable*, Eighth revised edition, London: Cassell and Co., 1963.

Encyclopedia of Ireland, Dublin: Allen Figgis, 1968.

The Random House Dictionary of the English Language, Second Edition — Unabridged, New York: Random House, 1987.

APPENDIX I

The Irish Language

Irish is one of the Indo-European languages going back in the linguistic stream to the fountainhead of the great Aryan family of languages. Ethnically the Milesians were of mid-European Aryan stock who came to Ireland via France in search of an island promised them as descendants of a leader, Gadelius. Whence the name Gaels and Gaelic. It dates from about 600 B.C. In time some of the Milesians wandered abroad again to France and Spain. Their Gaelic-speaking descendants — the Celts — came to Ireland ca. 300 B.C. bringing with them an advanced La Tène civilisation.

> The Celtic languages were *Gaulish*, which died out at the beginning of the Christian era; *Goidelic*, from which are descended Irish, Scottish Gaelic and Manx; and *Britannic*, from which are descended Welsh, Cornish and Breton. Cornish became extinct in the eighteenth century. Manx survived into the first half of the present century.[1]

Irish or Gaelic was spoken and there was an oral literature in Irish long before writing came in with Christianity in A.D. 432.[2] *Old Irish*, the oldest form of the language of which records survive belong to the period A.D. 600 to A.D. 900.

The Old Irish period was one of standardisation of Gaelic directed by the learned classes, who were based mostly in monasteries.[3] In time, a struggle was inevitable between standardisation and diversity.

The Middle Irish period, from A.D. 900 to A.D. 1200, represents the struggle between the evolving speech of the people and the older, rigid standards upheld by scholars. The latter won the day, for, we are told, 'the language was so rationally standardised in the 11th and 12th centuries that the final product had scarcely a dozen irregular verbs and was the most highly developed vernacular in Europe'.[4]

By the end of the 12th century a new type of learned layman had emerged, a literary and commercial entrepreneur who made his living (and his name), by writing and selling poems of praise to the aristocracy. For over four hundred years (1200-1650), this class maintained the standard language now referred to as Early Modern or Classical Irish.

> Patrick Power, writing on the poetry of the period, says:
>
> The term *classical* is particularly apt when speaking of Gaelic poetry between 1200 and 1600. During that time the language was standardised for literary usage and no deviation was allowed to the Bardic poet from rigid grammatical and syntactical rules. ... this kept the language virtually unchanged for four hundred years ... Elegant and subtly written praise poetry comprises the bulk of what remains from this era and its aristocratic and classical gait often hides a lack of originality and lyricism.[5]

In ancient and medieval Ireland the poets, who were the intelligentsia, were powerful, influential and respected.[6] Their power was curtailed somewhat by the Church, but they turned this to good account.[7] They survived the Norman invasion which began in 1179, for the invaders adopted Gaelic ways and supported the literary men. The Norman's contribution to Irish life and literature is noted by an historian thus:

> Because the early upper-class settlers spoke French and were the products of a French-oriented civilisation, they brought with them a code of chivalry and a vision of courtly love which was to leave its mark on the Gaelic literature of the period. This can best be seen in the new form of Gaelic love poetry which was born — the *dánta grádha* based on the *amour courtois*.[8]

The assimilation of Norman culture into Gaelic was complete by the end of the 14th century. The Earl of Desmond, Gerald Fitzgerald, wrote poems in Irish. The earliest of the new love poems preserved in the Irish manuscripts came from his pen.[9]

The end of the 14th century marked the beginning of a Gaelic literary renascence. The Gaelic poetry of praise composed by professional poets (they had had seven years of professional training), and the courtly or 'learned love poetry'[10] written by the Norman-Irish ruling romantics,[11] constitute the bulk of extant Gaelic literature down to the 17th century.[12]

The Gaelic prose writers of that period — the 14th to the 17th centuries — devoted themselves to the task of compiling compendia of old Gaelic literature — sagas,[13] history, genealogy, tales and other lore from earlier centuries. The fruits of their labour of love are preserved in such books as:

(1) *The Yellow Book of Lecan* begun in 1391 and completed in 1572. It contains the most ancient version of the *Tain Bo-Cuailnge* — The Cattle-raid of Cooley[14] — known to us. It also includes the *Amra Colaim Cille* — an elegy on the death of Colum Cille in A.D. 595, written by a contemporary poet named Dallán Forgaill.[15] Part of the MS of the *Yellow Book of Lecan*[16] is devoted to *Dindshenchas*[17] and other lore.

(2) *The Book of Ballymote*,[18] a celebrated Connacht manuscript, was compiled in A.D. 1391 by three members of the Gaelic literary school of the Mac Geoghans for Mac Donagh, a chieftain and owner-resident of the castle near Ballymote, County Sligo. It contains a copy of a Gaelic version of the *Aeneid*.[19] There is also a fine collection of Gaelic metrical tracts — a golden treasury for students of bardic poetry.

(3) *The Book of Lismore* (*The Book of MacCarthy Riabhach*), was written for a chieftain of the old Irish MacCarthy family in the province of Munster. Compiled between 1478 and 1506, the book contains a selection of the lives of Irish saints, some old Munster lore, and two interesting translations into Gaelic of two classics of European literature — *The Voyages of Marco Polo* and *The Conquests of Charlemagne*.[20]

Many of the prose writers of the period were scribes rather than creative literary men.

The books they compiled or re-edited were not for sale but for presentation to worthy chieftains, lords or earls. Drama is not represented in this period of Gaelic literature, though Irish folk drama was a feature of Irish life then, as it has been down the centuries.[21] The fact is 'that the market in original composition was for poems'.[22]

Later Gaelic Poetry

The sword is mightier than the pen — at least temporarily. Patrick Power writes: 'The flowering of Gaelic literature in the 17th century had reached its zenith by the time Cromwell came to convert the Irish by fire and sword and Bible.'[23]

In the 17th century the Gaelic system was ruthlessly destroyed, and the poets were among the conquered. Now without wealthy patrons, they became peasant poets, poor wanderers enjoying the old respect but nothing else.

The poets' plight is echoed in *Godot*:

Vladimir: You should have been poet.
Estragon: I was. (*Gesture towards his rags.*)
Isn't that obvious.[24]

The poets' frustration expressed itself in bitter verse, and occasionally in maledictions.[25]

Gaelic words for cursing are distinctive, almost poetic and mostly onomatopoeic. The most popular standard words are:

mallacht — malediction or to speak evilly;

escaine — to reduce the stature or prestige of someone. The word is used in a form of satirical verse, and is as old as written Irish. To render unclean;

conntracht — to speak against (from contradiction);

guíodóireacht— to pray for someone thus: 'To hell with him!' or 'God damn him!';

shorknesing — a tinker's curse meaning, 'Blast him!' or 'Wither him!' It derives from an old Gaelic word, *seargú* meaning to wither. Hence the English word 'sear', and the expression, 'searing criticism'.

Cursing was as natural and necessary as praying in a crisis for every stratum of society in Ireland long ago. Since 'The essential doesn't change'[26] the need and use of such a non-lethal weapon has not diminished down the centuries. Gaelic distinguishes between *mallacht* (a curse) and the more vehement *slua-mhallacht* or 'a string of curses'.[2.] Also, to forestall the indiscriminate use of these legally held weapons, there was a *Reverting Curse*. Like a boomerang, an unjust curse was said to fall on its originator. For curses were original — the cursing formula as personal as the right to use it.

To illustrate how personal and individual was the art of cursing there was an institution called *The Cursing Contest*:

It was a feature of maledictory practice in early Christian times ... the cursing contest was an attempt by two opponents to overcrow one another by strings of maledictions uttered in dialogue form ... It is clear that these contests were not always seriously intended and they have an element of humour sometimes which is rare whenever cursing is mentioned in the old stories and historical or pseudo-historical records.[28]

The Poet's Curse

While the Widow's Curse was a cry from the depths of society for Almighty justice on a cruel Landlord or whoever, the Poet's Curse was a plethora of searing satire from the pinnacle of the professional classes.[29]

> The position of the poet in ancient Ireland and even up to the present day
> has always been honourable and often surrounded with mystical signifi-
> cance. It is evident from the annals that poets were believed to be capable
> of cursing and ... they preserve an attitude which has been found true in later
> days ... It was considered a serious breach of courtesy and even more serious
> loss of face for a ruler to refuse a poet the fee he demanded in ancient Ireland.[30]

For the poet, the ruler's refusal to pay the fee implied rejection of his poem, with
consequent loss of honour as well as honorarium. Today's equivalent of the default-
ing patron is the literary critic. Adverse criticism of a writer's work often results in
loss of public interest and private income for the professional poet or playwright.
Samuel Beckett knew all about the vagaries of literary critics.[31] His response is a
piece of satire set in the Irish traditional mould of a *Cursing Contest* between Vladimir
and Estragon:

> Vladimir: Ceremonious ape!
> Estragon: Punctilious pig!
> .....
> Vladimir: Moron!
> Estragon: That's the idea, let's abuse each other.
> Vladimir: Moron!
> Estragon: Vermin!
> Vladimir: Abortion!
> Estragon: Morpion!
> Vladimir: Sewer-rat!
> Estragon: Curate!
> Vladimir: Cretin!
> Estragon: (*with finality*) Crritic!
> Vladimir: Oh!
> *He wilts, vanquished, and turns away.*[32]

Vladimir, the more intellectual of the two was 'vanquished' by the worst term of
abuse — 'Crritic'. It was a greater insult than 'Vermin' or 'Sewer-rat'. The vehemence
of that final epithet 'Crritic' indicates the degree of scorn Beckett wishes to pour on
the latterday rulers of professional writers.

Cursing Rituals

Cursing was often accompanied by certain rituals. It lent solemnity to the act and
provided the necessary drama for the malediction.

Cursing Stones

The most interesting rituals were those in which stones were used. An old Irish
custom is 'the fire of stones'. Water-rounded stones were heaped in the form of a
peat fire. The offended person knelt in front of the stones and cursed his victim,
invoking misfortune on him and his descendants for many generations to come. The
phrase 'until these stones go on fire' was added. Each stone was thereafter a cursing
stone in its own right.

On the use of cursing stones singly or in heaps, Patrick Power writes:

> This strange custom is recorded widely from the west of Ireland and concerned water-rounded stones which were preserved especially for the purpose of malediction. All the available evidence suggests that this custom is very ancient indeed.[33]

He gives the location of famous or infamous cursing stones in the west of Ireland. One of these is Castle Kirk near Lough Corrib in Co. Galway. It is said that the stones in Castle Kirk — Saint Feichin's Stones[34]— were 'the terror of the land'.

The Cursing Stones and the Cursing Ritual in Godot

We can relate this curious maledictory practice to Lucky's lengthy tirade -- which was in fact a kind of ritual cursing exercise, complete with cursing stones.

Pozzo insisted Lucky put on his hat before giving him drill commands, Stop! Back! Turn! Think! Lucky began to 'think', but not in the way his master had expected, as Pozzo's reaction indicated. Lucky's ranting speech has all the characteristics of a cursing ritual. He harangues the offender from a height:

> ... from the heights of divine apathia divine athambia divine aphasia ....[35]

> It appears that pronouncing a malediction from an elevated position was understood to emphasise the pouring down of ill-luck from heaven, as if Jove were hurling thunderbolts in the person of the curser. Even today one hears the expression 'He cursed her from a height!' when someone wishes to imply that someone was foully abused.[36]

Lucky was foully abused by Pozzo, but Lucky's tirade was addressed to society in general, which, despite sporting facilities and antibiotics, 'is seen to waste and pine ... to shrink and dwindle ....[37]

He speaks of 'the skull ... in Connemara ... abode of stones ... fire the firmament ... blast hell to heaven ... if that continues ... abode of stones ... the stones ....[38]

The 'stones' are certainly cursing stones of which there are plenty in Connemara and other parts of Galway. The *glám dícenn*[39] he delivered is a poet's satire.

It is interesting that Pozzo did in fact 'waste and pine' inso-far as he came back blind and bitter in Act II. Lucky, so articulate in his invective, came back dumb in the second act. Could this be an example of the *Reverting Curse*?

The Irish language had always been a barrier to total English rule in Ireland.[40] A phrase 'court without English' is a poet's apt description of the Crown 'presence' in his country. Brian O Cuív writes:

> The phrase 'court without English' is doubtless a wry comment on the fact that the business of the Parliament of 1541, which acknowledged Henry as King of Ireland, was conducted through the medium of Irish, as of the Lords present only the Earl of Ormond, who acted as interpreter, could speak English.[41]

Queen Elizabeth I reigned from 1558 - 1603. In Ireland, she turned her 'court without English' to good account. Seeing that Irish was the universal language of the country, she commissioned her bishops to prepare a translation of the Bible into the vernacular. Moreover, she provided the type to have it printed. It took the scholars some thirty years to complete this literary task.

The official translation of the New Testament in Irish was published in 1603: it is the Protestant version. The first printed work in Irish is Queen Elizabeth's Cathecism published in Dublin in 1571. The type-fount she provided for this was bought by the Franciscans and taken to Louvain in 1611. There the Irish priests in exile set up a printing press, and Louvain became a centre of Gaelic learning.[42]

In Ireland, however, neither the King's English[43] nor the Queen's Irish achieved their avowed aims, which were, respectively, to anglicise and to proselytise the Irish.

That the Queen's men were Irish-speaking aristocrats within the Pale[44] is clear from a complaint made in 1578 by Lord Chancellor Gerrard that 'all English, and the most part with delight, even in Dublin, speak Irish'.

Brian O Cuív continues:

> The Gaelic social system which was destroyed in the seventeenth century was essentially an aristocratic one in which the ruling and professional classes held a pre-eminent position. We know a great deal about the characteristics and careers of the chieftains from contemporary literature. They were men of breeding and culture, generous patrons of musicians, poets and literary men in general.[45]

The purity of the Gaelic language was preserved orally in the Hedge Schools brought into being by the suppression of all the legitimate means of education, first by the Cromwellian regime, and later by the Penal Laws imposed on Irish Catholics. The Penal Code operated with varying degrees of rigidity for almost a hundred and fifty years. It ended when the Catholic Emancipation Act was passed in 1829.[46]

On the literature of that era Patrick Power writes:

> Generally speaking, the output of literature in Gaelic between 1700 and 1850 was meagre and the bulk of it was in verse.... there are many manuscripts of old tales which were written down after being somewhat 'modernised' ... so one finds that Gaelic literature, as produced in the years between 1700 and 1850, is almost exclusively confined to poetry.[47]

It is interesting to note that in the Hedge Schools, where the bulk of the population received instruction, a high standard of education was the norm.[48] They had a more extensive curriculum than other 'private' schools. Forbidden by the current rulers of the country, they had 'full attendance' in winter and in summer. Not only the 'Three R's' (reading, writing and arithmetic) were taught, but as Patrick Dowling points out:

> Other subjects found their way into the curriculum according to the local needs ... history, geography, book-keeping, surveying and navigation. Latin and Mathematics were commonly taught; sometimes Greek; and in Irish-speaking districts instruction in all these subjects was given in the vernacular.[49]

Early in the 19th century, however, English began to replace Irish as a medium of instruction in the Hedge Schools. Soon, according to the official report, in many parts of the country the 'bare-legged peasant' spoke two languages fluently.

There were poets, too, in the Hedge Schools: Dowling devotes a chapter to 'The

Poet Schoolmasters'. He says:

> Nearly every Irish poet in the 18th and early 19th centuries appears to have been a schoolmaster; though, needless to say, but few of the great body of schoolmasters were poets. In teaching, the poets had excellent employment for their talents, but not of the kind that brought them any pecuniary reward ....[50]

Among the Irish loan words which have become part of the English vernacular in Ireland are the following:

Irish	English spelling	English meaning
Amhrán	auran	song or poem in syllabic metre
Abú[51]	aboo	to victory! Used in battle cries
Ádh	aah	good luck, luck
Aisling	aisling	a dream, a poetical description of a vision
Árd	ard	prefix to nouns: high, excellent, noble, tall
Ard	ard-oireactas	a chief convention or assembly
Asal	asal	an ass (literally and metaphorically)
Amadán	amadan	a foolish man
Amlóg	auloog	a foolish woman
Árdán	ardaan	a hillock, pulpit, or play-stage
A rún	aroon	a term of endearment, darling, dear one
Bán	bawn[52]	white, blond, or beloved (Molly Bawn
Báinín	bawneen	flannel, a white coat or jacket
Baile	bally	town or village, Irish placenames: Ballymena, Ballina
Bótharín	boreen[53]	short narrow road
Beansídhe	banshee	a fairy woman
Bladar	blather[54]	flattery, coaxing, wheedling, talking
Bróg	brogue	shoe, sport or walking shoe
Cailín	colleen	a young girl
Céilidhe	ceile	an evening musical entertainment, an Irish (traditional) dancing festival
Ceol	ceol	music, melody
Ciotóg	ciothog	left-handed, an awkward person
Clann	clan	sept, breed, clan
Dia	Dia	God
Dia dhuit	Dia dhuit	Good morning, day etc., (*Grüb Gott!*)
Dáil	Dail	The Irish House of Parliament
Deas	dheas	right hand, dexterous, expert, pretty, nice
Deo[55]	deo	an end, the last, the rear
Go deo[56]	godeo	(of future time) ever, forever, never, eternity

Irish	English spelling	English meaning
Deor[57]	deor	a tear, a drop (of water)
Deor	deor	happy, lucky
Go deo na ndeor[58]	go deo na ndeor	for ever and ever, to the end of tears
Faire go deo	faire go deo	Alas! alas!
Duidin[59]	dudeen	a short tobacco pipe, or clay pipe
Earrach	earrach	spring, the spring-time, *fig.* youth
Eolas	eolas	knowledge, learning
Eide	eide	uniform, vestments
Eitléan	eithlean	an aeroplane
Éire	Eire	Ireland (the whole country or island)
Fada	fada	long (of time or space)
Fâilte[60]	failte	welcome, joy, delight
Fáinne	fainne	a ring, halo, circle
Faire[61]	faire	alas! expression of disgust, or sorrow, or pity
Fánach	fanach	idle, useless, vain
Fios	fios	information, science
Fear	fear	man, masculine, male
Fir[62]	fir	men, gentlemen
Grádh	gradh	love, charity
Gramscar	gramscar	rabble, refuse, sl. small change
Gob[63]	gob	beak, mouth, snout
Gobadóir	gobadoir	a 'snouty' person, a miser
Hata	hata	a hat of any kind
Haibil	hobble	a fix or difficulty, in a hobble
Indé	inde	yesterday
Indiu	indiu	today, at present
Inis	inish	an island, placename
Íseal	iseal	low, calm, soft-spoken
Íosagan[64]	Iosagan	Jesus, Jesukin
Láidir	laidir	strong, powerful, to assert, positively
Lán	lan	full, perfect, the *Cruiscín Lán*, a well-known drinking song
Leabhar	leabhar	a book
Leor	leor	plentiful, sufficient, hence the expression: *Money galore, Whisky galore*
Mac	mac	son, boy, descendant
Maith	maith	good, kind, favour, blessing, benefit
Maol	maol	bald, bare, blunt
Mí-ádh	miadh	misfortune, mishap
Mac-mí-adh	mac-miadh	an unfortunate fellow, a mischief-maker

Irish	English spelling	English meaning
Naomh	naomh	a saint, holy, sacred
Nead	neadh	a nest, home, haunt
Nodlaig	Nodlaig	Christmas
Nós	nos	a custom, habit, rite
Nuadhacht	nuadhacht	news, a novelty, fresh
Obair	obair	work, a literary work
Óg	og	young, junior, new
Oide	oide	teacher, tutor
Ollamh	ollamh	a master (of science or art), professor, chief poet, also the Rector of a university
Poitín	poteen	home-made whiskey[65]
Póirín	poreen	small potato, bean
Púnt	punt	Irish pound note, 1 lb
Pus[66]	pus	the lip, mouth, a vexed look, pout
Raispín	raispeen	a miser, a mean person
Rann	rann	a quatrain, verse, or stanza
Rannaire	rannaire	a versifier, reciter of poetry, song-writer
Rince	rince	a dance, spinning, sparkling, gambolling
Sasanach	Sasanach	English, an English person, a Saxon
Seanchas	seanchas	history, lore, ancient law, a record, a pedigree
Sidhe[67]	shee or sidhe	fairies, fairy folk
Smidirín	smithereen[68]	broken pieces, fragments
Sinn Féin	Sinn Fein	We ourselves
Súgán	sugan	a hay or straw rope. *Sugan chairs* or hayrope chairs are fashionable
Taoiseach	Taoiseach	Irish Prime Minister
Tamaill[69]	tamaill	a time, a while
Tinteán	tintean	hearth, home, fire-place
Tromach-Tramach	tromach tramach	pell-mell
Trócaire	trocaire	mercy, compassion, a Welfare Fund Committee
Uachtarán	Uactharan[70]	President, Superior
Uallóg	uallog	a coquette
Uallach	uallach	haughty, vain, foolish
Uisce	uisce	water, rain
Uiscebeatha	uiscebeatha	whisky, (living water)

NOTES

1 *Encyclopedia of Ireland*, p. 115.

2 The ancient Irish at first had a form of writing known as *Ogham* which, while based on the Latin alphabet, was a simple system of strokes cut in stone or in wood. It was used to record short statements on gravestones, or to write names of people or places.

3 Greene, *The Irish Language*, p. 12.

4 Power, *A Literary History of Ireland*, p. 32.

5 Ibid, p. 111.

6 O'Connor, Frank, *A Short History of Irish Literature*, New York, p. 69.

7 Hughes, Kathleen, 'The Golden Age of Early Christian Ireland' in Moody, T.W. and Martin, F.X. (eds.), *The Course of Irish History*, Dublin, 1967, pp. 76 - 83.

8 Lydon, J.F., 'The Medieval English Colony', Ibid., p. 146.

9 O Tuama, Seán, 'The New Love Poetry' in O Cuív, B., ed., *Seven Centuries of Irish Learning 1000 - 1700*, published for Radio Eireann by The Stationery Office, 1961, pp. 102, 103.

10 Ó Tuama Ibid, p. 103.

11 Ibid., pp. 107 - 109.

12 Power, *A Literary History of Ireland*, p. 76.

13 O'Connor, *A Short History of Irish Literature*, p. 55.

14 This saga is the central tale in the Ulster Cycle of Irish mythology. A comprehensive account of the *Táin*, and other sagas from different cycles of mythology is given by Professor Brendan Kennelly in the section 'Mythology', *Encyclopedia of Ireland* pp. 400 - 402.

15 O'Connor, *A Short History of Irish Literature*, pp. 24, 25.

16 This, along with many other ancient Irish MSS., can be seen in the Library of Trinity College, Dublin.

17 Place-lore. The word *dind* means 'prominent place' and *senchas* means 'lore, ancient tradition'. *Dindshenchas* means 'lore of famous places'. O Cuív, *Seven Centuries of Irish Learning*, p. 33.

18 The MS is in the Royal Irish Academy Library, Dawson Street, Dublin.

19 This epic poem by Virgil (70 - 19 B.C.) was translated into Irish in the 12th century. It was the earliest translation of the *Aeneid* from Latin into another language. The *Aeneid* comprised twelve books dealing with the story of the wanderings of Aeneas after the destruction of Troy.

20 Power, *A Literary History of Ireland*, pp. 67 - 69.

21 Gailey, Alan, *Irish Folk Drama*, Cork, 1969, p. 9.

22 Mac Airt, Seán 'The Development of Early Modern Irish Prose', in O Cuív (ed.), *Seven Centuries of Irish Learning*, p. 128.

23 Power, *A Literary History of Ireland*, p. 77.

24 *Waiting for Godot*, p. 12.

25 See 'The Poet's Curse' in Power, *The Book of Irish Curses*, pp. 66 - 71.

26 *Godot*, p. 21.

27 *All That Fall*, p. 17. 'Mr. Barrell (... *roaring*) Tommy! Blast your bleeding body ....

28 Power, *The Book of Irish Curses*, p. 21.

29 The poet's title was *Ollamh* (Professor). The chief poet of Ireland was called *Ard-Ollamh* (Supreme Professor). In Irish universities today the Rector or Chancellor is *Ard-Ollamh* (Chief Professor).

30 Power, *The Book of Irish Curses*, pp. 62-3.

31 He wrote to Alan Schneider, his American director, after the disastrous opening of *Waiting*

for Godot in Miami: 'Success and failure on the public level never mattered much to me, in fact I feel much more at home with the latter, having breathed deep of its vivifying air all my writing life up to the last couple of years ....' Reid, *All I Can Manage, More Than I Could*, p. 13.

32 *Waiting for Godot*, p. 75.

33 Power, *The Book of Irish Curses*, p. 29.

34 The cursing stones usually lay in or near an ancient monastic or church site.

35 *Godot*, p.43.

36 Power, *The Book of Irish Curses*, p. 27.

37 *Godot*, p. 43.

38 *Godot*, p. 44, 45.

39 In his *Book of Irish Curses*, Patrick Power writes: (p. 66) '... there were many types of satire known to Gaelic poets but ... one of them at least, the *glám dícenn*, appears to have been formal cursing. Whenever ... one reads that a poet 'satirised' someone, it could vary from mockery and sly abuse to fearful malediction. We are not concerned here with the ordinary satire known to Gaelic and English literature.'

40 O Cuív, 'An Era of Upheaval', in *Seven Centuries of Irish Learning*, p. 137.

41 Ibid., p. 140.

42 Power, *A Literary History of Ireland*, p. 78.

43 Henry VIII's act of 1537 entitled 'An Act for the English order, habit and language'. O Cuív, *Seven Centuries of Irish Learning*, pp. 137 - 140.

44 The English Pale, so called from the 15th century, was an area within twenty miles around Dublin where English law prevailed.

45 O Cuív, *Seven Centuries of Irish Learning*, pp. 141, 142.

46 Dowling, P.J., *The Hedge Schools of Ireland*, Cork, 1968, p. 25.

47 Power, *A Literary History of Ireland*, p. 95.

48 Dowling, *The Hedge Schools*, pp. 42, 43.

49 Ibid., p. 43.

50 Ibid., p. 99.

51 *Amhrán Abú* means a song of victory or the national anthem: *The Soldier's Song*.

52 Samuel Lover (1798 - 1869) illustrates the sad poetry of the heart in his ballad, Molly Bawn.

53 Beckett, Samuel, *Cascando, Play and Two Short Pieces for Radio*, p. 40.

54 J.M. Synge, *The Well of Saints*, Act I; Beckett uses the words blather and blathering frequently: *Waiting for Godot*, pp. 10, 66.

55 *Deo* has many shades of meaning, all indicating terminal or final situations. *Go* used as a preposition means 'till' or 'until'.

56 *Go deo* means 'till the end of time'. Dinneen, *Irish-English Dictionary*, pp. 328, 556.

57 Beckett uses *deor* meaning 'tear' and 'lucky' in *Godot*.

58 *Godot*, p. 14, there is a subtle link between 'no more weeping' or the end of tears (the suffering of being) and *Go deo* / 'eternity'. The willow tree (weeping willow) illustrates it.

59 *Godot*, p. 35.

60 Bord Fáilte is the Irish Tourist Board. A common expression: *Céad míle fáilte* or a hundred thousand welcomes.

61 *Godot*, p. 44.

62 *All That Fall*, p. 39.

63 Ibid., p. 27. (Gobstopper is ambiguous here).

64 A famous short story in Irish by Padraic Pearse (1907). Pearse (1879-1916), poet, playwright, essayist, was leader of the 1916 Rebellion, and executed in 1916. *Iosagán* is described as 'the

most beautiful short story ever to come out of Ireland'. *Short Stories of Padraic Pearse*, translated by Desmond Maguire (1968).

65 Keane, J.B., *Letters of a Matchmaker*, pp. 19, 44.

66 *Godot*, p. 60. 'It's never the same pus from one second to the next.'

67 Yeats, W.B., *The Land of Heart's Desire* (1894) has a Faery Child as one of its characters. It concerns the *'Sidhe'*. His play *The Only Jealousy of Emer* (1919) has one 'Woman of the Sidhe'.

68 *Endgame*, p. 16.

69 Keane, *Letters of a Matchmaker*, p. 8.

70 *Aras an Uachtarain* is the official residence of the President of Ireland.

Stone in the Making, Mythology, and Folklore of Ireland[1]

Ireland is richly endowed with stone. The island rests on a solid bed of ancient rock, which rises to form an almost unbroken chain of mountains and hills along its 2,000 mile coastline.

The main types of Irish rock are: *Limestone,* a sedimentary rock, formed upon the bed of a subtropical sea long before a turn of nature's kaleidoscope set the Emerald Isle upon the raw edge of the Atlantic Ocean. It is 'among the softest of Ireland's rocks (it is only 350 million years old!)' and underlies almost half of the island. Limestone has one big flaw: it is soluble in rainwater. But it is protected from Ireland's rain by broad spreads of peat or great thicknesses of debris left by the glaciers of the Ice Age. Limestone landscapes in the west, the Burren, Co. Clare and the Aran Islands now instance how the ravages of rainwater has reduced the naked rock to 'the character of maggot-eaten cheese'. The larger the 'solution hollows' in the bare rock the longer the legends of their origin.[2] Forever brimming over with pure Irish rainwater, they have been hallowed into holy wells or wishing wells, by folklore and hopelore.

Granite, a plutonic rock, rises to form the Dublin and Wicklow Mountains; the well-sung Mountains of Mourne in Co. Down; and the Derryveagh Mountains of Donegal. It also underlies lowlands of scenic beauty north of Galway Bay, and in Co. Carlow. All over the country, granite boulders or standing stones have rock rights in popular sentiment, staunch as the rock rites in the ethos of the early Celts.[3]

Quartzite, a metamorphic rock, originated in a bed of sand on an ancient shore. The grains of sand consolidated to form a sandstone buried within the earth's crust. Through great heat and pressure the individual grains of sand were melted and fused together to form the hardest of all Irish rocks. It forms the conical peaks of twin Sugar Loaf Mountains in Co. Wicklow; the Devil's Backbone, Errigal, and Slieve League in Co. Donegal; the Twelve Bens in Co. Galway; and the pointed Heights of Achill Island. Appropriately, the hardest of all Irish rocks forms the famed and most frequently climbed Irish mountain, 'the supremely graceful Croagh Patrick towering over the island-studded waters of Clew Bay in Co. Mayo.'[4]

Old Red Sandstone, a sedimentary rock, older than the limestone, formed from rock debris washed into the 'mountain-girt basins', which 400 million years ago occupied the area where Ireland now stands. In time the rock debris fused to form the hard rock called Old Red Sandstone, although more frequently its colours are purple, yellow, or green.

This rock underlies only 10% of Ireland's area, but it builds over 90 of the 190 Irish peaks that rise more than 600 metres above sea-level. It forms Ireland's highest mountain — Carrantouhill, (over 3,000 metres), in the Macgillycuddy Reeks which rise above the Lakes of Killarney. The popular ascent of this famous mountain begins at the mouth of the *Hag's Glen* on the north of the Reeks, up the Glen and then via the Devil's Ladder to the summit.

At first the tough Red Sandstone lay in vast horizontal sheets, until earth-movements gradually bent its great expanse into ridges and furrows which today form the uplands extending from Co. Waterford, through Co. Cork into Co. Kerry. In Cork and Kerry they fan out into the Atlantic Ocean in the famed peninsulas of the south-west. Separating the hard ridges of Old Red are romantic rivers; and bays of enchanting beauty, celebrated in poetry, song, and true sea lore down the centuries to our own day.[5]

Basalt, a rock of volcanic origin, forms the north-eastern corner of Ireland. The basalt of Co. Antrim forms Torr Head coastline, the irregular plateau of hills and uplands dropping sharply to the sea on the north and east, and terminates in cliffs overlooking Belfast Lough. Basalt is much younger than the limestone of the midlands, which is younger than the rocks forming the upland rim of Ireland. It was poured out during eruptions of lava some seventy million years ago at a time when Ireland was a land of volcanic fires and earthquakes.

At the close of the Cretaceous period (140-65 million years ago) earth movements were gentle, the land was elevated, breaks occurred, and vast outpourings of dark, molten basalt lava covered the exposed chalk of Co. Antrim. On the northern coast of Antrim the *Giant's Causeway*, where the older basalt flows have cooled to form regular hexagonal columns, is a celebrated natural wonder.

The volcanic origin of basalt was first recognised in the 18th century by French geologists. Irish and British scientists were unwilling to accept the idea from France, because the French Revolution had made all ideas coming from the country suspect, if not abhorrent to them.[6] But prejudice does not invalidate nature's bed-rock facts, nor politics obscure their origin, for long. Truth will out.

> Nature's fiery revolution crowned white limestone (chalk) with black basalt, and in Antrim, left the *Giant's Causeway* the mark and marvel of her cooled fury.[7]

A large part of Celtic mythology is based on stone(s). The profusion of stones in Ireland is truly fascinating. The infinite variety of shapes and sizes is bewildering, mysterious, and strangely exhilarating. Here is the work of Creation — rocks, boulders, stones — not of mass production. Each stone has an individuality, even in the security of a stone wall.

A Cologne man writes, and his camera illustrates:

> In some parts of Ireland one is very conscious of stone: beautifully shaped stones on shores, smoothed and rounded by the constant rolling of the Atlantic breakers: stone walls everywhere, sometimes making the effect of lace against the sky.[8]

This is amplified in an essay on *Shapes*, by Stephen Rynne:

> God made a terrible lot of shapes ... I am only thinking now of the thousands

of miles of loose stone boundary walls all over Western Ireland ... Every
stone is a shape pattern to itself. I challenge all comers to discover identical
twins among those millions of stones ... it would be easier to name all the
stars in the Milky Way than to give shape names to all the stones you see in
a loose stone wall.[9]

If that can be said of 'utility stones', what about those unique stones carved to
serve another purpose long before the birth of Christ — the stone idols standing as
sentinels of a culture that pre-dates history, in the island of Ireland?

The Corleck Idol, the three-faced god of the Celts, a magnificent sandstone head
of Iron Age sculpture, discovered in Corleck, Co. Cavan, in 1934. It was originally
found in 1855 in a cairn attached to a portal tomb. The Iron Age Celts who carved
this head represented youth, middle-age and old age in the image of their venera-
tion, 'There's a young face, a sort of middle-aged face, and an ould face,' said the
lad who reported the 'find' in a barn of his home, to his schoolmaster in 1934.[10]

Two other Iron Age heads were found with the Corleck Idol in the cairn in 1855.
They are:

The Coravilla Head — a turnip-shaped head, given to the National Museum in
1966; and:

The Corraghy Head — the bearded head, turned over to the Museum in 1969.
Other stone-carved heads found in Co. Cavan include:

The Clannaphilip Head in Killinkere, north of Virginia, near to the Cavan/Meath
border. This medieval carving is set in the east wall of a Catholic church no longer
used as such. It is described thus:

> Highly stylised, the head breathes tremendous power. Deeply scored lines
> bind the forehead and radiate from the eyes, nose, upper and lower lips.
> Here is a face that waits, accepts, endures. And poses questions.
>
> The question is whether the Head is male or female. Local tradition has
> overruled the caution of scholars and declared it a *'cailleach'* or hag, one of
> the Mothers. When the rain water runs down the deep furrows of the face
> this stone image is 'one of the greatest depictions of *The Grieving Mother* that
> Ireland has to offer'.[11]

The Cavan Head, contemplative idol from the Cavan Lakeland, absorbed in the
wonder of Cavan's myriad lakes offering facilities for the contemplative and complete angler.

The Togher Heads, a pair of heads, male and female, found near Finea, on the
Cavan/Longford border, and given to the National Museum, Dublin in 1984. They
are Iron Age figures: the female of the pair carved in detail to express the serene,
tender gaze of the mother, and the pagan fertility cult. 'This idol caresses even as
she asserts her power.'[12]

The Tomregan Stone, is in Ballyconnell C. of I. Church, West Cavan. As part of the
outer face of a Romanesque window, it presents an elongated oval head set above
an arched opening. The top half of the face — sow-eared — has a striking animal
look. The bottom half represents a bearded old man — or woman. 'The Bearded Lady
— who is half *The Devouring Mother*.'[13] This stone has many unusual features. A pair

of arms with hands outstretched descend from both cheeks. Biting beast-heads meet the finger-tips, or so it seems. The *squat* of the design, and other aspects of its obvious representation of *The Fecund Mother*, give *The Tomregan Stone* a haunting and unique quality among the many stone idols standing as symbols and sentinels of Irish mythology.

The Turoe Stone (pronounced tew-roe) in Co. Galway, in the West, is one of the famous standing stones in the country associated with the Druids and pagan ritual, that was absorbed into Christian symbolism after the 5th century. The stone has artistic links with Germanic and Greek design of the period around 300 B.C.

> The Turoe Stone ... is a powerful piece of western granite about four feet high, its dome decorated in a great welter of swirling curves, like the tattooed spirals of a Maori head. Archaeologists tell us that its unending movement represents one of the earliest and yet very characteristic Irish examples of purely Celtic art (La Tène) — in a variant known as the Waldalgesheim style, which was developed in the Middle-Rhine area of Germany from classical Greek motifs some time around 300 B.C. The stepped pattern beneath the swirling curves .... is also of Greek origin.
>
> The Turoe Stone, therefore, is likely to have been carved around the same time as a Celtic tribe fell upon Delphi, the site of the great Greek oracle, in 279 B.C. There in Delphi, it finds a curious analogue in the similarly shaped Omphalos Stone, which marked the centre of the world for the ancient Greeks.
>
> Perhaps the four parts into which the swirling curves of the Turoe Stone's cap is divided, represent the four corners of the world. In our mind's eye, we should perhaps imagine the Turoe Stone as being the centre of some great pagan Celtic earth ritual, involving the giving forth of deep oracular divinations by the druids.[14]

The Turoe Stone was originally located beside a ring-fort or 'fairy ring',[15] which means that ritual and 'magic' were linked in the divinations. The name of the ring-fort is Rath of Feerwore or Rath of the Big Man. For 'reasons unknown'[16] the Turoe Stone was moved from the rath some hundred and fifty years ago.

The *Lia Fáil* stone, standing on the grass on the crest of the Hill of Tara, in Co. Meath, is the legendary coronation stone of the ancient kings of Ireland. Like the Stone of Scone,[17] which originally came from Ireland, the *Lia Fáil* is called the Stone of Destiny.[18] It is in fact a phallic symbol, the Irish legacy of a pagan fertility cult.

The Lia Fáil is a concrete link between Ireland's pagan past and her Christian culture that incorporated much of that past in its splendid ceremonial. Stone of Destiny can hardly be a misnomer for the Lia Fáil, for 'destiny' in the sense of 'divine pre-ordination'[19] is the equivalent in pagan religious belief of Christian centuries-long acceptance of 'kings by the Grace of God',[20] and 'the divine right of kings'.[21]

Granite was the favourite and favoured rock in ancient Ireland. It has the curative properties people now seek in the mineral waters of spas and springs, wherever they exist.

The ancient Celtic and megalithic people knew all about the energy given off by certain types of granite and other igneous or metamorphic stone of volcanic origin.[22]

Butterflies have always been attracted to the warmth of granite rocks. All over the world there are special rock places where migrating insects stop to rest and absorb some mysterious energy from the warmed stone. One such resting place is the butterfly rock on Slieve League, Co. Donegal. Others are found in the far-flung boulder-strewn slopes of the Rocky Mountains and the granite heights of Mount Gingera, Australia.

> The early Celts of Ireland also understood that the granite stone of Ireland emitted a healing force. Granite is highly paramagnetic (attracted to a strong magnet) and all over Ireland are standing stones utilised for healing and also as birthing stones for the Celtic lassies.[23]

Altogether, there are more magic stone structures in Ireland than anywhere else in the world. As well as healing stones there are fairy rings and stone forts, and the strong stone walls of old deserted cottages, and towers, inside which wild gardens grow in the glow of the surrounding rock energy.[24]

The Celts reciprocated the warmth of rock energy by giving its name to the locality it distinguished. Ireland is strewn with place names containing the Irish word for rock, *Carraig*[25] or Carrig or Carrick. The village of Carrick is a starting place for the ascent of Slieve League (630 metres), where the butterfly rock hosts the travelling insects.

History or legend or local prominence is also enshrined in such place names. There is Carrickfergus, *Fergus's Rock*, near Belfast, Co. Antrim. According to some medieval writers it is named after Fergus MacErc, ruler of the ancient Dalriada territory in Antrim, who became the first Irish king of Scotland. In Co. Monaghan, Carrickmacross — *The Rock of the Wooded Plain* — is famous for the exquisite Carrickmacross lace, which is still produced there.

A particular rock near a river lent its name to the village or town that grew up around it. We have Carrick-on-Suir or Carraig na Siúire — *The Rock of the Suir*, a town on a lovely stretch of the River Suir, lies partly in Co. Tipperary and partly in Co. Wexford. Carrigart or Carraig Airt — *Art's Rock* is a sea-side resort on an inlet of Mulroy Bay, Co. Donegal. Numerous finds have been made at the prehistoric habitation sites or 'kitchen middens' in the sandhills around Carrigart. There is an ogham stone nearby. The carrick places of Ireland and their ancient associations would fill a book.

Stone in the folklore of Ireland evolved from the myth, magic and mystery associated with stones in Ireland. From the pre-Celtic period dating back to 3200 B.C.,[26] down to present-day theories about 'lucky' stones, birthday stones, talismans, commercial and sentimental value of stone(s), this unique mineral has exercised the imagination and compiled a rich treasury of folklore.

Stone is the most enduring expression of identity in human history. Its significance as milestones in man's cultural development includes its use as his tribute to the dead. Ample evidence of this is seen in the 300 court cairns[27] and some 150 portal dolmens[28] that mark various places in the country, and provide unwritten volumes of its history.[29]

Alternatively, folklore is sometimes translated into stone in Ireland. This is done not only for its national heroes: poets, patriots, and politicians; but for a humble fiddler who 'died in action' in 1770.

A house musician is remembered in an appropriate monument of stone; and bequeaths a linguistic riddle to posterity. The story is told by Paddy Tunney:[30]

The Stone Fiddle

Below is part of the inscription on the Stone Fiddle at Castlecaldwell, County Fermanagh, which was erected to the memory of one Denis McCabe, fiddler, who fell out of a barge, the property of Sir James Caldwell, Baronet and Count of Milan, on the 13th of August, 1770, and was drowned. Denis McCabe was a celebrated fiddle-player who was employed by the good knight to entertain his guests. On this particular occasion the guests were too intoxicated to reach an oar or throw a rope to poor McCabe. The old people used to say that the fiddler was still sawing away when he came up for the third time.

After the sad event Sir James seems to have had remorse and ordered the monument to be struck from stone quarried near the spot. It was erected on the Rossbeg shore above the castle, near the spot where the drowning took place, and was supported by two stone pillars. Then a local stone mason, who set little store on antiquity or sentiment, removed the Fiddle and left it leaning against the great beeches near the Railway Station, and built its supporting pillars into gate piers for a local squireen.

In time a Fermanagh Historical Society, fearing that souvenir hunters would eventually chip off and bear away the entire fiddle stone, removed it to the old gatehouse leading to the Castle, where it remains to this day, cemented to the wall.

The inscription ends with the letters: 'D.D.D.' ... And to this day the controversy rages. What do the three Ds stand for? Is it Drink Drowned Denis or Denis Died Drunk?

The Stone Fiddle

Beware ye Fidlers ye Fidlers fate
Nor tempt ye deep least ye repent too late
Ye ever have been deemed to water foes
Then shun ye lake till it with whiskey flows
On firm land only exercise your skill
There you may play and drink your fill.

The most celebrated stone in Irish Folklore is the *Blarney Stone*, set in the wall of Blarney Castle, five miles north-west of Cork. Blarney Castle and the magic Blarney Stone with its traditional power of conferring the gift of eloquence on all those who kiss it are world-famous. Tourists come from everywhere to 'kiss the Blarney' and inhale a breath of its magic. They return happy at having accomplished the physical, acrobatic feat of reaching and kissing the Stone; and feeling spiritually elated by its spell.

The word 'Blarney', well entrenched in the English language,[31] is supposed to have originated in dealings of Queen Elizabeth's government with the then lord of Blarney, Cormac MacDermot MacCarthy. Repeatedly he was asked by the Queen's Deputy, Carew, to recognise the Queen's sovereignty, to renounce the traditional Irish system by which the clans *elected* their chief, and to take the tenure of his (own) lands from the English Crown.

While seeming to agree to this proposal, the lord of Blarney Castle put off the fulfilment of his promise from day to day 'with fair words and soft speech', until at last Carew became the laughing-stock of the Queen. Elizabeth declared, 'This is all Blarney; what he says he never means.' Thus 'Blarney' came to mean pleasant talk intended to deceive without offending.

Blarney Castle, originally a fortress of the Clan MacCarthy of south Munster, consists chiefly of a massive square keep or tower with a battlemented parapet 83 feet (ca. 25 metres) above the ground.

The Castle was built in two sections: the first, a tall, narrow tower containing a staircase and small rooms; the second -- adjoining and overlapping the earlier work — a massive keep of oblong plan, remarkable for the graceful batter (inclination) of its walls. The battlements crowning the keep are typically Irish in form.[32]

Below the battlements the famous Blarney stone is set in the wall. To kiss it one has to lean over backwards (grasping an iron railing) from the parapet walk of the battlements. For the very nervous, there is a 'guide' or attendant always present, to hold the kisser by the heels. With the new-found gift of persuasive flattery the latter can convince the helpful guide that it was all worth while.

The *Blarney Stone* is a cherished natural heritage. In a land where so many can 'give a tongue to a stone', the *Blarney* is the only *Stone* that can return the compliment. It has inspired poetry, song, and many colourful strands of folklore.

Stone in the Making, Mythology and Folklore of Ireland is poetry; crystallised in this poem:[33]

Stone
Opaque prism
Alpha of the universe
Molten birth cooling to caul, fragmented
Into fertile dust.
Petrified roots of oak, diamond hard,
Probe mantle-folded bog to be drawn down, down,
Back to the centre of origin and eternity —
The ultimate atom of stone.
High-cross and head-stone: granite, coaxing energy
From the cosmos, gifting those attuned to receive

And accept with second sight and ancient memories.
Stone caressed by the sea to silken sand
Fossil of fish, touch-stone of schist
Lintel, hearth and stepping stones
Quartz glittering in the pocket of a child
Hollowed font and hollowed quern
Pebble on the tongue of the dead.
Stone to mark tombs and the passage of dreams.

Dana Wynter
Glenmacnass 1984

NOTES

1   This theme is dealt with in a comprehensive and scientific manner by Professor Gorden L. Herries Davies of Trinity College, Dublin, in an article entitled: 'The Making of Ireland', *Ireland of the Welcomes*; Vol. 34, No. 1, 1985.

2   Robinson, Tim, *Setting Foot on the Shores of Connemara*, Lilliput 1984, pp. 17, 18.

3   Apart from the properties (energy and healing) which the Celts attributed to granite rocks, there is a long tradition of sentimental attachment to certain stones in localities. They are landmarks entwined in local history, legend, and personal memories. Whether they provide childhood hiding places, as in Beckett's *That Time*, meeting places, or the subject of song, their link with the land and the generations it bore give them an identity next to the hearth-stone called home. The Gaelic word for 'home' is *tinteán* or hearth-stone.

4   Herries Davies, 'The Making of Ireland', p. 24. Hundreds of pilgrims climb this mountain annually (the last Sunday in July each year), to commemorate St. Patrick's forty days and nights fast on its summit, when he christianised Ireland in the 5th century. According to legend, it was from the top of Croagh Patrick that he banished the snakes from the island of Ireland.

5   The most fascinating recorded sea lore is *The Voyage of Saint Brendan* (1976), translated by Professor John J. O'Meara from the Latin, *Navigatio Sancti Brendani Abbatis*, written in Ireland as early as A.D. 800. It describes in detail the voyage of a crew of monks captained by St. Brendan (489-570 or 583), and their discovery of North America almost a 1,000 years before Columbus. Sailing from Brandon Creek, Co. Kerry, a similar voyage via the 'Stepping Stone Route' of St. Brendan was made in 1976-77 by the famous explorer, Tim Severin and his crew of five. His book *The Brendan Voyage* (1978) proves that St. Brendan's voyage and discovery *'could* be the case'.

6   The Irish insurrection of 1798 was actively supported by France.

7   *Encyclopedia of Ireland*, p. 41.

8   Pfeiffer, Walter, 'Aspects of Ireland', *Ireland of the Welcomes*, Vol. 30, No. 6, 1981, p. 25. Pfeiffer, born near Cologne, Germany, visited Ireland many times with his camera, 'drawn by the light and the life-style', before finally settling in Ireland in 1966.

9   Rynne, Stephen, 'Shapes', *Ireland of the Welcomes*, Vol. 34, No. 1, 1985, p. 11.

10 MacIntyre, Tom, 'Sentinels of Secret Places', *Ireland of the Welcomes*, Vol. 34, No. 1, 1985, p. 31.

11 Ibid., p. 31.

12 Ibid., p. 32.

13 Ibid.

14 Harbison, Peter, 'The Turoe Stone', *Ireland of the Welcomes*, Vol. 34, No. 1, 1985, p. 26.

15 Ring-forts, dating from between the 6th and the 10th centuries were built round a home or other precious structure, to protect or defend it.

16 *Waiting for Godot*, p. 44.

17 The Stone of Scone on which the kings of Scotland used to be crowned, was brought to England by King Edward I, in 1296. Since then it has formed part of the Throne in Westminster Abbey which British monarchs occupy at their coronation. The Stone, then called the 'Lia Faill' or 'Tanist Stone', was brought from Ireland by Fergus son of Eric, who led the Dalriads to Argyllshire. It was removed to Scone (near Perth) by King Kenneth in the 9th century.

18 *Ireland of the Welcomes*, Vol. 34, No. 1, 1985.

19 *The Penguin English Dictionary*, p. 196.

20 *Brewer's Dictionary of Phrase and Fable*, p. 521. The notion prevailed from the reign of Edward the Confessor (1042-1066), to the reign of Queen Anne (1702-1714), that monarchs had divine powers of healing scrofula (tuberculosis of lymphatic glands), simply by touching the sick person ('the royal touch'). One of the last persons touched in England was Dr. Johnson, in 1712, when he was less than three years old, by Queen Anne. The French kings laid claim to the same divine power from the time of Clovis, A.D. 481. On Easter Sunday, 1686, Louis XIV touched 1,600 persons, using the words: *Le roi te touche, Dieu te guérisse*.

21 Ibid., p. 288.

22 Callahan, P.S., 'Butterfly Rock', *Ireland of the Welcomes*, Vol. 34, No. 1, 1985, p. 44.

23 Ibid., p. 45.

24 In *That Time*, Beckett tells how as a child he used to hide in the ruin of a tower, sitting 'all day long on a stone among the nettles' (p. 10).

25 Dinneen, *An Irish-English Dictionary*, p. 166.

26 Kearney, Richard, 'Mythopoeic Thought' in Kearney, ed., *The Irish Mind*, p. 15.

27 *Encyclopedia of Ireland*, p. 67. Court cairns were tombs used for collective burial by the immigrants to Ireland, around 3000 B.C. These megalithic chambered tombs were built of great unhewn stones beneath a mound of earth or stones.

28 The portal dolmens — also primitive burial tombs — date from about 2000 B.C. They were constructed as a single chamber entered through massive portals. A capstone of enormous weight covers the chamber. *Encyclopedia of Ireland*, p. 68.

29 Purcell, Brendan, 'In Search of Newgrange: Long Night's Journey Into Day' in Kearney (ed.), *The Irish Mind*, pp. 39-55.

30 *Ireland of the Welcomes*, Vol. 34, No. 1, 1985, p. 35.

31 The dictionary meaning of 'Blarney' is: 'To flatter, cajole, or wheedle. Wheedling flattery.' Funk & Wagnalls *Practical Standard Dictionary*, p. 135. *The Penguin English Dictionary* gives the meaning: 'blarney *n (coll)* persuasive flattery', p. 70.

32 *Illustrated Ireland Guide*, Bord Fáilte, Dublin, 1967, pp. 195, 196.

33 Published in *Ireland of the Welcomes*, Vol. 34, No. 1, 1985, pp. 18, 19.

INDEX

LITERARY TOUR OF IRELAND

Elizabeth Healy

'A passionate, intimate and often illuminating book.' *Irish Times*

Elizabeth Healy's route-by-route guide reveals a land which has for centuries inspired poets and storytellers.

Your guides are, among others, Yeats, Lady Gregory, Synge, O'Flaherty, O'Connor, the ancient Táin, Seamus Heaney, Goldsmith, O'Casey, Shaw, Swift, Joyce and Beckett.

Elizabeth Healy is a former editor of Bord Fáilte's *Ireland of the Welcomes*.

HB £24.99 Colour & B/W photos, maps and drawings 245 x 192 mm 320pp ISBN 0 86327 446 3

POEMS OF THE DAMNED:
Baudelaire's Les Fleurs du Mal –
The Flowers of Evil

Translated by Ulick O'Connor

First published in 1885, **Les Fleurs du Mal** was banned and Baudelaire was prosecuted for obscenity. 1995 sees the 140th anniversary of the publication of the poems.

PB £5.99 216 x 138 mm 32pp ISBN 0 86327 512 5

'Ulick O'Connor has managed to preserve the familiar Baudelairian cadence. His rhythm has such natural grace that one is bewitched by it. The poem is reborn before our eyes and is music to our ears, not translated but recreated.'
Michel Delon de l'Académie Francaise

WOLFHOUND PRESS
68 Mountjoy Square
Dublin 1
(Tel: 8740354 Fax: 8720207)